OFFICIALLY NOTED
Stains on fore edge.
SP 7/2/14

✓ W9-BXZ-594

Culture Wise
CHINA

The Essential Guide to Culture, Customs & Business Etiquette

Leo Lacey

WITHDRAWN

Survival Books • London • England

GENEVA PUBLIC LIBRARY DISTRICT

First published 2011

All rights reserved. No part of this publication
may be reproduced, stored in a retrieval system or
recorded by any means, without prior written
permission from the publisher.

Copyright © Survival Books 2011
Cover photo © Jack Qi (🖳 www.shutterstock.com)
Maps and illustrations © Jim Watson

Survival Books Limited
26 York Street, London W1U 6PZ, United Kingdom
☏ +44 (0)20-7788 7644, 🖹 +44 (0)870-762 3212
✉ info@survivalbooks.net
🖳 www.survivalbooks.net

British Library Cataloguing in Publication Data.
A CIP record for this book is available
from the British Library.
ISBN: 978-1-907339-27-1

Printed and bound in Singapore by Stamford Press

ACKNOWLEDGEMENTS

I would like to thank my many friends, family members and colleagues who provided information for this book. In particular, I wish to thank my wife, Guo Zhao Li, for her patience and assistance, and my sons for their encouragement. My heartfelt thanks also go to Su Su Gao, Han Fule and the very helpful Ms Zhong of the Zhengzhou Public Security Bureau for their assistance, together with Brian Merifield and David Leffman.

Thanks are also due to Robbi Forrester Atilgan for editing; Lilac Johnston for proofreading; Peter Read for final editing and proofing; Di Bruce-Kidman for desktop publishing and photo selection; and Jim Watson for the cover design and maps. Finally a special thank you to all the photographers (listed on page 270) – the unsung heroes – whose beautiful images add colour and bring China to life.

THE AUTHOR

Leo Lacey was born in the UK, where he trained as a civil engineer, and has lived and worked in Europe, Africa, Asia, Australia and the Pacific islands. In the '70s he became a citizen of Australia, where he also served as a Justice of the Peace. He first visited China shortly after the end of the Cultural Revolution to work on the construction of offshore oil platforms and in the late '90s began work on the building of a dam on the Yellow River. A widower, he met his second wife Guo Zhao Li while working on the dam project and they married in 2000.

Leo now acts as a consultant to an engineering design company in Henan province and teaches English at local schools and at one of Henan's universities. He has had a number of articles published in Australia and the UK, and has also been a regular contributor to the Chinese press, as well as writing for Lonely Planet and Rough Guides. In 2003, he was awarded the 'Friendship of the Yellow River' – the highest possible accolade for a foreigner – by the provincial government of Henan in recognition of his contribution to life and education in the province.

Leo and Zhao Li divide their time between China and Australia, spending summers in Zhengzhou, the principal city of Henan province, and winters by the beach in Manly, New South Wales. Leo's other passions, besides China, include rugby football – he used to play for London Irish – and motorcycle racing.

What Readers and Reviewers Have Said About Survival Books:

"If I were to move to France, I would like David Hampshire to be with me, holding my hand every step of the way. This being impractical, I would have to settle for second best and take his books with me instead!"
Living France

"We would like to congratulate you on this work: it is really super! We hand it out to our expatriates and they read it with great interest and pleasure."
ICI (Switzerland) AG

"I found this a wonderful book crammed with facts and figures, with a straightforward approach to the problems and pitfalls you are likely to encounter. The whole laced with humour and a thorough understanding of what's involved. Gets my vote!"
American Club of Zurich

"Get hold of David Hampshire's book for its sheer knowledge, straightforwardness and insights to the Spanish character and do yourself a favour!"
France in Print

"Rarely has a 'survival guide' contained such useful advice – This book dispels doubts for first time travellers, yet is also useful for seasoned globetrotters – In a word, if you're planning to move to the US or go there for a long term stay, then buy this book both for general reading and as a ready reference."
Swiss News

"It's everything you always wanted to ask but didn't for fear of the contemptuous put down – The best English language guide – Its pages are stuffed with practical information on everyday subjects and are designed to complement the traditional guidebook."
American Citizens Abroad

"A must for all future expats. I invested in several books but this is the only one you need. Every issue and concern is covered, every daft question you have but are frightened to ask is answered honestly without pulling any punches. Highly recommended."
Reader (Amazon)

"Let's say it at once. David Hampshire's Living and Working in France is the best handbook ever produced for visitors and foreign residents in this country; indeed, my discussion with locals showed that it has much to teach even those born and bred in l'Hexagone. It is Hampshire's meticulous detail which lifts his work way beyond the range of other books with similar titles. This book is absolutely indispensable."
The Riviera Reporter

"Covers every conceivable question that might be asked concerning everyday life – I know of no other book that could take the place of this one."
France in Print

"The ultimate reference book – Every conceivable subject imaginable is exhaustively explained in simple terms – An excellent introduction to fully enjoy all that this fine country has to offer and save time and money in the process."
American Club of Zurich

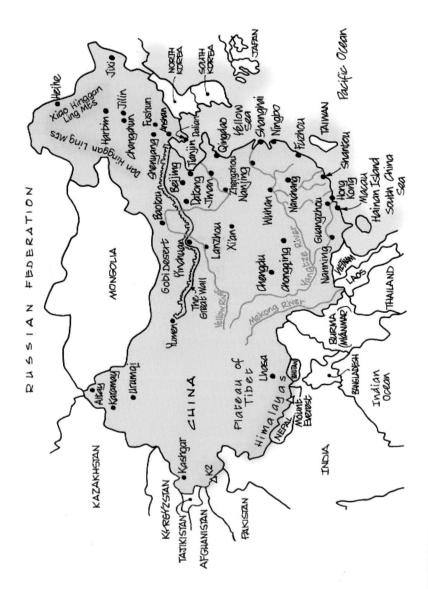

CONTENTS

9. RETAIL THERAPY

10. ODDS & ENDS

APPENDICES

INDEX

Mt Sanqing, Jiangxi

INTRODUCTION

If you're planning a trip to China or just want to learn more about the country, you'll find the information contained in *Culture Wise China* invaluable. Whether you're travelling on business or for pleasure, visiting for a couple of weeks or planning to stay long term, Culture Wise guides enable you to quickly find your feet by removing the anxiety factor when dealing with a foreign culture.

Adjusting to a different environment and culture in any foreign country can be a traumatic and frustrating experience, and China is certainly no exception. You need to adapt to new customs and traditions and discover the Chinese way of doing things, whether it's letting off firecrackers to celebrate the New Year or toasting someone's success with copious glasses of *baijiu*, learning how to cultivate your *guanxi* at work or deciphering the rules of *mah-jong*. China is a land of surprises and contradictions, where mountains are holy and crickets are kept as pets; where a smile can signify acute embarrassment and comparing someone to a turtle can cause great offence; where people burn money to honour their ancestors and wear pyjamas in the street.

China is so vast that the climate, customs and even the food vary enormously from one part of the country to the next. The way of life differs also, depending on whether you live in one of China's fast-growing metropolises or its still traditional countryside. In addition, you must grapple with the Chinese language which sounds and looks completely different from Western tongues. The key to living happily in China is to keep an open mind and cultivate your patience.

Culture Wise China is essential reading for anyone planning to visit China, including tourists (especially travellers planning to stay a number of weeks or months), business people, migrants, retirees and transferees. It's designed to help newcomers avoid cultural and social gaffes; make friends and influence people; improve communications (both verbal and non-verbal); and enhance your understanding of China and its people. It explains what to expect, how to behave in most situations, and how to get along with the locals and feel at home.

A period spent in China is a wonderful way to enrich your life, broaden your horizons, and hopefully expand your circle of friends. We trust this book will help you avoid the pitfalls of visiting or living in China and smooth your way to a happy and rewarding stay.

Hao yun! (Good luck!)

Survival Books
January 2011

Great Wall of China

1.

A CHANGE OF CULTURE

With almost daily advances in technology, ever cheaper flights and knowledge about almost anywhere in the world at our fingertips, travelling, living, working and retiring abroad has never been more accessible, and current migration patterns suggest that it has never been more popular. But, although globalisation means the world has in effect 'shrunk', every country is still a world of its own with a unique culture – and China is no exception.

> 'There are no foreign lands. It is the traveller only who is foreign.'
>
> Robert Louis Stevenson (Scottish author & poet)

Some people find it impossible to adapt to a new life in a different culture – for reasons that are many and varied. According to statistics, partner dissatisfaction is the most common cause, as non-working spouses frequently find themselves without a role in the new country and sometimes with little to do other than think about what they would be doing if they were at home. Family concerns – which may include the children's education and worries about loved ones at home – can also deeply affect those living abroad.

Many factors contribute to how well you adapt to a new culture: for example, your personality, education, foreign language skills, mental health, maturity, socio-economic conditions, travel experience and family and social support systems. How you handle the stress of change and bring balance and meaning to your life is the principal indicator of how well you'll adjust to a different country, culture and business environment.

> 'The Chinese have created the single most extensive and enduring civilisation in the world. Their language, spoken and written in the same form for some 4,000 years, binds their vast country together and links the present with the past, expressing a unified culture unmatched elsewhere. In contrast, the land of China is one of great geographical diversity. Bordered by mountains, steppes and deserts, the immense central plains are watered by great rivers, supporting a dense population, a large part of which has always been tied to the land, but which has proved extraordinarily skilled in the production of industrial goods of a high quality.'
>
> (notice in the British Museum, London)

CHINA IS DIFFERENT

Many people underestimate the cultural isolation that can be experienced in a foreign country, particularly one with a different language. While most foreigners have no problem accepting that China will be different from their own country, they may be surprised at just how different it is. Even if you've studied Chinese at length before arriving, you'll still find you have an awful lot to learn about the way the language is used, while dialects vary enormously throughout the country. If you speak no Chinese at all, you may feel at first as if you've just landed on the moon.

For foreigners, there are two very different Chinas. Firstly there are the four principal cities of Beijing, Guangzhou, Shanghai and Shenzhen, where expatriates have formed communities and where some aspects of life are similar to that of major cities around the world (except that all signs are in Chinese script). And then there's the rest of this huge country, from provincial capitals down to rural hamlets, where life is more thoroughly 'Chinese' – altogether unlike anything you may have experienced before.

At the same time, **you** are very different from the Chinese. There aren't, as yet, that many foreigners in China and they comprise a tiny minority. Even in a major city, if you venture away from the main shopping areas and tourist haunts, you can expect to be stared at and commented on. Your Chinese colleagues may ask a lot of inquisitive, relentless and sometimes very personal questions as they attempt to get to know you. Add to this the noise and the crowds of people you encounter in most public places – for such a large country, China can be incredibly congested – and you may find it physically and mentally exhausting.

China has many extremes of climate and weather, and you mustn't underestimate the effects that these can have on you. The heat of summer can lead to a lack of energy, poor sleep and dehydration; in some parts of the country, temperatures can rise to 38°C (100°F) and the humidity makes it feel even hotter. In the subtropical south of China it rains almost incessantly – far more than in Manchester (England) – and while winters aren't that cold, you'll certainly feel chilly and damp. Housing in southern China often lacks good insulation and central heating is rare anywhere south of the Yellow River. Further north it's fitted as standard, but is sometimes linked to a local government control centre which switches it on in November and off

again in March, leaving you freezing if the weather changes early or late.

Wherever you live in China, you'll be faced with a host of challenges – such as a new job and a new home – which can be overwhelming before you even begin to encounter the local culture. You may have left a job in your home country where you were in a senior position, competent at your job and knew everyone with whom you worked. In China, you may feel that you're initially almost a trainee, and don't know any of your colleagues or the local way of doing things. The sensation that you're starting from scratch can be demoralising.

Even if you move to a major city, many things that you're used to and take for granted in your home country may not be available, e.g. certain kinds of food (decent cheese is a rare treat), opportunities to enjoy your favourite hobby or sport, and books and magazines in your own language. International television is limited – you cannot use a satellite dish to beam in foreign channels – and most cinemas show films dubbed into Chinese. And if you're used to a media that reports everything, including amusing critiques of the government, you may find Chinese newspapers stuffy in the extreme.

This lack of 'home comforts' can wear you down. You'll also need to cope without your local support network. At home you had a circle of friends, acquaintances, colleagues and possibly relatives you could rely on for help and support. In China there's no such network, which can leave you feeling lost. You can and will make friends. There's likely to be a welcome from other expatriates and the Chinese

will want to get to know you also, but first you must overcome the barriers of language and culture.

The degree of isolation you feel usually depends on how long you plan to spend in China and what you'll be doing there. If you're simply going on a short holiday, you may not even be aware of many of the cultural differences; although if you are, it will enhance your enjoyment and may save you from a few embarrassing or confusing moments. However, if you're planning a business trip or intend to spend an extended period in China – perhaps working, studying or even living there permanently – **it's essential to understand the culture, customs and etiquette at the earliest opportunity.**

> 'If you reject the food, ignore the customs, fear the religion and avoid the people, you might better stay at home.'
>
> James A. Michener (American author)

CULTURE SHOCK

Culture shock is the term used to describe the psychological and physical state felt by people when arriving in a foreign country or even moving to a new environment in their home country (where the culture and, in some cases, language may vary considerably by region and social class). Culture shock is a common experience among those who travel, work or study abroad, when in addition to adapting to new social rules and values, it's necessary to adjust to a different climate, food and dress. It manifests itself in a lack of direction

and the feeling of not knowing what to do or how to do things, or what's appropriate or inappropriate. You literally feel like a 'fish out of water'.

Culture shock is precipitated by the anxiety that results from losing all familiar rules of behaviour and cues to social intercourse – the thousand and one clues to accepted behaviour in everyday situations; for example, when to shake hands and what to say when you meet people; how to buy goods and services; how to use a cash machine (ATM) or the telephone; when to accept and refuse invitations; and when to take statements seriously and when not to. These cues, which may be words, gestures or facial expressions, are acquired in the course of a lifetime and are as much a part of our culture and customs as the language we speak and our beliefs. Our peace of mind and social efficiency depend on these cues, most of which are unconsciously learned and recognised.

The symptoms of culture shock are essentially psychological. However, there are also physical symptoms, including an increased incidence of minor illnesses (e.g. colds and headaches), and more serious psychosomatic illnesses brought on by depression. Culture shock can even cause physical pain. You shouldn't underestimate the consequences of culture shock, although the effects can be lessened if you accept the condition rather than deny it.

The high levels of pollution in many Chinese cities are compounded by damp and humidity, resulting in poor air quality. As a result the Chinese are prone to coughs and colds, and you will be also, particularly if you suffer from a respiratory disease such as asthma. Just walking down the street can leave you feeling breathless, and that's before you try to cross the road or drive your car.

Stages of Culture Shock

Severe culture shock – often experienced when moving to a country with a different language – usually follows a number of stages. The names of these may vary, as may the symptoms and effects, but a typical progression is as follows:

1. The first stage is commonly known as the 'honeymoon stage', and usually lasts until a few days or weeks after arrival (although it can last longer, particularly if you're insulated from the usual pressures of life). This stage is essentially a positive (even euphoric) one, when you find everything an exciting and interesting novelty. The feeling is similar to being on holiday or a short trip abroad, when you generally

experience only the positive effects of a change of culture (although this depends very much on where you're from and the country you're visiting).

2. The second (rejection or distress) stage is usually completely opposite to the first and is essentially negative and a period of crisis, as the initial excitement and 'holiday' feeling wears off and you start to cope with the real conditions of daily life – a life that is nothing like anything you've previously experienced. This can happen after only a few weeks, and is characterised by a general feeling of disorientation, confusion and loneliness. Physical exhaustion, brought on by a change of time zone, extremes of hot or cold, and the strain of having hundreds of settling in tasks to accomplish, is a symptom of this stage.

You may also experience regression, where you spend much of your time speaking your own language, watching television and reading newspapers from your home country, eating food from home and socialising with expatriates who speak your language. You could also spend a lot of time complaining about the host country and its culture – not a good idea in China where loudly-voiced negative comments about politics, in particular, can attract the unwanted attentions of the Public Security Bureau. Your home environment suddenly assumes a tremendous importance and is irrationally glorified. All difficulties and problems are forgotten, and only the good things back home are remembered.

What Foreigners Dislike About China:

● the people – there are just too many of them;

● having to bake your own bread – only an addict of tasteless white bread could stomach Chinese bread;

● pollution of the air, the water and even the land;

● spitting – by both men and women;

● alcohol – the local Chinese spirit, *baijiu*, is vile and getting people drunk is considered fun;

● the struggle to find somewhere peaceful;

● being stared at.

---

3. The third stage is often known as the 'flight' stage (because of the overwhelming desire to escape) and is usually the one that lasts the longest and is the most difficult to cope with.

During this period you may feel depressed and angry, as well as resentful towards the new country and its people. You may experience impatience and frustration at not being understood, and feelings of discontent, sadness and incompetence. These feelings are inevitable when you're trying to adapt to a new culture that's very different from that of your home country, and they're exacerbated by the fact that you can see nothing positive or good about the new country but focus exclusively on the negative aspects. You may become hostile and develop an aggressive attitude towards the country. Other people will sense this and you'll find it even more difficult to communicate: Chinese people, especially, react badly to confrontation, equating it with a loss of face on both sides, and may respond by doing their best to avoid you.

You may have difficulties with the language, your house, job or children's school and transportation – even simple tasks like shopping may be fraught with difficulties – and the fact that the local people are largely indifferent to these problems only makes matters worse. Even if they try to help, they may be unable to understand your concerns, and you conclude that they must be insensitive and unsympathetic to you and your problems.

Relinquishing your old customs and adopting those of your new culture is difficult and takes time. During that time there can be strong feelings of dissatisfaction. The period of adjustment can last as long as six months, although there are expatriates who adjust earlier and a few who never get over the 'flight' stage and are forced to return home.

> **'Small ills are the fountains of most of our groans. Men trip not on mountains, they stumble on stones.'**
> Confucius (Chinese philosopher)

4. The fourth (recovery or autonomy) stage is where you begin to integrate and adjust to the new culture, and accept the customs of the host country as simply another way of living. **The environment doesn't change – what changes is your attitude towards it.** You become more competent with the language, and you also feel more comfortable with local customs and can move around without feeling anxiety.

   You still have problems with some of the social cues and you won't understand everything people say (particularly colloquialisms and idioms). Nevertheless, you've largely adjusted to the new culture and start to feel more familiar with the country and your place in it – more at home – and begin to realise that it has its good as well as its bad points.

5. The fifth stage is termed 'reverse culture shock' and occurs when you return to your home country. You may find that many things have changed (you'll have changed, too) and that you feel like a foreigner in your own country. If you have been away for a long time and have become comfortable with the habits and customs of a new lifestyle, you may find that you no longer feel at ease in your homeland. Reverse culture shock can be difficult to deal with and some people find it impossible to re-adapt to their home country after living abroad for a number of years.

The above stages occur at different times depending on the individual and his circumstances, and everyone has his own way of reacting to them, with the result that some stages last longer and are more difficult to cope with than others, while others are shorter and easier to overcome.

Reducing the Effects

Experts agree that almost everyone suffers from culture shock and there's no escaping the phenomenon. However, its negative effects can be reduced considerably and there are a number of things you can do before leaving home and immediately on arrival.

● **Positive attitude:** The key to reducing the negative effects of culture shock is to have a positive attitude towards China (whether you're visiting or planning to live there). If you don't look forward to a trip or relocation, you should question why you're going. There's no greater guarantee of unhappiness in a foreign environment than taking your prejudices with you.

It's important when trying to adapt to a new culture to be sensitive to the locals' feelings, and try to put yourself in their shoes wherever possible, which will help you to understand why they react as they do. Bear in mind that they have a strong, in-bred cultural code, just as you do, and react in certain ways because they're culturally 'trained' to do so. If you find yourself frustrated by an aspect of the local culture or behaviour, the chances are that they'll be equally puzzled by yours.

Why Foreigners Love China

● the people, their attitude and friendliness;

● the strangeness of life compared to the West;

● respect for the elderly;

● the endless variety of the street markets;

● the pace of change, which is extraordinary;

● the beauty of the countryside, the ancient architecture and the women;

● the history;

● the food; you'll never get fat on a Chinese diet;

● the fact that even the most intolerant people learn to be patient.

- **Research:** Discover as much as possible about China before you go, so that your arrival and settling-in period doesn't spring as many surprises as it might otherwise. Reading up on China and its culture before you leave home will help you to familiarise yourself with the local customs and make the country and its people seem less strange on arrival. Being aware of many of the differences between China and your home country will make you better prepared to deal with them. You're less likely to be upset by real or imaginary cultural slights, or to offend the locals by making cultural gaffes. Being prepared for a certain amount of disorientation and confusion (or worse) makes it easier to cope with.

  This book will help enlighten you about what to expect. For further information there are literally hundreds of publications and websites about China (see **Appendices B** and **C**). Some websites provide access to expatriates already living in China who can answer questions and provide invaluable advice. There are also 'notice boards' and 'forums' on many websites where you can post messages and questions.

- **Visit China first:** If you're planning to live or work in China for a number of years, it's advisable to visit the country before making the leap, to gauge whether you think you would enjoy living there and be able to cope with the culture. If that's not possible, try to find people in your area who have visited China and talk to them about it. Some companies organise briefings for families who are about to relocate abroad. If you're planning to go to China to teach English, there are a number of websites dedicated to this which provide information and advice, and you can pose questions to people with experience of teaching there.

- **Learn Chinese:** Along with adopting a positive attitude,

overcoming the language barrier will be your greatest weapon in combating culture shock and making your time in China enjoyable. The ability to speak Chinese and to understand the local vernacular isn't just a useful tool that will allow you to buy what you need and find your way around, but is the key to understanding China and its culture. If you can speak Chinese, even at a basic level, your scope for making friends is immediately widened. You may not be a natural linguist, and learning Chinese can take time and requires a lot of motivation. However, with sufficient perseverance, virtually anyone can learn enough Chinese to participate in daily life.

Certainly the effort pays dividends, and expatriates who manage to overcome the language barrier find their experience in China is much richer and more rewarding than those who don't. The Chinese accept that their language is difficult for Westerners and are honoured that you have made an effort to learn it, and are far more receptive to your needs.

- **Be proactive:** Make an effort to get involved in your new culture and go out of your way to make friends. Join in the activities of the local people, from celebrating an important festival such as Chinese New Year to learning to fly a kite or pick up the intricacies of mah-jong. There are often local clubs where you can play sport or keep fit, be artistic, learn to cook local dishes, etc. Not only will this fill some of your spare time, giving you less time to miss home, but you'll also meet people and

make friends. If you feel that you cannot join a local club – perhaps because your Chinese isn't good enough – you can always participate in activities for expatriates, of which there are many in the major cities. Look upon a period spent in China as an opportunity to acquire new skills, attitudes and perspectives. A change of culture can also help you develop a better understanding of yourself and stimulate your creativity.

Talk to other expatriates: Although they may deny it, most expatriates have been through exactly what you're experiencing, and faced the same feelings of disorientation. Even if they cannot provide you with advice, it helps to know that you aren't alone and that it gets better over time. However, don't make the mistake of mixing only with expatriates, as this will alienate you from the local culture and make it much harder to integrate.

- **Keep in touch with home:** Keeping in touch with your family and friends at home and around the world by telephone, email and letters will help reduce and overcome the effects of culture shock. The internet has made the world much smaller, and if you have access to a computer you can read newspapers from your home country online and even talk to friends in another country face to face.

- **Be happy:** Don't rely on others to make you happy, or you won't find true and lasting happiness. There are things in life which only you can change. Every day we're surrounded by situations over which we have little or no control, but to moan about them only makes us unhappier. So be your own best friend and nurture your own capacity for happiness.

Culture shock is an unavoidable part of travelling, living and working abroad, but if you're aware of it and take steps to lessen its effects before you go and while you're abroad, the period of adjustment will be shortened and its negative and depressing consequences reduced.

FAMILIES IN CHINA

Family life may be completely different in China and relationships can become strained under the stress of adapting to culture shock. Your family may find itself in a completely new and possibly alien environment, your new home

may scarcely resemble your previous one (it may well be smaller and have different amenities) and the climate may differ dramatically from that of your home country. The stresses of adapting to a new environment can strain family relationships – particularly an environment that's as different as China. If possible, you should prepare your family for as many aspects of the new situation as you can, and explain to your children the differences they're likely to encounter, while at the same time dispelling their fears.

> **'And that's the wonderful thing about family travel; it provides you with experiences that will remain locked forever in the scar tissue of your mind.'**
>
> Dave Barry (American writer & humourist)

Culture shock can affect non-working spouses and children more than the partner who works. The husband (it's usually the husband) has his work to occupy him, and his activities may not differ much from what he was accustomed to at home. On the other hand, the wife has to operate in an environment that differs considerably from what she's used to. She'll find herself alone more often, a solitude intensified by the fact that there are no relatives or friends on hand. However, if you're aware that this may arise beforehand, you can act on it and reduce its effects. Working spouses should pay special attention to the needs and feelings of their non-working partners and children, as the success of a family relocation depends largely on the ability of the wife and children to adapt to the new culture.

The fact that so many people live in high-rise apartments, and the lack of a neighbourly culture – the Chinese tend to keep themselves to themselves, at least initially – can make life very isolated for the partner who's left at home. There may be no garden for the children to play in and no familiar shops nearby. In China, perhaps more than in other countries, a network of expatriates who've been through the same experiences is vital, and you should ensure that the home-based partner has someone to turn to when the other is at work.

Good communication between family members is essential, and you should make time to discuss your experiences and feelings, both as a couple and as a family. Questions should always be invited and, if possible, answered, particularly when asked by children who will be going through a culture shock of their own, in an unfamiliar school and with playmates of different nationalities. However difficult the situation may appear in the beginning, it helps to bear in mind that it's by no means unique and that most expatriate families experience exactly the same problems, and manage to triumph over them and thoroughly enjoy their stay in China.

A NEW LIFE

Although you may find some of the information in this chapter a bit daunting, don't be discouraged by the foregoing catalogue of depression and despair; the negative aspects of travelling and living abroad have only been highlighted in order to help you prepare for and adjust to a new life. The vast majority of people who travel and live abroad naturally experience occasional feelings of discomfort and disorientation, **but most never suffer the most debilitating effects of culture shock.**

As with settling in and making friends anywhere, even in your home country, the most important thing is to be considerate, kind, open, humble and genuine – qualities that are valued the world over. Selfishness, brashness, anger and arrogance will get you nowhere in China – or any other country. Losing your temper will almost invariably be counter-productive in China, where patience and politeness will get you further than any other approach. Treat Chinese people with respect and they'll do likewise. Remember that people see you as a representative of your country, therefore you should try to be a good ambassador. It will pay dividends.

The majority of expatriates living in China would say that, overall, they enjoy living there. A period spent in China is a wonderful way to enrich your life, broaden your horizons, make new friends and maybe even please your bank manager. We trust that this book will help you to avoid the pitfalls of life in China, and smooth your way to a happy and rewarding future in your new home.

'Twenty years from now, you'll be more disappointed by the things you didn't do than by the ones you did do. So throw off the bowlines. Sail away from the safe harbour. Catch the trade winds in your sails. Explore. Dream. Discover.'

Mark Twain (American author)

2.

WHO ARE THE CHINESE?

The past century has seen more changes for the Chinese people than occurred in the previous two millennia, from the downfall of the dynastic Emperors to a Republican government and then to the current communist regime, encompassing partial occupation by foreign trading companies in their concessions, invasion and occupation by the Japanese, civil war between the communists and the nationalists, the trauma and chaos of the Cultural Revolution, and then opening up to the outside world and subsequent transformation into one of the world's great economic powers.

> 'Let her sleep, for when she wakes, she will shake the world.'
> Napoleon on China

For the Chinese people it has been a tumultuous century, and yet they have taken it all in their stride. Today, China has become a factory to the whole world. Fortune 500 companies vie for the opportunity to establish manufacturing and research facilities in China, and for most of its inhabitants China has become a far more comfortable place than in living memory.

Poverty has been reduced, proportionately more so than anywhere else in the world; people eat better and health standards have been raised. People feel more prosperous, although improvements have come at a price. The search for ever-greater production has led to serious pollution, and the desire for money has led to widespread corruption. Both problems are being tackled by the government, but they're so widespread that it will be many years before they're overcome. The people, meanwhile, don't let these problems stop them from enjoying the fruits of their labour. They simply get on with life, patiently and with humour. They are a proud people and nothing can break their indomitable spirit.

A POTTED HISTORY

China has one of the longest recorded histories in the world. The following timeline is a brief record of the main events, both ancient and modern.

The Prehistoric Era

ca. 1.8 to 2m years BC – Traces of very early hominids found at Dragon Hill in Sichuan give rise to the belief that these remains are those of the first hominids to enter and live in China.

Demographics

Full country name: The People's Republic of China

Capital city: Beijing

Population: 1,338m, including 23m in Taiwan (July 2010 estimate) – China has the largest population of any country in the world.

Population density: 143 inhabitants per km² (370 per mi²). Beijing has a density of 14,000 inhabitants per km² (36,260 per mi²).

Largest cities: Shanghai 18m; Beijing 17m; Guangzhou 12m; Shenzhen 8.6m; Tiajin 8.2m; Chongqing 7.5m. There are 61 cities with a population exceeding 1m.

Ethnic groups: There are 56 in all. The Han Chinese number some 1,230m and make up just under 92 per cent of the population, while the largest ethnic 'minorities' are the Zhuang (16.2m), Manchu (10.7m), Hui (9.8m), Miao (8.9m) and Uyghur (8.4m). The smallest minority are the Lhoba, of whom there are just 2,965.

Number of foreign residents: About 500,000, according to official figures. The largest expatriate groups are the Japanese (41 per cent), Americans (22 per cent) and Koreans (19 per cent). There are relatively few British expats living in China.

State religion: None, although religion is no longer forbidden.

Most followed religions: Buddhism, Taoism and Confucianism, followed by Islam and Christianity.

670,000 to 400,000BC – Human skulls and other bones – known as 'Peking Man' – discovered in 1923 at Zhoukoudian, outside Beijing. They clearly showed the presence of man and his hunting abilities at that time.

6,000BC – Excavations at Banpo near Xi'an uncover proof of the arrival of an agrarian society and the domestication of animals.

The Great Dynasties

2100-1600BC – The start of the first dynasty, the Xia dynasty, led by Yu the Great.

1600-1100BC – The arrival of the Shang dynasty during which the first written records appear, and people master the arts of working bronze and jade for both decoration and weapons.

1100-221BC – Society begins to form itself into cities, which gain earth ramparts under the Zhou dynasty, initially based near present-day Xi'an. The Emperor moves to a new capital in Luoyang in 771BC. This period sees the birth of Taoism and Confucianism, together with Legalism, a philosophy which exalts the power of the law. These three concepts still influence the way that the Chinese think.

221-207BC – The Qin dynasty is led by Qin Shi Huang, the emperor who's guarded by the famous terracotta warriors discovered in 1974 near Xi'an. The name *Qin*, which is pronounced 'Chin', is believed by scholars to be the source of the name China.

The Qin dynasty was the first to govern a truly united country. The Qin oversaw the start of a standard national currency and the creation of a revised system of writing using characters that still exists, little changed, today. During its rule, the earliest version of the Great Wall was built.

206BC-207AD – The reign of the Han dynasty. During this 400-year period of stability, the Hans create the various institutions and bureaucracies that will form the basis of the next 2,000 years of civilisation. Today, the vast majority of Chinese believe themselves to be descended from the Han.

207-581 – During the time of the Three Kingdoms, between 208 and 280AD, the leaders of the three states, the Wei, the Shu and the Wu, fight for supremacy. This period is followed by multiple short-lived dynasties, and China is racked by civil war for close on 400 years.

581-618 – Following a coup, the Sui dynasty takes control and re-unites the country. A massive new capital is constructed near Xi'an (the largest city in the world at that time), bureaucracy is simplified and a new legal code established. But the Sui dynasty is unpopular, and in 618 the Emperor Yang is assassinated.

618-960 – The era of the great Tang dynasty. During its almost 350 years of dominance, Chinese culture reaches new heights in art, literature, music and porcelain; the bureaucracy is reshaped, with entrance and promotion based upon merit rather than birth, and the current system of provinces and counties is established. During this time, China expands its influence into the regions and countries now known as Xinjiang, Tibet, Korea, Japan and Vietnam. However, the golden age doesn't last and after a period of anarchy and disunity known as the Time of Five Dynasties and Ten Kingdoms, the Song dynasty is formed.

960-1215 – Initially based in Kaifeng at the head of the Grand Canal, the northern Song emperors are forced to move south to Hangzhou following incursions by the Jurchen

Emperor Taizong (Tang Dynasty)

(Manchu) tribes from the north.
Once in Hangzhou, they establish the southern Song dynasty and China's cultural achievements increase, with the invention of gunpowder, the magnetic compass and moveable type printing, as well as great advances in agriculture, mining and porcelain manufacture. Confucianism becomes dominant and a new type of government official arrives: the scholar.

1215-1368 – Genghis Khan makes good the Mongolians' long-standing threat to invade China. He attacks, breaches the Great Wall and captures Beijing in 1215 to commence the Yuan dynasty, although it takes another 64 years for the Mongolians to overcome all resistance. On Genghis Khan's death, first his son and later his grandson Kublai Khan continue the expansion of the Mongol empire, which at its zenith stretches from Hungary and the Ukraine to Persia, and as far east as Korea and Vietnam. Trade routes to Europe by both land and sea are opened up and foreign traders welcomed to China, but the

people resent having foreign leaders and rebels seize the throne in 1368.

1368-1644 – Porcelain and furniture design reaches its apex during the Ming dynasty. Chinese ships explore the Indian Ocean, opening routes to East Africa and India, until the Emperor Hongwu commands them to stop any further exploration – the reason is unclear, although Imperial funds may have been needed to fight Mongolian invasions – and a long period of isolation from the rest of the world begins.

> **The Ming was the last great Han dynasty, and oversaw the building of some of China's greatest symbols such as the Forbidden City in Beijing. The Ming also supervised the rebuilding and strengthening of the Great Wall. Much of the wall which tourists stroll along today was built or repaired by the Ming.**

1644 – The Manchus invade from Manchuria and found the Qing dynasty. Among their many orders is one forcing all men to adopt their hairstyle – a shaven head and a long ponytail (or queue) at the back – or face the death penalty. Many thousands are killed for refusing to cut their hair.

1683 – Taiwan is annexed and declared a part of Fujian province.

1751 – Tibet is re-occupied and declared an autonomous protectorate, and the area called East Turkestan becomes a separately administered region renamed as Xinjiang.

1840 – Sales of tea and other goods from China to Britain far exceed Chinese interest in British products, leading to a

Genghis Khan

Qianlong Emperor

effectively ruling the country, at a time when a disintegrating China desperately needs a government with vision.

1894 – War breaks out with Japan, and China is humiliated. The peace settlement includes the handing over of Taiwan as part of reparations. The Japanese rename the island Formosa and occupy it until 1945.

1898 – The Germans are granted a concession over Qingdao. This indignity is one of the events fuelling an anti-foreign uprising known as the Boxer Rebellion, which in 1900 culminates in a siege of the foreign legations in Beijing. An international relief force finally breaks the siege, and the Empress Dowager Cixi flees to Xian.

The Republican Era

1908 – The Empress Dowager Cixi dies, and a two-year-old boy named Puyi is declared China's last Emperor.

1911 – Following a series of strikes originating in Wuhan, a nationwide uprising topples the Qing dynasty. A provisional Republican government is set up under the leadership of Sun Yat-sen, but military commander Yuan Shikai forces him from office and makes preparations to declare himself as a new emperor.

1916 – Yuan Shikai dies, and the country erupts into civil war as various warlords fight over territory. Sun Yat-sen returns and establishes control over southern China under his Nationalist Kuomintang party.

1921-27 – The Chinese Communist Party (the CPC) is formed in Shanghai. The communists and nationalists work together to suppress the warlords until Sun Yat-sen's death in 1925. Chiang Kai Shek becomes head of the Kuomintang.

vast trade imbalance in China's favour. In response, Britain begins to import cheap opium into China from its Indian colonies, feeding an increasing demand. Chinese attempts to stop this trade lead to the Opium Wars (1840-1858), with British gunboats shelling Chinese ports. China is eventually forced to cede Hong Kong Island and open up certain cities as Treaty Ports, where foreigners are allowed to reside and trade freely. One of these is Shanghai. Payment to Britain of a huge financial indemnity bankrupts the country, creating widespread poverty and popular discontent.

1850 – The anti-dynastic Taiping Rebellion breaks out in Guanxi and sweeps through the centre of China. An estimated 20m are killed in what is probably the most bloody civil conflict in history, until it's finally put down by combined Qing and British army forces in 1864. By this time the vain, arch-conservative Empress Dowager Cixi is

1927-33 – A general strike organised by the CPC breaks out in Shanghai, brutally suppressed by a militia raised by the Kuomintang. The leaders of the CPC are forced to flee the city. Civil war commences between the two parties, with the nationalists repeatedly mounting extermination campaigns against the communists.

1933 – Japan takes Manchuria from China, setting up the puppet state of Manchukuo under the last Chinese emperor, Puyi.

1934 – Under threat of annihilation, communist forces – the Red Army – retreat from eastern China in a series of withdrawals aptly named the Long March. During the retreat, talented guerrilla fighter Mao Zedong becomes head of the CPC, deposing an old order led by Russian advisors. After a year on the move, the surviving bands of communists find sanctuary together in remote, rural Shaanxi province, where they build a power base among the local peasantry.

1936 – Chiang Kai Shek ignores the Japanese occupation of Manchuria and instead focuses on fighting the Communist Red Army. However, Kuomintang general Zhang Xueliang, a Manchurian infuriated at the invasion of his homeland, kidnaps Chiang in what becomes known as the Xi'an Incident. Following mediation with CPC power-broker Zhou Enlai, Chiang is forced to agree to a United Front with the communists against the Japanese.

1937 – The Japanese stage an incident near the Marco Polo Bridge, declare war and invade much of eastern China, occupying most of the coastal areas and adjoining territory. The nationalists withdraw west up the Yangtze from their capital at Nanjing, eventually establishing their headquarters far inland at Chongqing in Sichuan. Meanwhile the Red Army remains based in Shaanxi and, finding the north of the country almost devoid of any government, the communists occupy it. The truce between the two Chinese governments is held for the time being, with the US providing supplies to the Chinese armies by flying them in over the Himalayas.

1945 – The end of the Second World War and the defeat of Japan. Almost immediately, fighting breaks out between the nationalists and the Red Army and develops into a full scale civil war.

1949 – The communists finally drive Chiang and the Kuomintang leadership to Taiwan, along with nearly 2m supporters, the entire stock of gold from the Chinese Treasury and many of the cultural relics from the Forbidden City. In Tian'anmen Square, on October 1st, Mao declares the foundation of the People's Republic of China.

> '**A revolution is not a dinner party, or writing an essay, or painting a picture or doing embroidery; it cannot be so refined, so leisurely and gentle, so temperate, kind, courteous, restrained and magnanimous. A revolution is an insurrection, an act of violence by which one class overthrows another.**'
>
> Mao Zedong

The Socialist Era

1949 – China is still torn by civil war, its resources exhausted, but people are full of hope for a new era as the

CPC sets about putting the country to rights. Drugs, gambling and prostitution vanish overnight and women are given equal rights with men. The peasants, for the first time, have their own land to cultivate and people feel in control of their destinies; they set to work with a will. Soviet Russia offers the new regime support. The US, meanwhile, bitterly opposed to communism, offers its backing to Chiang in Taiwan.

1950 – War breaks out in Korea as the communist North invades the South. The US sends troops to assist South Korea under the aegis of the United Nations, and the North Korean army is driven back to the Yalu River, the border with China, at which point the UN's General MacArthur threatens to invade China. Mao responds by sending troops to assist the North Korean army. By sheer dint of numbers, the UN forces are pushed back to the original border between North and South Korea on the 38th parallel and an armistice is declared.

1951 – Following the occupation of Tibet by Chinese forces, a rebellion breaks out in Lhasa. It's quickly suppressed by the Red Army and, after a second unsuccessful uprising in 1959 the Dalai Lama flees to India to continue his campaign for an independent Tibet from a safer distance.

1957 – China is now stable and the economy in better order. Mao decides to seek out the people's thoughts and asks them to express their feelings through the Hundred Flowers Campaign. The widespread critical response to the communist government is not at all to his liking and leads to the arrest and punishment of those who had dared to speak out.

1958 – Mao implements his Great Leap Forward, a scheme to collectivise farmers into vast communes and turn every village and township into a steel-producing unit, melting down any available iron, including pots, pans and tools, in an effort to show that China can equal steel production in the West. It's a disaster: the people have their newly-earned land torn from them once again, while the melting down of tools and farm equipment means that crops are neglected. This, combined with consecutive droughts in 1959 and 1960, results in mass starvation, while the steel is so badly produced as to be useless. It's only the intervention of Deng Xiaoping, who introduces a limited free market for surplus crops, which gets matters under control again. Meanwhile Mao, side-lined and discredited, looks for ways to regain his grasp on the CPC.

1966-76 – Mao's Great Proletarian Cultural Revolution. Its objectives are to get rid of the four olds: old ideas, old culture, old customs and old habits. The students love it; forming a quasi-military unit called the Red Guard, they

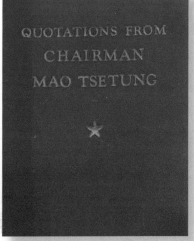

Little Red Book

set about destroying anything related, however remotely, to capitalism, the West or the Soviet Union (which had recently withdrawn support for the CPC). Teachers are attacked, books burned, all secondary schools and universities closed, temples ransacked and shops selling anything even remotely Western destroyed. Within a year the orgy of destruction is so out of hand that the army is instructed by Mao to arrest some of the Red Guard's ringleaders and to send millions to the countryside for re-education, but the core beliefs of the Cultural Revolution live on, particularly in the cities. As Mao becomes increasingly frail during his final years, some sort of stability starts to return under the guidance of Zhou Enlai, and links to the outside world are resumed.

1971 – China is admitted to the United Nations (replacing Taiwan as the legitimate 'China'). The following year, US president Richard Nixon flies to Beijing and meets with Mao. Restrictions in trade between the US and China are gradually lifted, and diplomatic relations eventually re-established in 1979.

> **'Every communist must grasp the truth. Political power grows out of the barrel of a gun.'**
>
> Mao Zedong

1976 – A massive earthquake rocks Taiyuan and over a quarter of a million die. Many people see this as an omen and, later the same year, Mao dies. Within a short time, the Gang of Four – Mao's wife and three senior Communist Party officials who, together, are held largely responsible for the chaos of the Cultural Revolution – are arrested.

1977 – Deng Xiaoping gently takes the reins of power. Pragmatic rather than dogmatic, his goal is a successful China and he doesn't mind picking other countries' brains for ideas as he starts to open up the country to the rest of the world, setting up free-trade zones and encouraging enterprise. It's a time of upheaval, but also one of great hope as people become capitalists within the framework of a communist state.

1979 – Concerned by a rapidly growing population, the government imposes the controversial one-child policy. Urban couples are limited to having only one child, and boys are often favoured, leading to the abandonment and even killing of many baby girls.

1989 – Troops open fire on students demonstrating in support of democracy in Beijing's Tian'anmen Square and many protestors and bystanders are killed. The death toll ranges from a couple of hundred to many thousands, depending on the source. Iconic images of 'Tank Man', a lone student standing in the path of the army tanks, are beamed around the world, but while they ignite anger in the West, many Chinese are less sympathetic to the students' demands. As a result of the incident, the government tightens up political control while accelerating economic reforms.

1992 – The Chinese tiger continues to roar as the International Monetary Fund (IMF) rates its economy the world's third-largest behind the US and Japan.

1993 – Deng steps down, leaving the legacy of a China firmly set on the road to modernisation. His position as Party Chairman is taken over by Jiang Zemin, ex-Mayor of Shanghai and very much one of the old guard, but development continues under his leadership. In particular, work begins on the Three

Three Gorges Dam, Yangtze River, Sandouping

Gorges Dam, a huge hydro-electric project across the Yangtze River with the aim of creating cleaner energy but at the expense of cultural artefacts and the local ecology.

1997 – Deng Xiaoping dies, and separatist bombs in Xinjiang on the day of his funeral leave over 90 people dead. In the same year, Britain hands control of Hong Kong back to the Chinese.

1999 – The accidental NATO bombing of the Chinese embassy in Belgrade, during the Balkan conflict, does little to improve US-China relations. Macau becomes a part of China once more but, like Hong Kong, it enjoys a high degree of autonomy under Deng's 'one country, two systems' principle.

2001 – China is accepted into the World Trade Organisation and wins the right to host the 2008 Olympic Games.

2002 – The Chinese Football team debuts at the World Cup Finals in Japan and South Korea but fails to score a goal.

2003 – Jiang Zemin steps down as leader and is followed by Hu Jintao. China is hit by the SARS virus. Scientists send China's first manned spacecraft into orbit.

2005 – Relations falter with Japan, but improve with Russia and Taiwan.

Taiwan's National Party leader visits China, the first time nationalists and communists have met since 1949.

2006 – As work on the Three Gorges Dam nears completion, environmentalists express concern over the country's high levels of pollution – China has overtaken the US as the world's largest emitter of greenhouse gases.

2008 – A massive earthquake in Sichuan province kills tens of thousands. Anti-Chinese protests in Tibet threaten, but fail, to disrupt Beijing's Olympic Games.

2009-2010 – In spite of concerns over the global economic crisis, China continues to forge ahead. China now manufactures more cars than any other single country; it has overtaken Germany to become the world's largest exporter and has the second-largest economy after the US (having overtaken Japan). Poverty has been massively reduced and health has improved significantly. As mass celebrations take place to celebrate 60 years of communist Power, China has made astonishing progress in the three decades since Mao's death and is now a world power to be reckoned with.

> **'Poverty is not socialism. To get rich is glorious.'**
> Deng Xiaoping

THE PEOPLE

For over two thousand years, the Chinese people's guiding philosophy and moral code has been based almost entirely upon the teachings of Confucius, which sets a social structure of obligations leading down from the ruler to the lowliest peasant. There have been regular attempts to purge his memory – including under the first emperor, Qin Shi Huang, and during Mao's Cultural Revolution – but so firmly has Confucianism become embedded in the Chinese psyche that all have proved unsuccessful.

Today, buoyed by the feeling that their country is seen by the world as a new powerhouse, most people are happy. Those younger than 35 have never known a time when daily life hasn't been improving, and all they see are the glittering opportunities that present-day China presents. Those aged 40 to 55 remember the Cultural Revolution, but with surprising fondness, as an exciting time when youth ruled the roost and old traditionalists were there to be mocked. It's only people aged 55 or older who remember the gross injustices that happened daily during the Cultural Revolution; the need to never, ever, let slip an unguarded word, the continual policy reversals and the lack of food. In contrast, they now live in a new, dynamic China, where things that they had never even dreamed of are commonplace. It's a world that many aren't comfortable with, and they're less optimistic than the young. As during the early days of the revolution, they tend to keep themselves

to themselves, constantly saving for the rainy day that they believe to be just around the corner.

People's attitudes may differ but Chinese cultural roots are deep, and there are some characteristics which cross generations and are common to many Chinese people. The main characteristics are described below.

Family Values

To understand the Chinese, it's necessary to understand the importance that they place on family relationships, Confucianism's strongest legacy. In the US, if someone wants to set up a business, they choose a partner and employees by finding people with the necessary skills and experience. They may, in time, become friendly with their partner and workforce, but it will always be a business relationship. This isn't the case in China, where people almost always go into business with a family member or someone who has a long history of friendship with the family. Their first employees will also be family members, no matter how remote the relationship, or long-standing friends.

Unlike in the West, with its cult of the individual, the Chinese family unit has always been largely mutually dependent; if someone wins the lottery or loses his business, his whole family shares his joy or shame. Family bonds are particularly strong when it comes to caring for elderly relatives. Compared with the West, where age is virtually a sin, old age is respected in China. Grandparents are revered, and sons regard it as their filial duty to ensure that their parents' life in retirement is a happy one and that they want for nothing. A common sight is that of middle-aged men and women pushing their parents around in wheelchairs. The elderly aren't packed off to an old folk's home when they become infirm, but move in with their son and his wife and are made to feel important. Grandparents develop a particularly strong connection with their grandchildren, and are a constant companion and teacher during a child's earliest years.

Guanxi

When looking for work or dealing with bureaucratic issues, the importance of knowing the 'right' people (connections) is paramount in China. The Chinese set great store by 'knowing someone who can help'. This is called *guanxi* which literally means 'connections'. People who can offer you *guanxi* may be relatives, friends who owe you a favour, or people who see that having you in their debt could be useful in the future. As China looks to the West and people are judged more and more on merit, *guanxi* is becoming a little less important, but it's still a considerable force and having good *guanxi* can often be the essential

requirement for success – even in a court of law.

> Although most Chinese look alike to foreigners, e.g. most have the same straight black hair and brown eyes, each has an individual and singular appearance. The idea that all Chinese people are inscrutable is another Western myth. Like any other race, they're capable of a wide range of facial expressions.

Intrusiveness

Almost the first thing that many Chinese will ask you is, 'How old are you?' or 'How much do you earn?' They're not being rude. Out of ordinary curiosity, Chinese people ask each other questions on subjects that are rarely brought up in the West, and they don't mind if you ask them similar questions. Go out for a meal with a group of Chinese and see how, at the end of the meal, the diners ask the host how much the meal cost – and he tells them.

Personal facts about foreigners are a source of great interest to most Chinese, and they see no reason why they shouldn't ask you the same questions they ask each other. With the family being so central to Chinese life, total strangers may strike up a conversation by asking whether you're married, and if not, why not. If you say you're married, they ask how many children you have. Should the answer be none, they'll blithely ask why.

Face

Much is written about this, and it's a fact that the Chinese don't like to

lose face or self-respect – although neither do most people in the West. Certainly the Chinese aren't nearly as obsessive as the Japanese about this, but nonetheless it's helpful if you can avoid situations where the aim is to make the Chinese person back down. Although most Chinese individuals are fairly relaxed about face, this isn't the case with business people or with the present ruling party. Face is very important to both.

Never lose your temper and/or say harsh things to a Chinese person in front of other people, Chinese or foreign. Not only will he lose face (and probably never forgive you), but so will you. If you really must reprimand or criticise someone, only do so when you're alone and out of both earshot and sight of others.

Face can also make it difficult to extract a 'straight' answer. If a Chinese person feels that the answer sought is one that would be unwelcome to the questioner, he may well prevaricate rather than say something negative. The Chinese don't like to rock the boat.

Self

As a general rule, Chinese people are polite and friendly, but courtesy is often reserved for people they know and they're in no way deferential to strangers. Living in a society with 1.3bn others cannot be easy, and politeness tends to break down in public, particularly in crowded situations, when people push and shove to hang on to their place. They often appear oblivious to others. A man may travel up an escalator, step off and stop right there, blocking everyone else's path, while teenagers walk three abreast along a narrow street and travellers crowd around a ticket office. The Chinese don't set out to be deliberately rude, but in such situations their sense of 'self' is paramount. It doesn't help that they're largely immune to the concept of personal space which Westerners hold so dear.

Chinese people are especially self-assertive on the roads, where the rule is 'every man for himself'. If you slow down to let someone change lanes ahead of you, the driver behind you will almost certainly sound his horn in annoyance. Similarly, no one waits at a pedestrian crossing to let people cross the road unless they're forced to stop by the sheer weight of the crowd.

> One unusual courtesy the Chinese have involves the passing of money, paper, a book or a business card to another person. To be polite, this should always be offered using both hands.

Privacy

The Chinese are often accused by Westerners of having no sense of privacy, but this reaction is mainly influenced by their attitude to bodily functions, in particular using the toilet, about which they're anything but coy. Most foreigners are shocked by their first visit to a Chinese public toilet, which is alarmingly public with either waist-high doors or partitions or none at all. The Chinese are very open about the subject: everyone knows that Chairman Mao suffered from constipation as he didn't keep it a secret. Go to a doctor with almost any internal problem and immediately you'll be asked, '*Ni dabien hao ma?*' ('Are you defecating well?').

Yet Chinese people do have a strong sense of privacy, particularly when it comes to their own home. It is a rare honour to be invited to someone's house, one which is normally only extended to family and very close friends. And this desire for privacy in their personal lives extends to their cars, a large number of which have blacked-out windows.

Harmony

Harmony is one of the tenets of the *I Ching*, one of China's old classic texts, and of Traditional Chinese Medicine, and the present government has expressed a wish for China to be a harmonious society. This builds on one of the strongest threads of the Chinese psyche: generally, they like conformity and prefer not to make themselves conspicuous. They aren't an aggressive people.

Art & Nature

The Chinese are artistic in many aspects of their lives, such as their script and their cooking, while they look to nature for treatments and cures. Both are important aspects of Chinese life. Everything from their porcelain to their gardens reflects their artistic nature; a copperplate Chinese script is far more attractive than a Western typeface, and graffiti in Chinese looks like a work of art rather than a splash of protest. The importance of nature is seen in their approach to medicine, which treats the body as a whole natural entity, and to food – bought fresh, cooked fresh – as you may expect from a nation with its roots so firmly embedded in agriculture.

Lucky Numbers

The Chinese aren't particularly superstitious, although they do put great store by certain numbers. The number 13 isn't considered unlucky but four, a word which is pronounced like the word for death, is avoided as much as possible. Numbers six, eight and nine are all considered lucky: six represents good fortune, eight indicates wealth and nine promises longevity. If you see a car with an 8888 number plate you can be sure that the owner has paid a fortune for it, possibly well over 100,000 RMB.

Noise

The Chinese seem to have a far higher tolerance of noise than Westerners. They love firecrackers, and the evening of Chinese New Year sounds like Armageddon. However, it's the loud conversations that amaze. Witness two men shouting at each other, face to face, and you expect a fight to break out at any minute, although they're probably only discussing the price of dumplings down the road. Even the opening of a new shop demands the hiring of a noisy 'band' of drummers and loud music.

Spitting & Hawking

Although now officially banned in some cities and increasingly the subject of criticism, spitting remains a common habit in China, for both men and women. Although not as prevalent as it was a decade ago, spitting seems to be due to a combination of the pepper and garlic in many people's diet, smoking and pollution, and you'll see it everywhere, in the street, on buses and trains, in the office and even in shops. Many taxi drivers find that stopping at traffic lights provides the perfect opportunity for them to open the door, lean out, and let loose spittle onto the road. Hawking, or clearing the throat noisily, sometimes as a precursor to spitting, is also common. To have someone walking behind you, making the most appalling noises in his throat, is unnerving to say the least. The best solution is to pause, look in a shop window and let them pass, praying that they don't let fly as they go by.

SENSE OF HUMOUR

Far from being inscrutable, the Chinese love a joke and it's a common sight to see a couple of old dears laughing in the street. Much Chinese humour is based on words with two meanings and they love 'cross talk' (*xiangsheng*), a form of repartee not dissimilar to the banter of comic duos such as Morecambe and Wise. The most popular exponent of cross talk is Zhou Ben Shan, and he's funny even if you cannot understand everything he says. He has many imitators.

As well as cross talk, the Chinese also love slapstick and ridiculous humour; Benny Hill and Mr Bean are both popular. Irony is lost on the Chinese, probably in translation. Chinese jokes tend to be a bit laboured. They do have risqué jokes – known as yellow jokes, rather than blue – but don't try telling a dirty joke to a Chinese audience, as their 'yellow' humour is quite mild and you may shock them.

> A typical Chinese joke and good example of *xiangsheng*: Wang was talking to Zhang and he said "Thank you" to Zhang. Zhang said "Thank you, too" to which Wang replied "Thank you, three." Immediately Zhang said "What are you thanking me for?" to which Wang responded "Thank you, five."

CHILDREN

Children have always been pampered by the Chinese, but the application of the 'one-child policy', effectively restricting many urban couples to having no more than one child, means that the only son or daughter is often spoilt. These 'little dragons' are among the few obese people in China; a result of too frequent excursions to fast food emporiums and their parents' inability to say no. If both parents are at work, the child is left with grandparents and is spoilt by them, too. Despite this, Chinese children are generally well behaved, helpful, respectful and diligent, although a few deserve the label 'little Emperor'.

Officially, couples are only allowed to have a single child, but while this is fairly rigidly enforced, there are

diverse range of people. Many pick up basic Chinese more quickly than adults; and in a world that's increasingly trading with China, this could be useful in the future. Not only that, but they'll have lived in a place where a little pocket money goes a long way.

Foreign parents soon discover than most Chinese children aren't 'wrapped in cotton wool' as they increasingly are in the West. Safety barriers are often non-existent, and just crossing the road is hazardous. As a result, spending their early years in China can lead to children becoming independent and self-reliant adults.

loopholes: ethnic minorities can have as many children as they like; if two 'only children' marry, they may have two children; and if a farming couple have a daughter, they're allowed to have a second child in the hope that it will be a son. Some couples find out their unborn child's sex during the pregnancy and then opt for a termination if it's a girl; there have also been well documented cases of baby girl children being killed or abandoned. As a result, there's now an imbalance in the numbers of young men and young women that will inevitably lead to an unnaturally large proportion of men unable to find a wife, as well as increased pressure on a new generation of 'only' children with no siblings who must look after their ageing parents.

Foreign children can benefit greatly from living in China. They learn that there's another world beyond their home environment, and how to get on with a

CLASS SYSTEM

There is no old money in China. The country where the peasants were once ruled over by Emperors and feudal lords disappeared forever in the early 20th century to be replaced by a society of equals, even if some were more equal than others. The nearest China has to an establishment or class system are the descendants of the Communist Party's hierarchy. They are treated with considerable respect – and often benefit from *guanxi* when it comes to finding a good job – but not to the degree that they are in North Korea, where a new dynasty of Emperors is emerging.

There is plenty of 'new' money in China, as the economic expansion of recent years has created a growing number of people who have suddenly acquired vast wealth and are struggling to handle it. Members of China's *nouveau riche* aren't a pretty sight. Frequently government employees, their 'girlfriends' or businessmen who have got lucky – through talent or corruption – they flaunt their newfound wealth in the most obvious ways, driving BMWs (particularly the more ostentatious four-wheel-drive models), smoking ludicrously expensive 'luxury' cigarettes and eating in exclusive restaurants. A whole industry has grown up to satisfy the demand for exorbitantly-priced 'luxury' goods for their consumption. As a result, China has become the second-largest market in the world for designer clothes and accessories, a trend that shows no sign of abating.

Ordinary Chinese people loathe the *nouveau riche*, and each time one gets his come-uppance they're delighted.

ATTITUDES TO WOMEN

Since 1949, women have officially been treated as equals to men, and salaries for a job are the same for both sexes. In China, you see women taxi drivers, bus drivers, labourers and masons, and women share agricultural work in the fields. There are also plenty of women running businesses and gaining high positions in the professions, such as law and medicine, although there are fewer female politicians and no women in the Communist's Party's high-ranking Politburo. However, equality has its downside: old-fashioned courtesies, such as saying 'ladies first' or opening a door for a woman, are no longer the custom. Chinese men really **do** see women as their equals: not as strong in some ways, perhaps, but otherwise the same. It's as common to see a woman pedalling a bicycle with her husband or boyfriend on the carrier as it is to see a boy carrying a female passenger.

> **'Women hold up half the sky.'**
> Mao Zedong

ATTITUDES TO MINORITIES

The majority of China's minorities live in autonomous regions, close to the country's borders, where they have (partial) control over their own government. Many speak their own language. There are some 56 separate ethnic minorities, which include:

- **Hui:** a Muslim people descended from the Persians, Islamic Arabs and Mongols, they're probably the most widespread of the ethnic minorities. The largest groups live in the northern Ningxia autonomous region, but there are also many in Beijing and in Gansu, Hebei, Henan, Heilongjiang, Jilin, Liaoning, Qinghai, Shandong, Shanxi, Tianjin, Xinguang and Yunnan provinces.

- **Tibetans:** most live in the Tibet autonomous region (annexed by China in 1950) and neighbouring Qinghai province. China has taken considerable steps to open up the country and modernise its cities and education system, and while there has been friction between the Tibetans and the Chinese, most visitors find Tibet to be a model (though remote) and peaceful community.

- **Uyghur:** a Turkic people, the Uyghur live principally in the Xinjiang Uyghur autonomous region; this was called East Turkestan until some way into the 20th century. They are now found in most parts of the country, often running restaurants serving Muslim food and speaking their own language, which bears a strong family resemblance to Arabic and Turkish.

- **Zhuang:** although they live mainly in the Guanxi Zhuang autonomous region, many are based in Guangdong, Guizhou, Hunan and Yunnan. They are distantly related to the people of Thailand and Laos.

- **Manchus:** originally from Manchuria in the northeast of China, they still live principally in the northern provinces of Heilongjiang, Jilin and Liaoning. Their religious beliefs include shamanism, a way of communicating with the spirit world.

- **Miao:** famous for their ornate hats, the Maio are one of the largest minorities in the southwest. They originally came from Hunan and Guizhou, but now live mainly in the Guangxi Zhuang autonomous region and in Sichuan and Yunnan provinces.

- **Mongols:** these are the descendants of the warring hordes who swept down from Mongolia to conquer China under Genghis Khan. For many centuries, China ruled Mongolia but in 1912, when China became a republic for the first time, Outer Mongolia became independent while Inner Mongolia remained within China. This autonomous region is where most Mongols now live. All Mongolians share a common language, and the written version is singularly lovely.

China is dominated by the Han Chinese, who account for over 90 per cent of the population, and feel that they treat the remainder very well. The government builds new schools, railways and roads for them, funds the refurbishment of their public buildings and temples, and allows them to practice their religions – albeit state-approved versions of those religions. Moreover, ethnic minorities are among those exempt from the one-child family planning policy. The Han often feel that the minorities are ungrateful for all that has been done for them. Many of the ethnic minorities see things differently. They appreciate the material gains that Beijing has provided and the opportunities for their children's education, but they also see the Han swamping their towns, owning most of the shops and businesses, and occupying positions of power within local government.

There is some truth to both viewpoints. The Han do dominate local economies and government, partly because they're better tuned in than the local indigenous people to the thinking of the central government in Beijing, but also because they tend to be sharper operators. It is a difficult dichotomy, and probably only time will smooth the relationships, although (hopefully) without any loss of identity for the minorities. Certainly, China is a more harmonious country than many Westerners believe it to be; despite occasional serious riots in both Tibet and Xinjiang, these areas are far more stable than the Western media reports.

> 'Throughout the ages, Chinese have had only two ways of looking at foreigners. We either look up to them as Gods or down on them as wild animals.'
>
> Lu Xun (writer & social critic)

ATTITUDES TO FOREIGNERS

The Chinese, both officials and ordinary citizens, are courteous towards Westerners, particularly to those that fit their image of someone from the West, i.e. white skin, blue eyes and fair hair. Marriages with Westerners aren't uncommon. Many people go to quite extraordinary lengths to help a foreigner, although not to the extent of compromising their privacy. Chinese people may entertain you at a restaurant but not in their home, but don't feel offended as they act the same towards their Chinese friends,

They can be less accommodating towards foreigners from other Asian countries and from Africa. In particular, the Chinese have never forgiven the Japanese for many of the things that happened during the Japanese occupation of China between 1933 and 1949, and some older people loathe them. There's also animosity towards ethnic Chinese who have taken up citizenship of another country. The patriotic Chinese are frequently critical of them, calling them 'bananas' – yellow on the outside and white inside – and even accusing them of being traitors to China.

Staring

Outside major cities such as Beijing and Shanghai, and places on the tourist trail such as Xi'an, foreigners are a rarity. In small towns and villages, people often stare and call out to get your attention; you may hear someone say loudly to their family '*laowai*' or '*waiguoren*' – both mean 'foreigner'. Policemen often wave your car down for no reason other than the fact that you're a foreigner. Country people are usually very curious, and some may never have seen a *dabizi* – 'big nose' (a not-quite-so-polite name for foreigners) – before.

Expect to be stared at or to find someone peering over your shoulder to see what you're reading. If you stop to examine something in a shop, you're likely to find a small crowd gathering around you, curious to know what interests you. Take a pair of trousers into a changing room in a department store and you may emerge to find a number of people waiting to see if you buy the garment. Even people who have seen plenty of foreigners are still fascinated to find out what makes 'big noses' tick. This is a large part of the attraction that US fast-food restaurants such as KFC and McDonald's have for the Chinese.

The easiest way to overcome all this attention is to address the onlookers in Chinese. Even a simple *ni hao* (hello), said with a smile, is sufficient in most cases.

NATIONAL ICONS

Every country has its icons – people, places, structures, symbols, flora and fauna, food and drink – which are revered or unique to that country and have special significance to its people. The following is a list of some of China's icons that you can expect to see, experience or hear reference to.

Icons – Confucius & Mao Zedong

The first two are so overwhelmingly important that they're listed separately.

Confucius (551-479BC) – Known in Chinese as *Kong Fuzi*, no other single person has had as much influence on the character of the Chinese people as Confucius. His teachings of 2,500 years ago ring as true today as they did when first written. A strictly moral man, he believed that every person had a role in life and a duty to perform that role ethically, and that every role is a part of a hierarchy. He taught, too, the importance of study and the overriding necessity for honesty

in all things, from individuals to governments.

> **'What one does not wish for oneself, one ought not to do to anyone; what one recognises as desirable for oneself, one ought to be willing to grant to others.'**
> Confucius (Chinese philosopher)

Statue of Confucius

Mao Zedong (1893-1976) – Born in Hunan, Mao grew up in a world where China was regularly humiliated by foreign powers. A largely agrarian society, its ports were foreign enclaves or concessions, its railways and major industries were foreign-owned, poverty was endemic and warlords ruled much of the country. By force of personality and clever thinking he united China with the support of the Communist Party of China (CPC) and, in uniting the Chinese he led them to believe in China, even if it was a China that he fashioned

Mao Zedong

from the feudal wasteland by revolution against the status quo.

Chairman of the CPC from 1943 to 1975 and known in the West as 'Chairman Mao', not everything he did was successful. His successor Deng Xiaoping acknowledged this, saying that Mao's ideas were '70 per cent right and 30 per cent wrong'. However, while the Cultural Revolution scarred the country for many years, Mao is still seen as the Great Helmsman, and his pictures and statues are everywhere.

Icons – Other People

Chen Kaige (b. 1952) – A member of the Red Guard during the Cultural Revolution, he trained as a film director at the same time as Zhang Yimou and achieved international recognition with his 1993 drama *Farewell my Concubine*.

Dashan (b. 1965) – A Canadian who studied Chinese at Toronto and Peking universities, Dashan – real name Mark Rowswell – was the first Westerner to become a national celebrity in China, thanks to his appearances on television, where his

mastery of Mandarin Chinese and the art of *xiangsheng* (cross talk) made him famous. Dashan, who has a Chinese wife, has done much to help open up China to the West and vice-versa. His Chinese name means 'Big Mountain'.

Deng Lijun (1953-1995) – Taiwan-born and never married, she became the ultimate Chinese pop singer before her early death at 42. Her old-fashioned romantic ballads are still enormously popular with all ages. She's sometimes better known as Teresa Tang.

Deng Xiaoping (1904 – 1997) – A native of Sichuan, Deng Xiaoping was treated alternately by Mao Zedong as his trusted deputy and then a potential enemy. He was downgraded and punished by Mao three times but kept bouncing back and, following the death of Mao and the end of the Cultural Revolution, took control of China from 1978 to the early '90s. Under his direction, China was opened up to the world and his period of leadership signalled the start of China's rise as an international power. Many people today feel that their present lifestyle is due to Deng Xiaoping's vision and pragmatism.

> **'We call it Socialism with Chinese characteristics.'**
>
> Deng Xiaoping

Deng Yaping (b. 1973) – Just 1.5m (4ft11in) tall, this diminutive table-tennis player from Zhengzhou in Henan dominated table tennis in the early and mid-'90s, winning six World Championships and four Olympic medals at Barcelona in 1992 and Atlanta in 1996. She has a Master's degree from Nottingham University and a doctorate from Cambridge and is still involved in Chinese sport today.

Genghis Khan (1167-1227) – When in 1215, the Khan's Mongolian forces overran the Great Wall and took Beijing at the start of his conquest of China, it signalled the foundation of the great Mongol empire which stretched from Hungary in the west to Vietnam in the east. His grandson, Kublai Khan, extended and stabilised the empire and founded the Yuan Dynasty which ruled China until 1368. Today, he's an icon among Mongols and his contribution to China's history is appreciated, although he isn't revered by all Chinese.

Gong Li (b. 1965) – The first Chinese film actress to achieve international fame, Gong Li was discovered by the director Zhang Yimou, became his paramour and starred in all his early films. She has won a clutch of best actress awards in both Chinese and international cinema, most recently for Rob Marshall's *Memoirs of a Geisha*. In 1996, she married a businessman from Singapore and has since taken up citizenship there.

Hu Jintao

Hu Jintao (b. 1942) – The current leader and President of the People's Republic of China and the General Secretary of the CPC. An engineer and technocrat, he was appointed by his predecessor, Jiang Zemin, and is a quietly progressive leader in the style of Deng Xiaoping.

Jiang Zemin (b. 1926) – Trained as an electrical engineer and one time Mayor of Shanghai, he followed Deng Xiaoping to become President in 1993. Very much one of the old guard, Jiang Zemin governed almost unobtrusively, but during his time in charge he oversaw the return of both Hong Kong and Macau from their Imperial 'owners' and Beijing's successful bid for the 2008 Olympic Games.

Lao Tse (*Laozi*, ca. 600BC) – Born a century before Confucius, he's said to be the founder of Taoism.

> There are many legends about Lao Tse who may – or may not – be a mythological figure. One recounts that he was born as a 62-year-old man, with a grey beard and long earlobes, both symbols of wisdom and a long life; another that he lived to the age of 999 and was a teacher of Buddha. His name means 'Venerable Master' and many Chinese people claim to be one of his descendants.

Li Ning (b. 1963) – A successful Olympic gymnast, he made his name at the Los Angeles Olympics in 1984 where he won six medals, and was chosen to light the Olympic Flame at the opening ceremony of the 2008 Beijing Olympics.

Li Yang (b. 1969) – Language entrepreneur Li Yang invented a unique method of teaching English, which involves learning sentences with the emphasis on pronunciation rather than on grammar or vocabulary. Known as Crazy English, it became wildly popular in the late '90s, and his lectures draw crowds of over 20,000.

Liu Huan (b. 1963) – Pony-tailed Liu Huan is China's King of Mandopop. He has had numerous hits, including *Asking Myself a Thousand Times for that* which topped the Chinese hit parade for several weeks. He sang the official theme song at the opening of the Beijing Olympics: a duet with English soprano Sarah Brightman called *You and Me*.

Liu Xiang (b. 1983) – Shanghai-born Liu Xiang literally leapt to prominence by winning China's first-ever track gold medal at the 2004 Athens Olympics in the 110m hurdles. Much was expected of him at the Beijing Olympics but injury forced him to retire from the competition. Following surgery in the US, he is back to hurdling in pursuit of more medals.

Marco Polo (1254-1324) – A Venetian merchant who travelled extensively through Asia for more than two decades, meeting Kublai Khan and countless others and providing the first detailed account of life in China by a European. The Chinese view him as sympathetic to their country and very different from later Europeans, who came to exploit rather than explore, and copies of his travels sell well in China.

Peking Man – Archaeologists excavating at Zhoukoudian near Beijing in the early '20s discovered remnants of an early human which they estimated to be between 230,000 and 400,000 years old. At the time, these were the earliest relics to have been found of

man. During the Second World War, the remains of Peking Man were taken from the site, with the intention of having them shipped to the US for safety, but somehow they vanished, never to be seen again.

The Soong sisters – A remarkable trio, the three daughters of Hainanese missionary and businessman 'Charlie' Soong were born at the end of the 19th century, and went on to become some of the most influential players in modern Chinese history by virtue of marrying famous men and using their wealth and power to help those less fortunate. Ai-Ling, the eldest, married finance minister H H Kang, then the richest man in China; middle daughter Qing-Ling married Sun Yat-sen, the first Republican leader of China; and the youngest, Mei-Ling, became the wife of Chiang Kai-Shek, leader of the nationalists.

> **It's said that Ai-Ling loved money, Mei-Ling loved power and Qing-Ling loved China. Although her sisters were nationalists, Qing-Ling sided with the Communist Party and is still very much an icon among the Chinese who visit her tomb and houses, now museums. Mei-Ling moved to the US and died there in 2004 at the age of 106.**

Sun Yat-Sen (1866-1925) – Uniquely worshipped by both the Communist Party of China and the Nationalist Kuomintang as the true founder of Republican China following the downfall of the Qing dynasty in 1911.

Sun Zhu (544-496BC) – Soldier famous for *The Art of War*, a 2,500 year old book that is still read today, not only by military strategists but also by business moguls and would-be political leaders.

Wang Chuanfu (b. 1966) – Billionaire businessman. His enterprise caught the eye of renowned US investor Warren Buffet, who invested heavily in Wang Chuanfu's BYD (Build Your Dreams) company – the largest manufacturer of mobile-phone batteries in the world – driving the share price up five-fold in 2009 and catapulting Wang into the position of the wealthiest person in China with a fortune estimated at over US$5bn.

Yao Ming (b. 1980) – At 2.29m (7ft6in) and 141kg (310lb), he was the first Chinese basketball player to crack the NBA, joining the Houston Rockets in 2002. He has played for the Chinese men's basketball team in the last three Olympics and is married to a member of China's women's basketball team, Ye Li, who's a mere 1.92m (6ft3in) and 83kg (183lb).

Zhang Yimou (b. 1950) – Film director. His first film was *Red Sorghum*, while more recent epics include *Hero* and *The House of Flying Daggers*. More recently he directed the opening and closing ceremonies at the Beijing Olympics and the choreography of the parade and carnival celebrating the 60th Anniversary of the People's Republic of China.

Zhang Yin (b. 1957) – Boss of Nine Dragons Paper and China's richest woman in 2009 with a US$5bn fortune, earned from importing waste paper from the US and Europe and turning it into corrugated cardboard.

Zhang Ziyi (b. 1979) – Actress who was discovered by the director Zhang Yimou and starred in several of his films, including the Oscar-winning *Crouching Tiger, Hidden Dragon*, *Hero* and *The House of Flying Daggers*. She also played the lead role in *Memoirs of a Geisha*.

> 'In China we don't see someone as truly beautiful until we have known them for a long time and we know what is underneath the skin.'
>
> Zhang Ziyi (Chinese film actress)

Icons – Places & Structures

The Bund – The best known image of Shanghai, the Bund is a waterfront area on the west bank of the Huangpu River. Built in the late 19th and early 20th centuries to the design of city buildings in the West, it was the centre of the International Settlement and still presents a fine impression of the world

The Bund, Shanghai

that existed in Shanghai before the Second World War.

The Forbidden City – Located at the precise centre of Beijing, the Forbidden City – also known as Beijing's Palace Museum – was the principal palace of the Emperors of China from its construction in the early 1400s until 1911, when the Qing dynasty collapsed. The world's largest palace complex, it contains 980 buildings within the boundaries of its 180 acres (73 hectares). Although many of its greatest treasures were spirited away to Taiwan by the nationalists in 1949, those that remain are magnificent.

The Li River (*Li Jiang*) – Every visitor to China should take a trip along this river. Shallow boats travel from Guilin to Yangshuo, passing through an amazing vista of near vertical karst mountains which looks exactly like all those Chinese paintings that you thought were wild exaggerations: an unforgettable experience.

The Olympic Green – Park in Beijing containing the stadia and other buildings constructed for the 2008 Olympics, including the National Stadium (the Bird's Nest), the National Aquatic Centre (the Water Cube), the National Indoor Stadium and Olympic Village. It's a popular attraction with Chinese people, who are proud that their country hosted the Olympics.

The Potala Palace – The winter home of successive Dalai Lamas, this massive building dominates Lhasa in Tibet. Although a palace has stood in this place since 637AD, the existing imposing building was built between 1649 and 1694. It was protected from damage during the Cultural Revolution by the personal intervention of China's first prime minister, Zhou

Enlai, and has recently undergone major refurbishment. Named after the mountain is clings to, the Potala Palace is an awesome structure, comprising 13 storeys and over 1,000 rooms, and rising 300m (1,000ft) above Lhasa. In places, its walls are 5m (16ft) thick. A UNESCO World Heritage Site, it receives 6,000 visitors a day in the peak summer months.

The Great Wall of China (*Changcheng*)

From as early as the 5th century BC there has been a wall to keep out the raiding tribes from the north, but the present structure largely dates from the time of the Ming dynasty. The wall stands around 6m (20 feet) high and is wide enough in sections for four horsemen to ride abreast. Many famous places disappoint when visited but this doesn't, particularly if you visit a lesser-known (and less touristy) section of the wall. In its entirety, the Great Wall stretches for 8,852km (5,500mi), although not all of it is wall. Trenches and natural barriers such as rivers make up some of its length. There is an enduring myth that the wall is visible from the Moon and some astronauts orbiting the Earth claim to have spotted it.

The Temple of Heaven (*Tian Tan*) – Built by the Emperor Yongle in the early 15th century, the temple complex was where the Emperors would pray to Heaven for a good harvest. The main building is probably the most perfect example of ancient Chinese architecture still in existence.

Terracotta Army

The Terracotta Army – Known in China as the Terra Cotta Warriors and Horses (*Bingma Yong*), this much-visited collection of statues was discovered in 1974 not far from Xi'an in Shaanxi province by villagers digging a well. The spectacle, which dates back to 210BC, consists of some 8,000 full-size soldiers together with their horses and chariots, which were buried there to guard the tomb of Qin Shi Huang, the first Emperor of China. When unearthed, most of the statues were either intact or capable of being re-assembled and the attention to detail is amazing – each man has individual features. The Emperor's tomb remains unopened, and its contents can only be guessed at.

Tian'anmen Square *(Tian'anmen Guangchang)* – Tian'anmen means the Gate of Heavenly Peace and refers to the structure on the north side of the square which forms one of the main entrances to the Forbidden Palace. The square itself is enormous and has been the site of some momentous events in recent history (including the 'Fourth of June Incident' in 1989). It contains several important buildings, including the Chinese National Museum and the Chairman Mao Memorial Hall, where you can view the embalmed remains of the 'Great Helmsman'.

Yangtze River (*Chang Jiang*) – Rising in Tibet and entering the East China Sea just north of Shanghai, the Yangtze flows for about 6,400km (3,920mi) making it the third-longest river in the world after the Nile and the Amazon. The source of much of China's riches as well as many of its devastating floods, the Yangtze is home to dolphins and alligators as well as the world's largest hydroelectric dam. Visitors can travel on one of the regular passenger vessels up and down the river; the most popular cruise, between Yichang and Chongqing, includes the passage through the scenic area around the Three Gorges Dam.

Yellow River (*Huang He*) – Famously yellow from the extraordinary amount of loess (fine silt) that it carries down from the plains, much of which sinks as sediment and raises the river bed. This has led to the river flooding over 1,500 times in the last 3,000 years. Despite this, most Chinese regard it as the 'Mother of China', the place where their nation was nurtured and grew.

Starting in Qinghai province in the west, it flows steadily across the central plains of China and reaches the sea in Shandong at Bohai Bay. At 5,464km (3,398mi), it's the sixth-longest river in the world.

Yu Gardens (*Yu Yuan*) – This picturesque corner of old Shanghai is exactly how most foreigners imagine old China to look. First established in 1559, some of its buildings and attractions have since been rebuilt and some are almost a pastiche, but it's great fun to wander around. In the middle is a footbridge across a small lake and, perched in the middle, a teahouse selling expensive tea where celebrities quench their thirst.

Icons – Symbols

Bicycle – You see them everywhere, except in Chongqing where it's very hilly. With the advent of electric bicycles and other motorised vehicles, bikes became a little less common; however, as traffic jams become more frequent, people are using them again in city centres. Most bikes are of the single speed, sit-up-and-beg variety.

Chopsticks (*kuaizi*) – China's answer to the knife and fork, usually made from wood; plastic chopsticks may be more hygienic but are slippery and not easy to use. Left-handed people frequently use chopsticks with their right hand.

Feng shui – A system of aesthetics – it translates literally as 'wind and water' – *feng shui* is employed to ensure that the best orientation is chosen for new offices, homes and even tombs. It's normal to contract a practitioner for his advice, and this is taken very seriously.

Gunpowder – This Chinese invention is used in firecrackers and

rockets to celebrate the completion of new buildings, events such as weddings and other family occasions, and in enormous quantities during the Spring Festival which accompanies Chinese New Year in early February,

Dragons

Thought to be terrible creatures in the West, dragons (*long*) are regarded quite benignly in China. They are considered to be capable of controlling the seas and rivers and the weather, so are seen as creatures of power and strength.

Jade – An ornamental stone which has been treasured and crafted in China for over 8,000 years. Beware of plastic copies.

Junk (*chuan*) – An ancient design of sailing vessel first used around 1,000 years ago. Largely replaced by steam or other powered vessels, although a few are still in use.

Kung Fu – Kung Fu is called *Gongfu* in China and is most famously taught at Shaolin Temple in Henan province where the resident monks are said to have invented it to defend the temple. Former pupils from Shaolin have set up similar schools throughout China and in many overseas countries.

Mao suits – The Great Helmsman wore a signature suit with a high, stiff collar and, as recently as the '80s, everyone in China, men and women, wore a copy of this suit in either dark blue, dark green or dark grey. Some are still about, worn mainly by farm workers, although excellently tailored examples of Mao's suit are sometimes sported by senior government officials.

Pagoda (*ta*) – This quintessential Chinese structure was traditionally built within or alongside a Buddhist temple for the safekeeping of religious relics or writings, or placed at 'unlucky' points of the compass to protect temples or towns from misfortune. Usually octagonal with seven or nine storeys, they may be made entirely of wood, brick or stone, although some 'restored' pagodas are made of reinforced concrete designed to look like wood.

Porcelain – Ceramic ware was developed in China hundreds of years before it was made in Europe, but the manufacture and design of porcelain reached a peak during the Ming dynasty between the 14th and 17th centuries, with new colours and ornamental techniques; it was the Ming rulers who

oversaw exports to the West on a massive scale. In Jingdezhen, the home of porcelain, even the lampposts are clad in blue and white porcelain.

Qipao – A beautiful, skin-tight, high-collared traditional Chinese dress made of embroidered silk, with a split side to the skirt that seems to rise to an inconceivable height. Foreigners often refer to *qipao* dresses as *cheongsams*. This has evolved from a misunderstanding of the Chinese words *chang shan* which are used to name a traditional garment worn by men – the words mean 'long shirt', and that's exactly what it is. The *chang shan* is still worn by some men, particularly on hot days, when their design makes them pleasantly cool.

Rickshaws – Originally from Japan, these human-powered 'taxis' were first used in the late 1800s, and by the '20s it was estimated that one in six men in Beijing earned a living pulling a rickshaw. Manual rickshaws were banned by Mao in 1949 – he regarded them as a symbol of the oppression of the working classes – and they're now rarely seen in China, although you can take a ride in a three-wheeled pedicab (bicycle-powered rickshaw).

Silk – Possibly China's first export, silk first made its way to Europe during Roman times via the Silk Road, although it had been made as long ago as 6,000BC. It's still

relatively inexpensive in China, where Suzhou is one of the main centres of production.

Traditional Chinese medicine – As well as the herbal and other natural remedies, TCM also includes the practices of acupuncture, cupping and massage, and is as much concerned with maintaining health as with curing illness. Every town has a pharmacy dispensing the appropriate herbs and materials.

Icons – Flora & Fauna

Cicada – Common in all parts of China that have a hot summer, these insects are regarded as a delicacy and people hunt for them at dusk. They aren't particularly tasty!

Dove Tree – The Dove Tree (*Davidia involucrate*) grows in western China, particularly in Sichuan province, and the many large white blossoms on it are said to look like a flock of white doves perched in the tree. Examples have been transplanted to botanical gardens throughout the world, including Kew (London).

Ginkgo biloba – Also spelt *gingko* and known as the Maidenhair Tree, the Ginkgo tree is a unique species with no close living relatives. It's widely cultivated in China and has various uses as a food and traditional medicine.

Kumquat – A fruit which resembles a miniature orange and is eaten skin and all. Miniature kumquat bushes are frequently given as gifts at Chinese New Year, the little round fruits being said to look like golden money.

Magpie – There are two types of magpie, the beautiful, smaller Azure-winged Magpie and the more common black and white variety. Both are regarded as lucky omens – the Chinese word for magpie translates as 'bird of joy'.

Giant Panda

Pandas (*da xiong mao* or big bear cat) are loved by everyone because they look like great stuffed toys. Now listed as an endangered species, the few thousand remaining giant pandas live mainly in the wilds of Sichuan. Although equipped as a carnivore, its diet is 99 per cent bamboo. The Chinese have worked hard to ensure the panda's survival, and it's a capital offence to kill one. Captive-bred giant pandas are regularly hired out by China to foreign zoos on a ten-year lease at an equally giant US$1m a year and on the understanding that any cubs born overseas must be handed back to China.

Peony (*mudan*) – Esteemed as one of the most exquisite flowers, the peony is a symbol for nobility and value, and regarded as the national flower of China. It became popular in the imperial palaces during the Sui and Tang dynasties, and earned the title of the 'king of flowers.' A symbol of spring, it's also used as a metaphor for female beauty and reproduction.

Peony

Pictured in full bloom, the peony symbolises peace.

Père David's Deer (*milu*) – This species was first identified in the 19th century by a French missionary, the eponymous Père David, and was once numerous in the wild. It was hunted to extinction by 1900, but survived due to breeding programmes in zoos and parks overseas, including Woburn in Bedfordshire. In recent years, Lord Bedford arranged the dispatch of several breeding pairs to China, where it's hoped they may be reintroduced back into the wild.

Plum Blossom (*mei*) – Along with the peony, the flower of the plum tree (*prunus mume*) is considered to be one of China's national flowers, and has long been a beloved subject in traditional painting.

Red-crowned Crane – Although China doesn't officially have a national bird, the red-crowned crane (*Grus japonensis* – translates as Japanese or Manchurian crane) comes closest. It is noted for having one of the most beautiful dances in the bird world and is a symbol of luck, longevity and fidelity. It's an endangered species with only an estimated 1,500 remaining in the wild,

most living in the Yancheng Coastal Wetlands.

Icons – Food & Drink

Beijing roast duck (*Beijing kao ya*) – Sometimes called Peking Duck, this iconic dish is prepared to a closely guarded recipe, and any restaurant wanting to sell it in China must pay a licence fee to the Quanjude restaurant chain which owns the trademark for the name. Ducks are roasted whole over a fire of pear wood, and the golden bird is then wheeled to your table where a cook carves it into thin slices in front of you. You eat it in folded pancakes with shredded shallots and plum sauce.

Dumplings – These delicacies come in a wide variety and bear little resemblance to British suet dumplings; they're more like a cross between large ravioli and small Cornish pasties. The people of Guangdong eat dumplings for breakfast, but further north the most popular varieties, such as *boazi* and *jaozi*, are eaten at lunch or dinner and are delicious, filled with savoury meat or prawns with vegetables.

Moon cake (*yue bing*) – A special treat, moon cakes are eaten at the time of Mid-Autumn Festival when they're given as gifts in ornate boxes, with the wrapping often costing more than the cakes. Although they resemble a small pork pie, moon cakes have various fillings; a description of their contents in Chinese script is pressed into the top of the cake before baking.

Noodles – These Chinese staples are made from wheat in northern China and rice in the south, and are served either boiled in a tasty soup or fried. They have existed in China for thousands of years – archaeologists have found them in tombs dating back to 1,200BC. Glass noodles are made from starch, and are served as a vegetable.

Rice – This essential grain was first cultivated in the Yangtze River basin some 7,000 years ago, and is eaten boiled or fried. It's been estimated that a third of the world's rice is grown and eaten in China. Despite growing so much rice themselves, the Chinese also import it, and some supermarkets sell rice from Australia, Thailand and the US.

> **'I wouldn't do it for all the tea in China.'**
> This popular saying illustrates the huge scale of tea production in China.

Tea – Grown in many parts of the country, and by far the most popular drink in China. Sold by the *liang* (about 2oz or 50g), the best tea is expensive by any standards. Tea (*cha*) is served in most restaurants to accompany your meal, normally free of charge and with limitless top ups. Many Chinese can immediately tell you where a particular cup of tea originates from. Green tea is by far the most popular, but there are a whole range of types including fermented, semi-fermented and unfermented varieties, although Indian-style black tea (curiously known in China as *hong cha*, red tea) is comparatively rare. Chinese tea is never taken with milk, though Tibetans drink it churned with butter and salt.

Tofu – Known as *doufu* in China, *tofu* is produced as a curd from soya beans and is enormously popular as a source of protein. Its subtle taste means it can be prepared in a variety of ways, e.g. fried, or boiled in stews. In Sichuan it's served heavily spiced and peppery, much like the rest of Sichuan food, while in Henan it's left to go rancid before being fried to make *chou doufu,* which creates an appalling smell.

Jin Mao Tower, Shanghai

3.

GETTING STARTED

One of the most difficult stages of adjustment to a new country is those first few days, when you a have a million and one things to do. This is stressful enough without the addition of cultural differences. China is almost certainly very different from anywhere else that you have been. In the larger cities you may find some similarities to your home country, but elsewhere almost everything will be dissimilar; the huge gulf between big-city China, where Western influences are creeping in, and rural China, which appears stuck in a past century, shouldn't be underestimated.

> Life is really simple, but we insist on making it complicated.
> Confucius (Chinese philosopher)

Arriving in and adapting to China can be a stressful experience, and this chapter explains what to expect and how to overcome some of the challenges, including those posed by obtaining the correct visa and documentation, finding accommodation, hiring or buying a car, opening a bank account, obtaining healthcare and utilities, arranging for your children's schooling, getting online, staying informed and coping with Chinese bureaucracy.

IMMIGRATION

Visas

Citizens of almost every country need a valid and appropriate visa in order to enter mainland China, the only exceptions being citizens of Brunei, San Marino, Singapore and Japan, who can visit without a visa for up to 15 days. Citizens of Hong Kong or Macau can enter China, provided they possess a Mainland Travel Permit: a credit-card sized plastic ID card which allows free passage to and from the mainland. These are valid for ten years for adults and for three years for children aged 17 or under. All other foreign citizens must possess a current visa in their passport, which must be valid for at least six months after the date of entry.

Visas consist of a pale green form glued into your passport, and have their type clearly indicated at the top: e.g. 'L' for tourists, together with details of the period of validity, which starts from the date of entry into China and not from the date of issue of the visa. The types of visa issued are as follows:

Visa Classes

C Crew visa for crews of aircraft, trains and ships temporarily in China.

D Permanent residence visa.

F Business visit or visit to lecture, for a cultural or scientific exchange or for a short-term study period of less than six months.

G Transit visa, for those entering China on a necessary stop over. Persons transiting over a period of less than 24 hours, and who won't leave the airport or port, don't require a visa.

J Journalist's visa.

L Tourism or family visit.

X Student visa to undertake study for a period exceeding six months.

Z Work visa, for those with a firm offer of employment, together with any accompanying family members.

Visas can be obtained from embassies and consulates of the People's Republic of China throughout the world. Application forms are available from embassies, or online at embassy websites, and you can apply by post, in person or online. Applications must be accompanied by your passport, a colour passport-style photograph sized 30mm x 40mm, and any supporting documents, e.g. a copy of a letter from the organisation that you'll be visiting or joining, a letter of invitation from a family member, etc.

Visas are normally issued for periods of 30 days for tourists and for three months for other types of visa, but can be for six months or a year. They are issued as single-entry, double-entry or multiple-entry visas. The cost varies and depends not only on the type of visa and the period that you want it for, or how many entries it covers, but also on which country you come from. China bases its visa charges on reciprocity, i.e. the amount a Chinese citizen has to pay for a similar visa to visit your country; therefore the fee paid by someone from the UK may be different from that paid by an applicant from the US or Australia.

It's important to remember that rules regarding visas and immigration are subject to frequent change and you should check the latest situation with your nearest Chinese embassy.

If you're issued with a multiple-entry visa, you should check it carefully, as some allow you to stay in China for no more than 30 days on any one visit. If you want to stay longer you must leave China temporarily before 30 days are up; most people fly down to Hong Kong for a day, once a month. For each day that you overstay, even though your visa is valid for many more months, you're fined 500 RMB (around £50).

Residence & Citizenship

Provided you hold the appropriate visa, e.g. to study or work, you can stay long

term in China. The Chinese authorities
don't issue residence permits, although
a few foreigners can obtain residence
cards (see below), and it's almost
impossible to apply for citizenship.
A small number of non-nationals
gain Chinese citizenship, usually via
marriage and long-term residence, with
citizenship being granted following the
death of their partners. However, it's
important to note that China doesn't
recognise dual nationality. Chinese
citizens who acquire a foreign passport
must give up their Chinese citizenship,
and foreigners who gain Chinese
citizenship are required to renounce
their previous citizenship.

Foreigners' Residence Card

Under certain, highly-restricted
circumstances it's possible to be issued
with a Foreigners' Residence Card.
These are available to foreigners
working in Shanghai (only) and are
valid for up to five years. In a few
rare cases, a Foreigners' Permanent
Residence Card may be issued to
foreigners working elsewhere in China,
although the word 'permanent' is
misleading as they're only valid for up
to ten years. Possession of either card
makes visas unnecessary and allows
holders to work without obtaining a
work permit. However, even if you're
someone exceptionally important to
China or a famous business personality,
fulfilling the requirements for either of
these can take two or three years.

Details of how to apply are available
from the Foreign Affairs desk at the
principal Public Security Bureau (PSB)
in Shanghai or, for the 'permanent' card,
at any major PSB office in your region.
Neither of these cards can be obtained
outside China.

ARRIVAL

It's possible to enter mainland China by
train, either from Hong Kong or from
Russia via the Trans-Siberian or Trans-
Mongolian railways or from Vietnam;
on foot across borders with Hong Kong,
Macau, Laos, Burma, Vietnam, Russia
or the central Asian republics; or by
boat from Thailand, Japan or Korea.
The overwhelming majority of visitors,
however, arrive in China by air – over
10m a year – and this information applies
mainly to them.

Almost all international flights
arrive in China at one of three
principal airports in Beijing, Shanghai
or Guangzhou, although there are
international airports at several other
provincial capitals such as Chengdu
and Kunming. All are good, well-
organised airports, although finding
someone who can speak English can be
difficult. Shortly before landing you're
given a Customs form and entry card to
complete plus, sometimes, a health card

(only necessary during periodic health scares, such as bird flu).

You should expect a fairly lengthy walk to the first barrier where a member of the police takes your entry card and examines your passport and visa; you then proceed to the health check, and hand in your health form – any other checks are rare. After collecting your baggage, you exit via the green and red channels of Customs, where you would be unlucky to be stopped, and hand in your Customs form. Then it's out into Arrivals. If no one is meeting you, follow the signs marked 'taxis' and join the line – it may look long but will move surprisingly fast. Don't, whatever you do, accept the offers of taxi touts – they're usually a short cut to being ripped off.

> **Taxis are unlikely to accept anything other than Chinese RMB (*renminbi*, literally 'People's Money', also known as *yuan* or *kuai*), therefore if you haven't already got some, stop at a currency office in the Arrivals hall. The rate offered is normally as good as you'll get anywhere.**

Registration

All foreigners are required to register with the Public Security Bureau (PSB) within 24 hours of arriving in China. Failure to do so can result in a fine of up to 5,000 RMB. If you're staying in a hotel or serviced apartment, the management usually takes care of this, but anyone staying in a private apartment or someone's home must attend a PSB office and register in person. Take along your passport and any other documents supporting your visit

BUREAUCRACY

Although Chinese bureaucracy dates back several thousand years, it operates remarkably smoothly. The Chinese are generally helpful towards foreigners and so, while you may need to produce a lot of paperwork and attend various offices to achieve your aim, this shouldn't be an unpleasant experience, even if it's sometimes a time-consuming one. There is less red tape than in many Western countries, and some licences and documentation common in other countries don't exist in China, e.g. there's no such thing as a television licence and there also are no council taxes, as such. The biggest headache most foreigners face is with the Chinese language, as even the simplest forms are a challenge when written in Chinese.

Your main bureaucratic dealings are likely to be with the Public Security Bureau's Foreign Affairs office. As well as registering with the PSB on arrival, you must inform them within one month of changing your address in China. The PSB can extend your visa, and this is a simple procedure provided you take along the necessary documents. This is also the place to go to apply for a 'permanent' residence card (see above), although the process is not for the faint-hearted.

If you want to drive, there's more red tape to negotiate, as you need a Chinese driving licence. If you own a car you must tax it annually with the local traffic police and obtain compulsory third party insurance. Once the car is eight years old it will need to pass a road fitness test each year, again with the traffic police. And if you have a dog you must obtain a dog licence, and have it inoculated against rabies annually.

Chinese bureaucracy becomes far more complex if you start a business, which is where the advantages of having a Chinese partner come to the fore, as he'll know precisely which licences and permits are necessary.

> **The Chinese prefer to own their own homes, rather than rent, and some sources put the percentage of citizens who are home owners at over 80 per cent.**

ACCOMMODATION

Renting a Home

It isn't difficult to find a place to live in China, although finding somewhere to

your taste may be more of a challenge. Most Chinese city-dwellers live in high-rise apartments; suburban houses with gardens are a rarity, although there are top-end villas, often in gated communities, with top-end rental prices to match and, more rarely, historic and interesting old houses.

If you're going to China to work for an established business, organisation or educational establishment, then accommodation is probably part of the deal and you'll be met at the airport and whisked to your new home which will probably be a one-bedroom or sometimes a two-bedroom apartment in a block of similar apartments. Foreign teachers and lecturers usually live on campus and, while foreign students may be offered on-campus accommodation, Chinese university students are obliged to live on campus – for them, sharing a flat off campus with a girlfriend is forbidden by universities.

Depending on its age, a foreign teacher's apartment will be adequate or possibly very nice indeed; some executive apartments in Shanghai are as luxurious as any you'd find in the West. Accommodation usually comprises a living room, kitchen, bedroom(s) and bathroom and has basic furnishings and equipment: expect some gas rings for cooking – ovens are rare in private homes – and a small fridge but no washing machine, although a television, telephone and possibly a computer are usually provided. It will have air-conditioning and/or central heating, depending on the location.

When accommodation is provided as part of a job package, utility bills (electricity, gas and water) are usually paid by your employer. Sometimes, internet access is also included, although you're expected to pay for overseas or long-distance telephone calls. This all tends to make the modest salary that many universities and schools offer look a lot less unreasonable. It's a similar situation if you go to work on a major construction project; there's likely to be a well-equipped construction camp located near the project works, quite possibly complete with various entertainment facilities such as a bar or even a swimming pool.

If, however, you arrive in China to set up a new branch office or business, or to establish a new factory, the onus is on you to find somewhere to live. Most people move into a small hotel on a long-term basis at a discounted rate while looking for somewhere to rent. Many Chinese buy property as an investment, and everywhere there are many empty apartments that you can rent, provided you can locate the owner or their representative.

Apartments are let both furnished and unfurnished. If yours is unfurnished, or you don't like the landlord's taste in furniture, it's easy and inexpensive to buy your own.

> While Chinese beds are adequate in length for all but the tallest foreigners, the mattresses can be on the hard side. Often they're no more than 7cm (3in) thick, which may take some adjusting to if you're used to a fully sprung Western-style mattress.

There are two prime sources of accommodation. Check out the classified advertisements in free magazines such as *City Weekend* which are aimed at expatriates and frequently have (sometimes expat-owned) properties for rent. Alternatively, use an agent. One of the best-known is Century 21 (🖥 www.century21cn.com/english), which is an 'estate agency' franchise with branches throughout China, dealing in both sales and rentals. Several major UK and US estate agencies operate in the major cities of Beijing, Shanghai, Guangzhou and Shenzhen, but they primarily deal in commercial property or top-of-the-market accommodation, much of which is out of the price range of 'ordinary' expats.

If you rent through an agency, you're expected to enter into a proper contract, usually for a year, and to pay one or two months' rent in advance plus a similar-sized security deposit against possible damage to the property. Make sure that

yourself in a dispute which goes to court, it's highly unlikely that the ruling will go against the Chinese party.

Buying a Home

It's possible for foreigners to buy property in China, and with the value of houses trebling over the past ten years, it's usually considered to be a good investment.

you understand what you're signing – have it translated if necessary – and that the condition of the property is noted in the contract so that there's less chance of the landlord inventing 'damage' to try to hang on to your deposit. An agent can be useful in helping you to have utilities connected. The downside is that agents charge tenants a fee equivalent to a month's rent.

Rental payments are subject to VAT at 5 per cent, and you'll have to pay for your utilities in a privately rented property. There may also be an extra charge for parking.

As in the West, many apartment dwellers pay a monthly fee to the management organisation responsible for the day-to-day cleaning, gardening and maintenance of the block or estate. This is rarely as expensive as service charges in the West – in an average apartment, the monthly charge works out at around 8 to 10 RMB per square metre – but it's as well to know the cost and who's responsible for paying it before signing a lease.

China has no rules regarding rent control, and landlords are free to set their own rent. Most are unwilling to haggle over the rent and should you find

There's a wide range of property on offer, including apartments, houses and villas. Many new builds are sold off plan or as shells, which you complete to your own specifications. Prices vary according to location. Outside the main cities, shells are priced between 6,000 and 7,000 RMB per m², whereas in Beijing or Shanghai, the average price soars to 25,000 RMB or as high as 70,000 RMB per m² in a sought-after apartment block.

Certain aspects of property purchase are likely to be different from those in your home country, including the following:

● You must have lived in China continuously for at least one year and may only buy one property. If you wish to buy more, it's necessary to set up an investment company, which is a complicated process.

● Mortgages are available and the interest rate in 2010 was just under 6 per cent. Many developers can offer a purchase plan. Mortgages in China are generally for no more than 20 years.

● There are a number of additional costs on top of the purchase price.

Expect to pay stamp duty at about 3 per cent of the property's value, plus a maintenance fund of 2 per cent. There are no compulsory legal costs as few Chinese purchasers bother to consult a lawyer! If you're buying a shell, you should budget about 20 per cent of the developer's sales price to complete the internal fixtures and fittings to an average standard, i.e. without granite worktops and gold taps.

● There's no true 'freehold' property in China, where all land belongs to the state and your purchase entitles you to live on the land for 70 years, after which the state can reclaim it with no guarantee of compensation. Reparation is usually payable if the government requires your land earlier, e.g. for redevelopment.

BUYING OR HIRING A CAR

Many foreigners, when they first see the traffic conditions in China, decide that it's both safer and easier not to drive, and either hire (rent) a car with a driver or stick with public transport. However, for those who want the freedom of their own car, there's more information on driving in China on page 153.

Car Hire

Self-drive car hire (rental) is uncommon, and the few rental companies – most located in major cities – do their best to persuade you to hire a driver as well. To rent a car and drive it yourself, you must leave a substantial deposit and possess an International Driving Permit (IDP); although China isn't a signatory to the agreement that governs the use of IDPs, rental agencies and most police expect

you to have one. If you do manage to hire a car and drive it yourself, it will have special number plates and may only be driven within a restricted area within the city boundaries. The cost is likely to be very high indeed.

Renting a car with a driver is a more straightforward, cheaper and far less stressful option. You can rent a chauffeur-driven car from an agency, or hire a taxi or, if there's a group, a minibus. This is as simple to arrange as flagging down a taxi, or heading to a transit point, such as a bus or train station, for a minibus. Rates are set by haggling, and depend on the length of rental and distance covered, but 350 RMB a day should cover it. On overnight trips you're also expected to pay for your driver's accommodation and food.

> Private car ownership only became legal in China in 1994. Since then, the Chinese love affair with the car has become an unstoppable force, with 13.6m cars sold in 2009 alone.

Buying a Car

Because private car ownership is a relatively recent event, the secondhand market for cars is almost non-existent outside Beijing and Shanghai. In each of those two cities there's a single, but large, secondhand car mart, but elsewhere there are very few dealers in used cars, and most cars on the road have not done a high mileage anyway. Dealers don't offer trade-in prices as a general rule, but just occasionally you can find a dealer who has, as a favour, done a deal with a regular customer and has one or two immaculate secondhand cars available for sale; but it's rare. Instead, when someone wants to change their car, they offer or give their existing car to a relative or friend and then buy a new one for themselves. There is no means of verifying satisfactorily whether or not there remains any finance owing on a secondhand vehicle or whether it has been involved in a major accident – judging by the way many Chinese drive, it will not have received much TLC. If you buy secondhand, you'll have to undergo a merry-go-round of costly bureaucracy to get it legally registered in your name.

Virtually every international car manufacturer has representation in China, and a large number make certain models in the PRC through joint ventures. China has a number of indigenous car manufacturers, including BYD, Chery, Dong Feng and Geely. Cars have come down in price since China joined the World Trade Organisation, and any car manufactured by a joint venture within China now costs much the same as it would in Europe, but more than in the US. Locally designed cars cost less, while imported models of foreign cars are subject to import tax and cost more than in their original country of manufacture.

There are a number of copies of overseas cars, such as the copy Smart – there's even a 'copy' of the Rolls-Royce – while there are several different copies of Honda's CRV. In Shanghai, the new owners of Rover and MG are now making well-engineered cars under the name Roewe, including an excellent new, Chinese-designed, mid-sized saloon called the Roewe 550. However, the Western system of having a basic car to which you can add a wide variety of extras doesn't exist. At best, you're offered a choice of two specifications: a basic model with cloth seats, manual gears and simple heating arrangements, or a top of the range model with leather upholstery, an automatic gearbox, climate control and the rest. You cannot, for example, have a car with cloth seats and an automatic gearbox. There's a choice of colours, however, and you can have a sunroof installed for around 10,000 RMB.

Finance is usually available, and manufacturers' agents will handle all the on-the-road paperwork for you, including road tax, registration and licence

plates. These added extras will come as a shock! In most cities, the cost of initial registration and number plates is around 10 per cent of the purchase cost of the car, but in Shanghai, where the local authorities are trying to limit the number of new cars joining the scrum on the local roads, they auction the right to register a car, and the price for registration is even higher – in 2007 it reached 50,000 RMB! Once registered, you receive a registration certificate, a little blue booklet, which must be carried in the car at all times, and are issued with a set of number plates. These may take two or three weeks to arrive; therefore in the meantime, you're permitted to drive with no number plates and with just a small paper sticker on your windscreen.

Importing a Car

It's possible to import a car into China – some countries' ambassadors drive specially imported cars from their home countries, which serve as mobile advertisements for their automotive trade – and you can ask a dealership to import a new model for you, but it's a complex process and, with the wide range of cars now available in China, probably not worth the hassle.

EMERGENCY SERVICES

China has a number of emergency services, including police, fire and ambulance. There are numbers which you can call for assistance, but bear in mind that Chinese operators are unlikely to speak English so you should memorise some useful phrases (see box).

Emergency Numbers

110	Police
119	Fire
120	Ambulance
122	Traffic police (traffic accidents)

Emergency Phrases

accident (car) – *che huo*

allergic reaction – *guo min*

attack (armed) – *zao dao gong ji*

bleeding (a lot) – *liu xie*

broken arm – *ge bo huaile*

broken leg – *tui huaile*

burglary – *dao zei*

fire – *zhao huo*

heart attack – *xin zang bing*

I need an ambulance – *Wo xiu yao jiu hu che*

I need a doctor – *Wo xiu yao kan yi shang*

intruder – *dao zei*

mugging – *kong he*

not breathing – *mei yo hu xi*

(I am) on the road to X – *Wo zai qu X lu shang*

overdose – *guo liand de*

unconscious – *wu yi shi de*

wounded/injured – *shou shang*

HEALTH MATTERS

The Chinese believe strongly that the most important factor affecting their health is what they eat and drink. Over the years they have developed a comprehensive knowledge of the effects that different kinds of food and drink have on their well-being, both positive and negative. Aside from diet, the Chinese look to three other factors to maintain their health – exercise, massage and traditional treatments such as acupuncture – and these four elements are combined in Traditional Chinese Medicine or TCM (see below).

People live as long in China as in many developed countries – the average life expectancy is just over 73 years – and suffer from many of the ailments prevalent in the West but to differing degrees. Breast cancer is not the major problem that it is in the West, but tuberculosis is more common in China than in more developed countries. Hepatitis, in all its forms, is a real concern, as is heart disease. Interestingly, despite the rampant air and water pollution, the Chinese don't appear to link this to bad health, although they're tackling the issue of smoking by banning it in certain areas, such as on most public transport.

In such a vast country, with more than half the population living in remote

rural areas, the provision of good health services for all is difficult, which is reflected in China's lowly position in the World Health Organisation's rankings, with the lack of good services in most rural areas dragging down the results.

The biggest single problem is that of affordability of treatment, which although usually very cheap by Western standards, is still far too expensive for most of the rural population. There's now a health support scheme for most of the rural masses, but it only provides a total of 50 RMB of expenditure a year – just five pounds or eight dollars' worth! – and even then the patient must pay 20 per cent of all costs.

Most expatriates find China a healthy place to live, and in 2010 no vaccinations were required by Chinese authorities. Medical services are more than adequate in the larger cities, and you'll find them accessible and generally remarkably good value if you use local services. However, before you leave for China you should visit your doctor and check the latest vaccination requirements. Most importantly, ensure that your tetanus protection, which only lasts ten years, is up to date.

If you take prescription medicines, bring an initial few months' supply with you, and discuss with your doctor how you can obtain further supplies in the unlikely event that you cannot buy them locally; in the larger cities, virtually everything is available. If you take vitamins or food supplements, these are widely available in most pharmacies and supermarkets at similar prices to those in Europe – many are made by overseas companies in China. Be aware of your blood group. Rh negative blood is rarely available in China, or in most of the Far East, therefore you could face serious problems if you need a transfusion.

Most hospitals in major cities have sterile needles, and if you're having an injection they'll show you the needle, in its sealed packing, before opening it. Sealed sterile needles are not necessarily available in more rural areas, so bring some with you if there's a chance you might travel off the beaten track.

Traditional Chinese Medicine (TCM)

TCM has been around for over 2,000 years. Many Chinese, particularly the elderly, believe in Chinese medicine implicitly, although younger people tend to prefer the faster results provided by orthodox Western medicine. TCM aims to cure the source of the problem and therefore eliminate the symptoms, whereas Western medicine focuses on treating

the symptoms which may then return at a later date. Both therapies are taught in Chinese universities, although there are now more colleges specialising in Western medicine than in TCM, but there are quite a few that teach both. Chinese doctors, even in TCM hospitals, prescribe whichever form of medicine they deem to be most appropriate.

Health Issues

China is still a developing country, therefore you should be aware of the following dangers and precautions:

● **Coughs & colds:** No one in China puts a hand or handkerchief in front of their face when they cough or sneeze and, because of the sometimes bad pollution and heavy smoking, many also spit openly in the street (and even indoors, such as in supermarkets). As a result, many people – expats included – suffer from almost

continuous colds in winter. Cough mixture and other cold treatments are available and effective, but if your symptoms are bad, it's worth seeing a doctor who will probably recommend 'dropping'. This means lying down with a needle inserted into a vein on the back of your hand, and having a sterile saline solution dripped, drop by drop, into your blood system. It may seem drastic by Western standards but is very common and surprisingly effective.

● **Hepatitis:** There are several different types of this viral infection that causes inflammation of and sometimes permanent damage to the liver. Hepatitis A is the most common, while hepatitis B is more serious and can be passed on by dirty needles, unprotected sexual contact or other direct contact with body fluids. All types are comparatively common in China, where the disease is believed to affect one in ten of the population. Many hepatitis carriers have no symptoms but can infect others. To stay safe, never share a drink or a cigarette in China, and observe general recommendations on safe sex. There's a combined vaccination called Havrix, which can provide protection against both hepatitis A and B, and which requires two initial injections plus a booster.

● **Infectious diseases:** As in most developing countries, there's a small risk of catching cholera, typhoid, giardiasis (particularly in Tibet), bird flu, dengue fever (in tropical areas) and tuberculosis. There have been no (reported) cases of SARS in China since 2005.

● **Rabies:** A mammalian virus, usually transmitted by the bite of an infected animal such as a dog, although you can also catch it from simple contact with animal saliva or other body fluids. Unfortunately, rabies is common and is the top killer among infectious diseases in China. Most cases are reported in Guizhou, Guangdong, Hunan and Sichuan provinces, with the worst area being Guangxi; and rabies is a particular hazard in Tibet, where packs of feral dogs roam towns and monastery complexes. About 3,300 cases were reported nationwide in 2007, with more than 200 cases reported in Beijing alone, despite the local requirement to have all dogs vaccinated. To put these statistics in an international perspective, rabies claims an average of one death a year in the US, while the last death from rabies contracted from an indigenous animal in the UK was in 1902.

Rabies

Rabies, or hydrophobia, is a serious condition, and you should avoid close contact with animals, even pets, particularly dogs. The incubation period ranges from a few days to over a month, but once symptoms appear the disease is invariably fatal; so if you're bitten, even slightly, wash the wound and get to hospital as fast as possible and ask for the Human Diploid Cell Vaccine.

● **Sexually-transmitted diseases (STDs) & HIV:** The government may claim that STDs, HIV and AIDS are less common in China than in the decadent West, but they exist all the same. If your employer discovers you've contracted a serious STD, such as syphilis or gonorrhoea, or are HIV positive, he'll be compelled to report it to the police and you'll be deported immediately, with your passport marked accordingly.

- **Swimming:** At swimming pools you're usually provided with sandals to wear when walking in the changing room and around the pool, and the management may insist that you wear a swimming cap in the water (these are sold at pools). To a large extent, these two simple precautions minimise the risk of catching an infection. There's a small risk of catching a foot infection, such as a verruca; and in China, there's a fairly common fungal infection called grey nail, which causes your toenails to turn black and fall off! Fortunately it can be treated and, while not pretty, isn't usually serious.

- **Tropical diseases & ailments:** If you plan to live south of the Yellow River, check whether you need to take anti-malarial medication and/ or be vaccinated against Japanese encephalitis, a potentially lethal disease carried by mosquitoes and present in areas of southern China.

Healthcare

China has two public health systems: one for the rural population which provides some, but very little, financial support in the event of sickness or injury, and the other a form of social insurance that employers are obliged to take out for their employees (although many don't). This, too, is limited and mainly confined

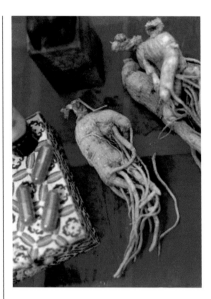

to in-patient treatment only. Wealthy Chinese can take out private health insurance to supplement these. Neither system is open to foreigners, who must fend for themselves, sometimes with the support of their employers, or take out their own insurance.

Fortunately, healthcare isn't expensive by Western standards, with a consultation with a doctor costing just 5 to 10 RMB. As an example, an operation to clean out debris from a knee joint (an arthroscopy) costs about 2,000 RMB, including three days' post-operative treatment in hospital.

Pharmacies

If you're ill, your first stop should be a pharmacy or chemist's *(yaodian)*, which can often be identified by a green sign with the pharmacist's name in white letters. Pharmacies are found in every town, and can often help with minor injuries or ailments. Larger pharmacies sometimes have a separate counter offering diagnosis and advice, although most attendant doctors only speak Chinese, so take along a phrase book or a Chinese-speaking friend.

The selection of Asian and Western products available (sometimes in a familiar packaging) is vast and improving all the time, although aspirin (*aspilin*) can be elusive. Many drugs that are prescription only in the West, such as antibiotics, can be bought over the counter in China; and you can also buy condoms, although these are probably more easily purchased at a supermarket. It's also possible to treat yourself with traditional Chinese remedies, and many pharmacies have a separate section for this.

Doctors

Chinese doctors are well trained and patients are often seen by a team of doctors; the most experienced one diagnoses, the others are there to learn. Around half of all doctors are female, therefore there's no difficulty finding a female doctor if this is your preference.

China doesn't have a GP system. Doctors mostly operate out of hospitals or clinics – sometimes their own private clinics – and there's no need to make an appointment; you just turn up and wait to be seen. Most Chinese people visit a state hospital if they need to see a doctor, a system which works surprisingly well (see below). If you need or want to consult an English-speaking doctor, you'll probably need to visit a private clinic or hospital in one of the major cities.

Clinics

Many schools and universities have their own clinics, as do the larger hotels, housing estates and workplaces. There are also many small clinics that are, in effect, doctors' private practices. Clinics

are identified by the sign of a white cross on a red background.

Public Hospitals

Most large towns and all cities have a variety of hospitals. Some are general hospitals, while others specialise in a particular area, e.g. bones, eyes or stomach complaints. There's an official rating system for hospitals, but ratings aren't easily accessible to the public, and aren't necessarily a good guide to the quality of treatment.

> Many Chinese people treat hospitals like a doctor's surgery, turning up with ever more minor ailments, therefore 'outpatients' can be crowded and confusing, although waiting times are surprisingly short. If your Chinese isn't good, you'll find it much easier if you attend with a Chinese-speaking friend or interpreter.

Unlike in the West, where a doctor refers you to a specialist, in China you select your own practitioner. The reception area displays a series of photographs of all the doctors working at the hospital, with details of their background and areas of expertise (in Chinese). Patients pick the one they feel will help them best and queue up at a payment counter. On payment you're given a receipt and told where to find your chosen doctor. Wait outside their room until it's your turn, hand over your receipt, describe your problem and you're then examined. Once the doctor has diagnosed your problem, he prescribes treatment, which may be orthodox medicine or, possibly, a traditional Chinese treatment. A trainee doctor will write a prescription which you take to the reception area. You pay for your prescription at a different counter and are given another receipt, which you then take to the hospital's pharmacy to collect your medicine.

If your prescribed treatment includes an injection, you take the medicine back to the doctor to administer it – a new, sterile needle is included with the prescription. If you need an x-ray, the doctor will give you a request to the x-ray department and you follow the same procedure, paying in advance, having your x-ray and then taking the results back to the doctor. The x-ray negatives will be given to you to keep.

It sounds a bit chaotic, but the system usually works very well. Everything is paid by cash and, provided that you're reasonably mobile, you're diagnosed and treated quickly. Fees are low: a consultation costs around 5 or 10 RMB and medicines are often cheaper than in the West.

A consultation with a doctor isn't very private. The door is often left open and patients passing by will look at you out of curiosity. Your doctor will have at least two trainee doctors and a couple of nurses sitting around the consulting table, too. Chinese people don't mind this at all – their concept of privacy is different from that of Westerners – and are more concerned that doctors are bumping up their meagre income by taking payments from drug manufacturers in return for prescribing their drugs. You may well be prescribed more medicine than you need, and there's a tendency for doctors to prescribe expensive Western drugs rather than cheaper herbal remedies.

Staying in Hospital

Hospitals range from thoroughly modern facilities to shabby, out-dated buildings. The best hospitals are spotless and the standard of service and equipment is every bit as good as in Europe or the US – even their payment systems are computerised and efficient – while prices are satisfyingly low by expatriate standards. Even in older, less hi-tech hospitals, service is good. If you need inpatient treatment or surgery, you're provided with pyjamas and usually share a well-equipped room with up to three other patients. Nursing care is attentive and visitors are permitted throughout most of the day. Families often bring food in for patients, but the hospital can provide meals as well.

Private Hospitals

If you have private medical insurance and/or wish to be treated by an English-speaking doctor, there are international and private clinics in the major cities. The best choice is in Beijing and Shanghai, but there are excellent hospitals in other cities as well. Many medical insurance schemes have agreements with nominated hospitals and require patients to use those establishments. If you don't have insurance, expect charges to be ten times what it costs to use a state hospital. There are some modern private hospitals in China, but most are a far cry from the Western image of a hotel-style building staffed with scores of white-clad doctors and nurses. Some so-called international hospitals are tucked away in scruffy back streets and staffed by people whose English is by no means fluent. Some private clinics specialise in traditional Chinese medicine (see below).

Emergencies

In a medical emergency, you should dial 120 for an ambulance. The Chinese ambulance service is reliable, although ambulances are staffed only by a driver and a nurse – there are no paramedics. You may need to help to get the patient on board, and it may be quicker to call a taxi or drive to the nearest hospital. Larger hospitals have an A&E department (emergency room), and patients needing emergency care are treated immediately, without having to pay in advance.

Women's Health & Childbirth

The authorities encourage women to give birth in hospital, and it's only in the most remote areas that children are born at home. Caesarian sections are used when necessary, but pain relief, such as epidurals, is uncommon. Chinese mothers get a great deal of advice and support from their families, but medical services such as pre and post-natal classes are available. Women should be aware that while sanitary towels are sold in supermarkets, it may only be possible to buy tampons in shops serving the expat community.

Dentists

Dentists are available in all towns and cities. There's no need to make an appointment and, as with hospitals, there's usually little waiting.

Dental clinics vary from a one- or two-chair dentist, practicing on his own, up to dental 'hospitals' which may well have 20 or more dental chairs. Larger operations offer a choice of dentist, and employ the latest equipment, techniques and materials. However, you may find yourself being treated in a line of other patients having treatment and, as in hospitals, there will be one or two trainee dentists attending each fully qualified dentist and doing some of the work, such as scaling and polishing teeth.

The standard of treatment is generally good. As a foreigner, you may be asked whether you want a Western-manufactured injection or filling materials or the cheaper Chinese versions, but these are similar and there's rarely anything wrong with the techniques employed. The cost is reasonable: a filling costs just 200 RMB, while a crown or set of false teeth will set you back around 1,000 RMB.

If you're genuinely apprehensive, try a children's dentist – they couldn't be more gentle and caring.

Opticians

Chinese people tend to suffer from poor eyesight more than Westerners, and a surprisingly high proportion wear

will then work on your feet using what look like miniature chisels to gently trim nails and hard skin.

Massage

Therapeutic massage is considered to have many health-giving properties, and is available in specific 'massage' clinics or TCM hospitals. It costs just 20 RMB for 45 minutes of skilful and relaxing massage.

INSURANCE

Overseas insurance companies have entered the Chinese market in quite a big way, and there are also a number of Chinese companies now competing for business. However, insurance is quite a new concept, and the only compulsory insurance for individuals is third party cover for your car.

Most Chinese, even the wealthy, shun insurance as they feel that they should look after themselves by saving for a rainy day, turning to the family for help if their savings are insufficient. They are highly suspicious of whether an insurance company would pay out unless they had good connections (*guanxi*), and their distrust of insurance companies is mirrored by their high savings rate. When disaster strikes, be it earthquake or flood, people trust to fate, feeling that acts of God cannot be predicted and that if they do happen, the government and their relatives will help.

spectacles. Full eye tests using the latest equipment are free, and the optician will tell you honestly if you need glasses or not. Glasses cost about 300 RMB, although designer frames may be five times as much. Contact lenses are popular, although those with coloured irises are difficult to find. Accessories such as contact lens fluid are available, but optician chains are rare.

> The only people who wear sunglasses in China are holidaymakers and *huai dan* (members of the criminal classes).

Chiropody

The Chinese look after their feet and a chiropody service is available at many public baths and steam rooms. You're expected to bathe your feet immediately prior to treatment, and the chiropodist

Health Insurance

Many employers, particularly foreign companies and joint ventures, have company insurance policies covering their employees and providing access to private medical services. It's possible to take out medical insurance via one of the private health funds, such as BUPA and AXA PPP, but some rate China as an expensive area – not least because they insist on patients being treated in the most expensive private hospitals – and premiums are high for the not so young. Another option is to take out medical cover with a local insurer; if you exclude the option of repatriation (flying you home, possibly in an air ambulance), the cost is substantially less. Medical insurance is beyond the pockets of many Chinese, and most people who aren't covered by an insurance scheme at work rely on local medical services and fund the actual costs, if any, themselves.

Car Insurance

For a medium-sized car, worth around 250,000 RMB, you can get comprehensive insurance cover for about 7,000 RMB, but the majority of drivers settle for third party insurance only. This became compulsory in 2006 and costs around 1,500 RMB a year, depending on which car you drive. Cover can be bought from a Chinese insurer. Proof of insurance, i.e. a sticker, must be displayed in the top right-hand corner of your windscreen.

Household Insurance

Insurance for your home and its contents is available from local insurers. Chinese people rarely insure their home, although some insure the contents; most rely on deterrents such as steel front doors and bars on the windows of lower floor dwellings. Most policies issued by local insurers are written only in Chinese, therefore you need to understand what is and isn't covered.

Claims

Chinese insurers are no more eager to settle your claim than insurers in the rest of the world, but having a police report and following the company's requirements to the letter can help. Knowing someone with influence at the insurance company will help even more.

EDUCATION

For the majority of urban Chinese, education is seen as the only way in which an individual can achieve a good lifestyle in a nation of 1.3bn, unless he's blessed with good *guanxi*. Many rural people feel the same way, but the pressures of keeping the farm going and income coming in often overrule their objective. Virtually all urban parents, and many parents in the countryside, go to extraordinary lengths to ensure that their child gets all possible assistance to enable him to obtain good results. As for the children, they are, with few exceptions, diligent, keen to learn and well behaved, and do their utmost not to let their parents down. Teachers,

throughout the system, focus on guiding students towards passing the all-important examinations, and they're judged almost solely on how well their students do in them.

Formal education begins at the age of seven and is compulsory until the age of 15. Core subjects include Chinese, mathematics and English. English is China's official second language and is taught from the first term of primary school all the way up to university level. At age 16, students have the option of spending a further three years in high school, in preparation for university, or going to a vocational college. There's no apprenticeship system allowing students to study while they work, and most tradesmen are self-taught.

Many parents seek to get their children into learning as early as possible, and there are a large number of state and private kindergartens throughout the country, many of which are bi-lingual. For a child aged from three to seven, Chinese kindergartens can be an excellent way of easing a foreign child into the Chinese education system, as they make friends and pick up many words and expressions of simple Chinese quickly. If possible, choose a kindergarten that's been recommended by a friend or acquaintance.

Education options for foreign children become trickier from the age of seven. In smaller cities and towns, there may only be a Chinese primary school where all the classes are conducted in Chinese, other than teaching English, and there's no guarantee that they'll accept a foreign child. Alternatively, you can teach your child at home or send him to a boarding school in your home country. In the largest cities, the choice is greater. There are international schools in Beijing, Shanghai, Guangzhou and elsewhere, where all classes are conducted in English, although the pupils will be from many countries.

> If you want to save money on schooling, consider offering to teach lessons yourself. Many private schools will leap at the chance to have you work for them and it's sometimes possible to get free, or at least discounted, tuition for your child in exchange for a few hours' teaching each week. However, it's imperative that it's legal, and that you obtain a working (Z) visa in order to do this.

State Schools

There are no rules or regulations preventing foreign children from attending a state school, although some Chinese schools are reluctant to accept foreign children for reasons of responsibility and security. State schools may be tougher at first, but give children a better chance of learning the language and assimilating into the community. Younger children are more adaptable, but children aged ten or over may struggle to cope with such a different culture and language. If your stay in China is relatively short, an international school (see below) will provide better preparation for their next destination.

International Schools

There are over 80 state-approved international schools in China, of

school bus. There's also likely to be a one-off admission fee of around 2,000 RMB. Tuition for seven to 18-year-olds at an international school is even more expensive, and costs between 150,000 and 180,000 RMB a year, plus fees for lunches and the school bus. Expect to hear the odd disgruntled parent muttering, "I'll be glad when Joe goes to Cambridge University – it'll be a darned sight cheaper than school here."

which 20 are in Beijing and 18 are in Shanghai. However, just because a school calls itself 'international' doesn't mean that it truly caters for expatriates' children. The Chinese like to incorporate Western branding into their businesses, therefore don't assume that, say, the Harvard International School has any connection with Harvard University.

There are, however, at least three international schools in China that do have genuine links with parent foreign schools. These include two branches of Dulwich College, one in Beijing (with more than one campus) and the other in Shanghai, and the Harrow International School in Beijing. There are also schools with connections to foreign educational establishments, including those in Australia, Canada, Singapore and the US.

International schools aren't cheap. A full day's attendance at an international kindergarten, e.g. one using the Montessori system, costs around 100,000 RMB a year in Beijing, and you must add a further 5,000 RMB for the cost of lunch and trips in the

While many international schools offer the UK National Curriculum, others are aligned with the curricula of other countries, with American, Australian, Canadian, French, German, Japanese, Pakistani, Spanish and Swedish schools all available in Beijing (where embassies are located). Some offer entry to the UK's GCSE and A-level examinations, while others offer the International Baccalaureate or the national examinations of a particular country.

Finding a good school is rarely easy. Expatriate magazines can be helpful, as can the internet, and schools are always happy to show prospective parents around their facilities, but the best way is to obtain recommendations from other parents.

University

In 2009, there were 2,236 higher-learning establishments in China, teaching 18.9m undergraduate and 1.2m graduate students. The standard of teaching and achievements is high and, in some subjects, particularly sciences, higher than in many developed nations. Chinese bachelor's degrees are accepted abroad in American, European and Antipodean universities. Many Chinese students travel overseas, some to continue their studies, but many because their exam results aren't good enough to gain them a place in a premier Chinese university.

LOCAL SERVICES

There are no local councils in China. Certain services such as street lighting are provided by local government, but there's no equivalent to local council or municipal tax. Rubbish collection is done by private contractors, and the cost is usually included in your apartment's monthly service charge.

The Chinese are committed to recycling, and every public waste bin has compartments for both recyclable and unrecyclable materials. Old ladies collect empty plastic bottles (they get

Solar energy panels, Guangdong

one *jiao* a bottle). Newspaper deliverers collect used newspapers. Virtually everything is recycled and nothing is wasted – although the practice of using 'night soil' as fertiliser has ceased.

UTILITIES

In China, many older homes use coal-fired boilers for heating and cooking, hence the large amount of pollution in many cities. However, newer properties usually have central heating; either gas-fired radiators or electrically-powered under-floor heating. Many people use oil-filled radiators as a booster. In some cities, both public and some residential buildings get their hot water and heating from a central system provided by the local government; in this case, heating systems are usually switched on in mid-November and off again in mid-March, and residents have no control over it.

If you live in a serviced apartment or accommodation provided by your employer, it's likely that utilities such as electricity, gas and water, will be included. However, if you rent your own house or apartment, you must pay your own bills. Services are usually handled by the management company (in a complex) or your landlord, who keeps the bills in his name, but on rare occasions you may need to take out a subscription. Your estate agent or landlord can help with this.

Electricity

Electricity isn't expensive, although you pay more if you're living in a rented flat as landlords tend to 'round up' the bill. Power cuts are comparatively rare. Electricity is 220v AC and the plugs in mainland China are either of the two or three flat pin type. You cannot use a UK-style three pin plug in mainland China. Most people buy a multi-plug extension, which usually accepts almost any plug.

Gas

Natural gas is available in most parts of China, but not every property is connected; older homes rely on bottled gas instead. Gas meters often operate with a gas 'credit card', which is inserted and left in a slot in the top of the gas meter. This card can be 'refilled' by taking it to a gas company office, where you pay to have gas units added to the card.

Water

Water is supplied by the local municipal water company, and its usage is metered. You should never drink water straight from the tap anywhere in China – all Chinese people use boiled or bottled water.

Paying the Bills

Usually your landlord or management company will handle the utility bills and then charge you for usage. If you're handling your own bills, you can arrange for utility services to bill your bank account direct and for the bank to pay their charges.

COMMUNICATIONS

Telephone

China has an extensive and reliable telephone system which covers the whole country. There are some 100m landlines in use, and the network includes some of the latest fibre optic technology. Calls to the UK or other overseas countries connect immediately, and reception is excellent.

China's international telephone code is 86. If you're dialling a number in China from abroad, you need to dial the international code then omit the 0 prefix from the area code, e.g. to call someone in Beijing (area code 10), you dial 0086 10 1234 5678. If calling the number from another Chinese city, dial 010 1234 5678.

Installation

To get a land line installed, visit the nearest office of China Telecom (🖥 www.chinatelecom-h.com), have your passport handy, along with some cash to provide a deposit, and ask for a connection. You'll be expected to provide the handset, which you can buy from China Telecom or any electrical goods shop. There's a standing charge of 20 RMB a month, which covers line rental; however, China Telecom doesn't send out bills. You put down a deposit to cover future calls, and then must visit one of their offices periodically to check your account, pay what you owe and top up your deposit. You can also get an itemised list of all calls made. Alternatively, give your bank the necessary cash, and ask them to settle your account for you. If you overrun your deposit by a fairly large sum, say 300 RMB, you'll find your phone can still receive calls, but outgoing calls will be blocked. When this happens, simply ask your bank to transfer cash to China Telecom and your phone will be re-connected.

China Telecom has occasional offers which allow you to cut the cost of calls, while international phone cards reduce the cost of long-distance calls substantially by routing them through a call centre. However, you're usually required to dial a lengthy prefix number before the number you want to call and you may end up dialling between 24 and 30 digits in total, so it's easy to make a mistake.

The cheapest way to make calls in China and abroad is to use internet telephony such as VOIP (🖥 http://voip.com/index.aspx) or Skype (🖥 www.skype.com/intl/en-gb/home), using a computer and headset, a popular system in China. Calls to other computers are free, and those to landlines and mobiles are hugely discounted.

Mobile Phones

China has over 600m mobile phone users. There seem to be as many mobile phone shops as there are restaurants, and young people treat their handsets like fashion accessories, changing them frequently. The three mobile phone network providers are China Mobile – the largest in the world, with over 550m subscribers – China Unicom and China Telecom, and you can visit one of

their shops to get connected. Take your passport with you as ID. A SIM card costs about 200 RMB and you have a choice of numbers. Mobile phone contracts are available, and are relatively simple to decipher, although most Chinese prefer the simplicity of pre-paid (pay-as-you-go) phones, which can be topped up to the value of 50, 100, 300 or 500 RMB. Top-up cards usually expire after six months, but can be extended when you recharge the account.

> **Mobile phone numbers are priced according to how many lucky or unlucky digits they contain. Six, eight and nine are lucky numbers, and phone numbers featuring these digits cost considerably more. You're unlikely to obtain a number including an eight, which is associated with wealth, as all of those numbers have been snapped up by superstitious businessmen.**

You can take your own handset to China and slot in a Chinese SIM, provided it operates on a 900MHz frequency band; European phones work on the Chinese network, but those from North America don't. Mobile phones are cheap in China, where prices start at just 99 RMB, and are on sale everywhere, even in supermarkets (Nokia, Motorola and Ericsson predominate). One interesting variation on the mobile theme is a phone that can only be used to contact other

telephones within a limited local radius. They only cost around 140 RMB and are brilliant for youngsters who want to chat or text their school friends.

Chinese mobile phone etiquette is rarely subtle. Every public space is full of people shouting into their mobiles, but at least they have the decency to leave if their phone rings in the cinema. Using a mobile on aircraft is forbidden, but the instant the engines are switched off, every phone on the plane is in use!

Internet

The internet is hugely popular in China, where some 500m people are regular users – at least 30 per cent of the population are online and the figure rises to over 60 per cent in Beijing and Shanghai. Social networking sites are popular, as in online shopping, and many users access the internet via their mobile phone.

The internet is a controversial subject in China, where the government has a reputation for censoring and blocking access to websites according to a complex set of rules, designed to 'protect' the state and its citizens. Websites can only be accessed if they're cleared by government censors, and popular sites such as Facebook, YouTube and even Hotmail are periodically rendered inaccessible. The Chinese public aren't entirely comfortable with some of the Western content which is accessible, and there's considerable pressure on the government to find a way to keep pornography off the internet.

An on-going dispute over censorship between the Chinese government and internet search engine giant Google means that the main Google website (🖥 www.google.com) now redirects

to the Hong Kong version, which is all in Chinese. However, you can access other countries' versions, e.g. Australian Google (🖥 www.google.com.au). Chinese techno-geeks also have ways of getting around internet censorship; there are clones of many websites, e.g. Tudou (YouTube) and Fanfou (Twitter).

If you want to be able to access uncensored foreign websites, you should install a proxy browser such as TOR (🖥 www. torproject.org) on your laptop <u>before</u> your arrival. Tor is free software, and an open network that helps you defend against a form of network surveillance that threatens personal freedom and privacy.

Internet cafes are also under government scrutiny. China isn't immune to the global phenomenon of young people becoming addicted to computer games, and internet cafes are seen as a major cause of this. A fire in an internet café in Beijing, in which nine people died because they couldn't escape, has further damaged their reputation in the eyes of the authorities, and customers under 18 are officially banned, while there are regular police inspections and checks to make sure that fire exits are open and accessible. Despite this, there are internet cafes in every city; some are vast and most are full to bursting. If you can find a spare seat, an hour's surfing costs as little as 2 RMB.

Most people use dial up to connect to the internet, but in the cities you can get China Telecom to install an ADSL (broadband) connection. The charge for unlimited usage is 100 RMB a month.

Faxes

If you need to send something by fax, such as a document showing your signature, you can use the business centre in any fairly upmarket hotel. You don't need to be a resident. This isn't a cheap option – it costs 30 to 40 RMB to send a single page overseas – but it's cheaper than buying a fax machine. If you have a printer/scanner, you can also scan a document, sign it and send it as an email attachment.

Postal Services

The postal service is run by the state-owned China Post and is generally reliable and fast, with letters taking a day in the same city and two days to reach other major Chinese cities. Airmail takes around seven to ten days to Europe, the US or Australia, but posted items can take as much as four to six weeks to arrive if sent by sea mail (surface).

It costs just 0.80 RMB to send a standard letter to any destination in China, or 6 RMB via airmail overseas. Airmail stickers aren't used, therefore you need to use an airmail envelope and/or make sure that the desk clerk stamps your envelope 'airmail'. As

well as stamps, you can buy ordinary and airmail envelopes cheaply at post offices – cheaper than in supermarkets – but Chinese envelopes have no adhesive and must be glued (glue is available at post offices). Stamps have adhesive on them (but aren't self-adhesive) – the Chinese use a damp pad to moisten these, rather than licking them.

Extra services include recorded delivery for sending important documents, and the Express Mail Service (EMS), which operates to most countries as well as within China. As well as reducing delivery times, EMS ensures that a letter or parcel is sent by registered post for extra security. EMS overseas can be relatively expensive, with an A4 letter containing up to 20 sheets of paper costing around 140 RMB to Australia, the UK or US, although this is substantially cheaper than using a private courier service such as DHL. However, not all expats vouch for EMS' reliability.

Main post offices usually open from 8am until 8pm, even during public holidays, and in many cities there are one or two post offices offering a 24-hour service. Smaller branch offices may have shorter business hours, and occasionally shut at lunch time. Post boxes are dark green with a white roof, and have the China Post logo on them in yellow. They contain two slots, one for local and one for long-distance and overseas mail.

Posting Parcels

Sending a parcel is a little different in China. The post office won't accept a sealed parcel – they want to ensure that it's correctly packed – so you must present your goods at the counter where staff will help you to pack them in an approved box. You pay for the box, tape and paper, which isn't expensive. Once the parcel is packed, but before it's sealed, it must be checked at the Customs window. During this procedure you must complete a number of forms, so don't expect to post a parcel in few minutes. It's always a complicated business and takes time.

Postal deliveries are made at least six days a week; twice on weekdays and once on Saturdays (and occasionally on Sundays). People are justifiably proud to work for China Post and there are as many postwomen as there are postmen, all neatly dressed in their dark green uniforms. In addition to delivering the post, they also deliver Chinese newspapers and magazines; you pay the postman in cash for, say, one year in advance and he'll deliver your newspaper each morning with your mail. Delivery of letters and parcels to and from overseas is fairly reliable, but delivery of overseas magazines or newspapers, many of which rely on private courier services, tend to be less satisfactory. Large or heavy parcels may have to be collected from a local post office, and you'll need your passport to prove your identity.

In addition to postal services, the post office offers an efficient money transfer service (see page 90).

STAYING INFORMED

The main Chinese news agency Xinhua is owned by the state and has an office in every province, as well as owning the main bookshops in every city. Xinhua has a total monopoly on all news within China, or affecting China, therefore everything that you read in Chinese newspapers or on Chinese television has a pro-government slant, whatever the context. If you read an item about a government official up to his neck in corruption, it's because the government **wants** you to read it, perhaps to make an example of the culprit. You will read nothing that the government **doesn't** want you to read. A second news service, the China News Service, serves mainly Chinese people living overseas.

If you want to learn more about events overseas, or to see how foreign news agencies report events in China, you can occasionally pick up a copy of *The Times* or a similar overseas newspaper at a five-star hotel, but the quickest way to garner such information is via the internet.

Newspapers & Magazines

The Chinese are keen newspaper readers, and some 25 Chinese newspapers are included in the

World Association of Newspapers' worldwide top 100. China has a great many regional newspapers which report both national and local news, although there are probably only two truly national newspapers: the *People's Daily* and the *China Daily*.

One of the most widely read Chinese-language newspapers is the *People's Daily* with a daily circulation of about 2.8m – a similar figure to that of the UK's top-selling daily *The Sun*. It has online editions in several languages, including English (⌨ http:// english.peopledaily.com.cn), but as it's essentially the voice of the Communist Party of China (CPC), don't expect to read any controversial or anti-government content.

The largest national daily English-language newspaper is the *China Daily*, published in Beijing, but available countrywide as well as online (⌨ www.chinadaily.com.cn).

Free copies are frequently provided to foreigners staying at hotels or travelling on Chinese airlines. It costs just 1.5 RMB a day, and is published six days a week (except Sunday). Universities and schools often provide free copies of the *China Daily* to foreign teachers. Owned by the CPC, it isn't the most exciting paper to read, with a heavy emphasis on political and business news, but it also has a fair bit of international news, including two or three pages of sport. More recently launched, but not as widely available, is the *Global Times* which is owned by the *People's Daily*.

In addition to the national press, China has a vast number of regional newspapers, some of which are published in English. Shanghai has an English version of the *Shanghai Daily* published online. In Guangzhou it's easy to obtain copies of the *South China Morning Post,* a newspaper published in Hong Kong. Although not censored as rigorously as the mainland press, this is probably even more turgid than the *China Daily*, and so slanted towards Hong Kong news that it provides astonishingly little of interest to any readers in mainland China.

There are a number of magazines available, such as *Beijing Review, Business Beijing* and *Beijing this Month*, as well as *Beijing* and *Shanghai Metro* which are published by *Global Times*. Both cities have a version of *Time Out* magazine. In Beijing, Guangzhou and Shanghai you can read local editions of *City Weekend*, and there are also a number of free expat-produced magazines. The emphasis in these is on forthcoming and recent events and classified advertisements, particularly accommodation. Copies can usually be found in bars and restaurants frequented by expatriates.

In larger branches of the Friendship Stores (see page 204), and in most upmarket hotels, it's possible to buy copies of overseas newspapers and magazines, such as *Time*, *Newsweek*, *The Times*, *Economist*, *The Asian Wall Street Journal* and *USA Today*, but they can be expensive and may be a few days or a week old.

Books

There's only one large bookseller in China, Xinhua, which is government owned and run. There's a Xinhua store in every town or city, and most have a foreign language section, but the choice of English-language books is often limited to dictionaries, books for teaching English and copies of famous works by long dead authors such as Mark Twain, Arthur Conan Doyle and Shakespeare. The best way around this is to bring as many books as possible with you (if you use an eReader, you can bring a year's supply!), or arrange for a friend, a book club or a bookshop in your home country to keep you supplied, or make the most of online stores such as Amazon.

Some popular novels and books are published in Chinese, but English-language versions are rarely available, although a few can be obtained from hotel bookstalls or shops at major tourist attractions such as museums – Shanghai Museum is a useful source – and, occasionally, in Friendship Stores. The Foreign Language Bookstore in Wangfujingdajie, Beijing is a good source of modern novels in English, plus lots of books on China including translations of Chinese classics such as *The Three Kingdoms*. A far-sighted expatriate has opened a small chain of shops called The Bookworm (🖳 www.chinabookworm.

com) in Beijing, Chengdu and Suzhou with, hopefully, more to follow.

If you have access to a university library, these frequently feature an English-language section, including recently published magazines and books donated by foreign teachers.

There's still censorship of books and magazines, but it isn't as stringent as in the past. It's possible to buy a copy of *Mao's Last Dancer*, which includes a controversial exposé of the communist system, in the Shanghai Museum bookshop. However, at the same time, copies of the latest version of Lonely Planet's guide to China have recently been confiscated from travellers entering China overland at the Vietnam-Guangxi overland border. Allegedly, this is because the publishers have coloured the map of Taiwan in a different shade from mainland China, which the authorities have interpreted as promoting Taiwan as an independent country!

Dictionaries

Buying a functional English-Chinese dictionary is difficult in China. There are many dictionaries on sale in China, but most are useless unless you can read Chinese script. Ensure that you bring a dictionary with you that includes pinyin – the official system used to transcribe Chinese characters into English – as well as English and Chinese, such as *The Times Essential English Chinese Dictionary*, **published by Federal Publications in Singapore but available in the UK or from Amazon. Such a dictionary is the most useful book you can own in China!**

Television

China's state broadcasting service is China Central Television (CCTV), which transmits 11 regular channels and a multitude of additional specialist channels, most of which are entirely in Chinese. There are no publicly released ratings, therefore it's impossible to work out which are the most popular shows, although soaps (many of which are made in Korea) and sport are watched avidly. Many drama serials are Mills & Boon type romances or stories based on the Chinese-Japanese war, in which the Chinese are always the winners!

The main channels of interest to foreigners are shown in the table below.

There are further channels specialising in finance, legal and agricultural issues, as well as those broadcasting programmes in foreign languages such as Russian and Spanish. A TV guide magazine, China Central Television, lists television programme schedules.

Cable television is available in larger cities, but is heavily slanted to its Chinese

Television Channels	
Channel No.	**Programmes**
1	the main news channel
3	music, cross-talk and shows, including some circus performances
4	news channel, plus the occasional English-language programme
5	sport, including a number of Premier League and *Bundesliga* football matches, particularly on Sundays. There's a round-up of all the European league results on Monday evenings, together with American football, hockey and basketball results – all in Chinese.
6	films, most of which are ancient, although a few are transmitted in English with Chinese subtitles
8	documentaries
9	branded as CCTV News, this is the only real English-language channel. It shows a mixture of news, travel documentaries and excellent business and arts programmes, but is frequently only available on cable at a cost of around 600 RMB a year.
10	documentaries and educational programming including wildlife series
11	mainly Chinese opera
14	children's programming
15	music, from classical to rap

subscribers, so you may be offered a package consisting of 20 Chinese channels plus, if you're lucky, the Discovery Channel or National Geographic Channel, and even these may be dubbed into Chinese. ESPN, Star Sport and HBO are unavailable in many provinces for private subscribers, although some hotels pay an exorbitant cost to show them. Star Sport alone can cost a hotel US$25,000 a year.

Satellite dishes are available, but you cannot use them to pick up foreign TV channels. This isn't because the Chinese authorities want to stop you viewing other countries' TV programmes, but because local government has a monopoly on cable television and wants to sell you its service.

It may be possible to pick up some foreign television channels via the internet. Pirate channels abound, and while they're regularly shut down, they often pop up again. University students invariably know where to find them!

Radio

Chinese radio broadcasts a mixture of soft, gentle music and rabid advertisements. The programming is entirely in Chinese, although English language broadcasts can be heard in some areas of China, or online, broadcast by the state-owned China Radio International (⌨ http://english. cri.cn). Overseas services such as BBC World Service and Voice of America can be received with a short-wave radio, although it's easier to listen to most foreign radio stations via the internet. Radios are available in China or you can bring one with you.

MONEY & BANKING

The Chinese are born businesspeople. When a Chinese person sees something new, his first thought is not 'that's nice!' but 'how can I make money from it?' The older generation is more careful with money, but even though they're big savers, they're constantly on the lookout for opportunities to make money.

Money is, in many ways, an obsession with a large number of Chinese. Banks lend generously, and people enter into borrowing, seemingly without a thought. The Chinese are also big gamblers, not merely pennies at mah-jong but also on the stock exchange, where each so-called investor is a day trader, often gambling on stock that has a good number, i.e. one containing an eight in its number on the stock exchange register. Eight is believed to be a number that will make you rich.

Chinese Currency

China's currency is officially called the *renminbi* (RMB), which means 'people's money'. It's sometimes called the *yuan*, while the slang name is *kuai*, which means 'piece'. The symbol for

RMB is written in two ways; one is similar to the Japanese Yen, a capital letter Y with either one or two lines crossing the stem (¥), but it's more commonly written as 元. One RMB breaks down into ten *jiao – mao* in slang – and each *jiao* breaks down into ten *fen,* so that there are 100 *fen* to 1 RMB. The *fen,* nowadays worth about one thousandth of a UK pound, is effectively no longer in use, although you can still sometimes find a five *jiao* coin in your change.

Paper money was invented in China in about 650AD, and cash is still by far the most common form of transaction. Cheques aren't usually provided for personal use, and credit or debit cards are a relatively new phenomenon. The largest denomination notes have a value of 100 RMB – this is only worth about £10 or US$15. Even though the cost of living is considerably cheaper than in the West, this is becoming a problem, as many businesses have to deal in huge wads of money. The smallest note is 1 RMB. A 1 RMB coin has been introduced, but isn't very common outside major cities and may even be treated with suspicion in rural areas. The smallest coin is one *jiao.*

Shop assistants examine 100 RMB notes carefully as there are occasionally fake notes in circulation, some of which are remarkably good. You should also check fresh-looking notes before accepting them.

The RMB's value currently floats within a fairly narrow range set by a basket of currencies. It has appreciated by around 25 per cent against the US dollar since 2005, but this has still not been fast enough to satisfy the US or the European Union, who want it to rise even higher to render Chinese goods less competitive in their markets.

Use of the RMB outside China is limited, although it's increasingly possible to exchange RMB in countries with whom China trades, such as Australia, Singapore and the United Arab Emirates. You may find you get a better rate of exchange from a 'dealer' in a local 'Chinatown' in your home country than with an official exchange bureau or bank.

Banking

Banking has a long history in China, dating back over 1,000 years to the Song dynasty, but while it's becoming increasingly sophisticated it's still, like many things in China, firmly in the hands of the state. The five major banks are all government-owned: Bank of China, China Construction Bank, Industrial and Commercial Bank of China, Agricultural Bank of China and Communications Bank of China. There are many other banks to choose from, including those run by provincial or city governments, such as the Bank of

Beijing, and few private banks, but the vast majority of Chinese people and businesses bank with one of the big five. The central bank, overseeing China's finances, is the People's Bank of China.

Foreign banks are slowly being established in China but they're few and far between. Unless there's one near you and it has the authority to conduct RMB business, they're of little use to private customers, although businesses may find them useful. Building societies don't exist in China, but China Post operates a savings bank.

Bank of China

The vast majority of private transactions are conducted in cash, including car and home purchases, so literally tonnes of notes move between banks every day. You'll often see armoured cars travelling between banks, with steel-helmeted guards armed with shotguns and assault guns standing guard. This is a good time to cross the road and avoid any possibility of them thinking that you may be a threat to the money.

In 2007, guards were delivering money into a Chinese bank and told the bank's customers not to move. One customer, with business to attend to, began to walk out of the bank, and was promptly shot dead. The guard who shot him wasn't punished because the authorities said he was just doing his job.

In larger cities, banks open seven days a week and from 9am until 5pm, but not all transactions are available at any time. Banks close for three or four days during Chinese New Year, and have reduced hours for the following 11 days. They may also close during other holidays, but there are no 'bank holidays' as such. They are open on Christmas Day and on other Western holidays, such as Easter or Thanksgiving.

Opening a current account isn't difficult and, if you're studying or working in China, you'll need one. All you need is your passport and a sum of money, say 100 RMB, as an opening deposit, plus the help of a Chinese-speaking friend. To keep control of your account, you initially have the choice of a bank book in which each transaction is recorded, or a bank card that you can use in an ATM. If you choose a bank book, you'll have to queue at the counter each time you want to draw or deposit money, while with the card you can withdraw money 24 hours a day, seven days a week by using an ATM at the bank. These are placed in a separate room located at the front of the bank, and you gain entry by swiping your bank card through a slot on the door frame. You cannot usually deposit money via an ATM.

Most students and young people opt for the bank card, but having a bank book gives you a continuous picture of your account (you receive no monthly statements) and you can always ask for a card once you have a bank book. What you won't receive is a cheque book, as these are rarely used in China (only businesses receive cheque books). If you want a debit card, you must ask for one. Debit cards (see page 91) are useful for withdrawing cash from your bank's ATMs, and can also be used at larger hotels and at a limited number of supermarkets and department stores.

Electronic banking is in its infancy in China, although the Chinese love for technology means it's likely to catch on fast. Some banks have websites allowing customers to conduct some transactions online. Bank of China has an English-language option to its website (🖥 www.bankofchina.com/en/pbservice).

There are a number of other quirks to Chinese banking which you should be aware of:

● **Changing money** – The bureau de change service is often restricted to a single branch of the Bank of China in any city, one which often closes at lunchtimes and weekends. Fortunately, many ATMs are compatible with foreign credit/debit cards, allowing you to draw funds from an overseas account, although most foreign banks charge a fee for this. Travellers' cheques aren't always easy to change in China. If you're staying at a four or five star hotel or go to a major branch of Bank of China, they'll probably cash them for you, provided that the cheques are from a well-known

issuer, such as American Express, and you can show your passport, but it's doubtful whether anyone else will accept them. There are American Express offices in Beijing, Shanghai, Guangzhou and Xiamen.

> Don't be tempted by people who loiter outside branches of Bank of China and offer to change your foreign notes. Not only is this illegal – it's often a scam whereby corrupt businessmen launder 'hot' money – but you may also end up with counterfeit RMB.

● **Transactions** – Almost all bank transactions require you to enter a six-digit 'password' into a machine on the counter; you'll be reminded to do this by the cashier pressing a buzzer, and may need to repeat the process several times to complete just one transaction. Even the simplest transaction can require your signature on several forms. Most counters have a machine for counting banknotes so that you can check that your large bundle of bank notes adds up to the sum you requested.

● **Interest** – All accounts, whether current or deposit, in *renminbi* or in foreign currency, earn a small amount of interest – between 2.5 and 3 per cent on deposit accounts – which is paid automatically each year, less income tax of 20 per cent.

● **Transfers & payments** – Even without personal cheques, you can still send money to an individual or organisation by using the post office transfer service. There is a special counter for this in all post offices. On payment of a small fee, you're given a receipt, and the recipient receives the money in around two days. This system works well, and a number of the embassies ask you to use it to pay for visas. To make larger payments, e.g. when purchasing a property, your bank can transfer funds between accounts but it's a complicated business. A tremendous amount of banking work relies on manual processes and anything out of the ordinary is difficult. However, you can set up direct debits for regular payments, e.g. for certain utility bills.

● **Foreign transactions** – Sending money to or from your Chinese account can be done by electronic transfer such as SWIFT. Each transaction costs about 200 RMB and takes less than 24 hours to complete. However, if you wish to deposit another currency with your bank, or a foreign organisation wants to pay funds to you in China, you must open

a separate account for that currency. Withdrawing money from one of your foreign accounts in *renminbi* involves the completion of several forms under an anti-money-laundering scheme introduced in 2007.

> **To reduce the risk of fraud, the Chinese have a set of numerical characters which are reserved for financial documents. Ordinary Chinese characters for numerals can be altered by adding a couple of strokes, e.g. by modifying a one so that it looks like a three, or a ten which can be changed by a single stroke into a thousand, but these special numbers cannot be altered. You should be aware of these characters, as they must be used on many banking forms.**

● **Credit & debit cards** – Among a population of some 1.3bn, there are believed to be only some 90m cards in circulation. They are popular among young people as a means of drawing money from ATMs at any time of the day, but few shops, other than the largest department stores or perhaps the major supermarkets, will accept them and, when they do, it can be a long drawn-out process. Almost all cards are debit cards, rather than credit cards which are rarely issued in China.

Some banks issue Visa and MasterCard cards in addition to their own cards, but these are also debit cards and can only be used in branches of the issuing bank or in certain areas in China. They aren't valid for use abroad – the *renminbi* is not an officially interchangeable currency, therefore

isn't legal tender in many parts of the world, making credit calculations difficult – although there's a local credit card called Union Pay, which is gradually becoming accepted in other countries around the Pacific Rim.

You can usually use your overseas credit card, provided it's from a well-known issuer, e.g. Visa or MasterCard, backed up by your passport, to draw cash from a bank in China or from an ATM. Credit cards attract a 3 per cent service fee from the Chinese Bank **in addition** to any charges the issuing bank imposes, while using a foreign debit card in an ATM will also incur fees on your home account. However, either is still a life saver if you run out of cash in a strange town.

- **Loans & overdrafts** – Loans are available, including to foreigners, although there's a set-up fee and interest is charged at around 6 per cent. Banks require collateral. Overdrafts are rare, and banks exert pressure on people to pay them off quickly.

TAXES

The Chinese tax year runs from January to December. Tax avoidance is fairly rare, at least among ordinary people, as penalties are severe – fiddling your taxes can result in a lengthy prison sentence. Foreigners are taxed on their Chinese income and, after five years' continuous residence in China, their worldwide income. However, China has double taxation agreements with many countries, therefore it's unlikely that you'll be taxed twice.

The main taxes that you can expect to pay are as follows:

- **Income tax:** This is applied to Chinese citizens earning just 24,000

RMB a year; however, foreigners are allowed to earn up to 60,000 RMB a year (or 5,000 RMB a month) before any income tax is due. If you're liable for tax, your employer will deduct it from your salary each month. There are no allowances that can be used to reduce your income tax, and the tax rate increases incrementally quite fast.

Property taxes: Stamp duty is payable on property transfers.

- **Motor vehicle tax:** This covers highway and bridge maintenance. It costs around 1,200 RMB a year and is payable at the local Motor Vehicle Taxation Office run by the traffic police.

- **Capital gains tax:** This is levied when you make a gain on anything, be it property or shares, if the gain is more than 50 per cent of the original value. Tax starts at 30 per cent and increases to 60 per cent for gains of 200 per cent or more.

- **Value added tax (VAT):** This tax is applied to everything, including food, at varying rates.

COST OF LIVING

This can vary enormously, depending on where you live. Rental costs in Beijing, Shanghai, and Shenzhen and, to a lesser extent, Guangzhou are astronomical compared to the rest of the country. You may pay between 6,000 and 8,500 RMB a month to rent a one-bedroom apartment in Shanghai, whereas a similar property in Xi'an would cost between 1,000 and 3,000

RMB. In some cities, such as Beijing, there are no commuter suburbs, as there are in London, so everyone pays city-centre prices. Almost everything in the major cities costs more – food, clothes and household goods – because the rents for shops are also higher. Even in smaller cities, where salaries and rents are proportionally lower, you may still have to pay up to half of your income to keep a roof over your head.

Your lifestyle also has a major bearing on the cost of living in China. If you want to drink Corona beer and eat Western food, your expenses will be twice as high as if you shop in markets, eat local food and drink Tsingtao beer (which is excellent). Local produce is exceptionally cheap compared to prices in more developed countries. A kilo of Chinese fillet steak costs 35 RMB from the local meat market, Tsingtao beer is 3 RMB for a 375ml bottle and petrol costs around 6 RMB a litre. One major anomaly is coffee: a cup of coffee in a nice coffee bar costs between 30 to 40 RMB, which may be why a lot of Chinese don't drink it.

For most expatriates, China is an astonishingly cheap place to live, and labour charges are low. A standard car service costs 150 RMB (including oil and filters), while to have your car hand-washed and cleaned (inside and out) costs 15 to 20 RMB. Teachers, who have their accommodation provided free, can easily live on a salary of 4,000 RMB a month – a standard wage for an expat teacher – even in Beijing, and still have money left over to travel or to save. However, if they want to go to a Houhai or Sanlitun bar every evening, it won't go anywhere near as far!

4.
BREAKING THE ICE

One of the best ways of conquering culture shock and feeling a part of life in China is meeting and getting to know the Chinese. Fitting in with a society that's very different from the one you've been used to is rarely simple. Everyday things are done in unexpected ways, people's priorities are unlike yours and it's easy to misinterpret someone's words or actions. Although the Chinese are generally friendly and welcoming, this chapter will make you aware of the difficulties you may encounter and how to deal with them. Some knowledge of even basic spoken Chinese minimises the problems of social interaction to a considerable degree, but understanding why the Chinese do things the way that they do and understanding (a little) about how they think is just as important.

'Love your neighbours, but don't pull down the fence.'
Chinese proverb

This chapter provides information about important aspects of Chinese society. It advises on how to make friends and acquaintances and behave in social situations, as well as topics to steer clear of in conversation. It also provides guidance on handling confrontations and dealing with officials.

COMMUNITY LIFE

The Chinese define a city as an urban community of over 200,000 people, while a town is classified as having a population of between 20,000 and 200,000; communities smaller than this are classed as villages. Over half the population still lives in the countryside, largely in villages, although the trend towards urbanisation is increasing, as literally millions of rural people flock to the cities each year seeking employment as migrant workers.

In the villages people live in one or two-storey houses, but in the cities and towns almost everyone lives in a high-rise apartment. There are still some old two-storey homes on the outskirts of most cities, but these are being demolished as more and more land is developed to create yet more high-rise estates. New houses are rare; where they're built they're known as 'villas' and only wealthy Chinese can afford them.

Apartments, and villas, are almost invariably built within large estates which house several thousand people. The majority of foreigners live in this kind of estate, although a limited number working on construction projects or in agricultural industries are based in rural China. Although a few estates are populated almost exclusively by embassy staff, the majority house a mixture of Chinese and foreign residents.

Each estate is enclosed by a wall and is, effectively, a self-contained area – almost a village in itself. Within the estate there are often a number of small shops, located on the ground floor of apartment blocks, and there may be other facilities such as a club, restaurant or even sports amenities. Individual properties are owned by their occupiers in most cases, although some purchasers may have bought them as investments to rent out. 'Owned' doesn't mean the same as it does in the West: in China, where all land belongs to the state, there's no freehold property, and purchasers can only buy the use of the land their property stands on for 70 years. What will happen to these estates in 60 or 70 years' time is anyone's guess!

Those who cannot afford a home on an estate live in far less luxurious surroundings. Local government doesn't provide social housing at subsidised rents. There is, however, a move towards building low-priced apartments for the poor, but they're for sale, not for rent, and because they're cheap they're snapped up by buyers with local government connections who don't need them to live in and usually sell them on at a profit.

Despite providing the workforce for its factories and construction projects, driving China's extraordinary rise in the world, most migrant workers live on the lowest rung of the community. There are no hostels or camps for them to live in – many share cramped and overcrowded rented rooms or even sleep on the streets or under flyovers. China has a fairly inflexible arrangement of residency permits – the *hukou* system – whereby you must be resident in an area to benefit from local services. It's difficult to transfer your *hukou* from area to another, and so migrant

workers who move to a new city to work don't enjoy the same benefits as local residents. Their children are often barred from attending local schools, and if a migrant worker suffers an accident in the streets, he receives far less compensation for his injuries than a local resident would.

Community Regulations

Estates are run by management companies that maintain facilities, set rules and arrange services; residents have little or no contact with local government. It's the management company which maintains the estate's infrastructure and security, arranges for waste to be carted away to the city's disposal area, keeps roads swept and gardens tidy, and ensures that the street lighting works. Residents pay a monthly 'service' charge; commercial entities such as shops and restaurants on the estate also pay rent.

Rules and regulations are few, although there may be restrictions on where you can park and rules about the use of security cards for the main entrance gate. There's usually a charge for parking your car, whether it's in a covered car park or on the estate's roads. Most management companies forbid the erection of satellite dishes or the altering of the external appearance of the block, although people get away with enclosing their balconies to gain extra living space.

If your sink overflows or the lifts don't work, the management company is your first port of call – they usually have an office on site and employ a little army of tradesmen to solve all your problems.

NEIGHBOURS

In rural China, people live and work in close proximity, and being a good neighbour is an important part of village life. However, if you live in an apartment in a Chinese city, you may find it difficult to get to know your neighbours. You could live there for years and never meet them, other than the occasional fleeting glimpse as you pass on the stairs or a quick *ni hao* in the lift. The Chinese don't expect to be on close social terms with the people who live on the same floor, and most regard their home as strictly private. If they want to socialise with people, they rarely invite them home, but prefer to meet them at a restaurant.

Even the fact that you're a 'big nose' is unlikely to pique their curiosity enough for them to approach you, although they'll most likely discuss you between themselves.

You're more likely to get to know the people who run the estate and the neighbourhood shops and services, and you may well exchange pleasantries with them about the weather or events – just like at home – but it will be an acquaintance rather than a friendship. Possibly the most likely way of striking up a friendship with a neighbour is if they have a pet, such as a dog or a caged bird, that they take out for exercise or to a nearby park. Admire their pet and you'll soon get talking.

SEXUAL ATTITUDES

The Chinese attitude to sex is low key compared to that of many Western countries, and Chinese sexual customs would appear unbelievably old fashioned in London or New York. Sex isn't treated as a commodity: television advertisements feature housewives or older (and wiser) women rather than glamorous models. Sex is very much a private matter between two people, and you rarely see a couple holding hands, unless they're friends of the same sex (and this doesn't suggest homosexuality, which is even more discreet than heterosexual sex – see below).

> During 2009, a professor from a well-known university was jailed for three years for organising 'swingers' parties on private premises. He was charged with 'disturbing social administrative order' which prohibits sexual activities where three or more people are involved.

Many Chinese regard the act of two unmarried people sleeping together as offensive. If one of them is a foreign man, it may be seen as insulting to China. There have been numerous instances of people reporting a foreigner for sleeping with a Chinese girlfriend, resulting in the police breaking into their apartment or hotel room and hauling the couple down to the police station, putting them in cells overnight and fining them as much as 10,000 RMB each. Presumably, they're charged with an 'offence against public order'. A foreigner trying to rent an apartment, accompanied by a Chinese girl, can expect to be told that there are no apartments available.

The 'one-child policy' also affects sexual attitudes and makes people think long and hard about contraception. Breaking this law is taken seriously.

Fines for having a second child can amount to around 10,000 RMB, if there are no mitigating circumstances: some couples are allowed to have a second child (see page 38), and the law isn't applied to ethnic minorities. In rural areas, people can even be driven from their homes and have their houses demolished. Many villages still have public notice boards listing all the women in the village capable of child-bearing, and whether or not they have the allowed one child. Not everyone abides by the rules – rich urban couples can afford to pay the fines – but overall, the one-child policy has enabled China to slow the increase in its population.

Young people find it difficult to indulge in casual sex, particularly in cities and towns. School hours are so long and lessons so intensive, particularly for those hoping to go to university, that they have little time free for anything other than eating and sleeping. Once they get to university the pressure is off, and at the start of the academic year there's a deluge of dating as every student tries to find a boyfriend or girlfriend; although most of this is due to their new-found freedom away from home and/or sheer loneliness, and it results in plenty of hand holding and surreptitious kissing but not a lot else. The largest problem facing students is not a lack of willing partners but a lack of opportunity. All are required to live on campus, where their accommodation is a bed and a small desk apiece in a six-bed dormitory. The dormitories are in single-sex blocks and there's a 10 or 11pm curfew. There simply is nowhere private where they can enjoy any intimacy.

This is less true in the countryside, where many children don't progress beyond primary education and thus don't face the pressures of studying for the future. Rural children are more likely to have sex at an earlier age, and there are the occasional unplanned pregnancies, although these often result in early marriages due to parental pressure.

Arranged marriages are rare in modern China – those that do occur are mainly in rural areas – but families still have considerable influence on a child's choice of partner. The state also has a 'say' in when and how young people form relationships, and many Chinese people concur. The government recommends girls not to have a serious relationship before the age of 21, and boys are expected to wait until they're at least 23. It isn't a law, as such, but it's a bold or foolish young person who doesn't conform.

There's one way around parental and state controls, if young lovers are really persistent. Many tourist locations have 'love houses' in their grounds that can be rented by the hour. They are fairly basic, but serve the purpose if there's no alternative.

> According to official statistics, there are around 8 marriages – and 0.8 divorces – per 1,000 people each year. Some 10 per cent of all marriages end in divorce. It's a much lower figure than in the UK or US, but this is probably down to the Chinese belief that marriage is for life rather than any stigma attached to separation.

Men

Although Chinese men are 'allowed' to have a serious relationship as soon as they're aged 23, most don't marry until they're 30 or a little older. By this time, they're starting to feel the pressure from society and their parents to settle down. Friends and family try to push them into marriage by setting up 'romantic' situations with the opposite sex, or organising a 'partner' for meals out and other occasions. If a man has problems finding a mate he can turn to a matchmaker; these are usually women who've been successful in finding partners for other young men but they rarely advertise their services.

Although divorce is surprisingly common in China, most young men – and women – look on marriage as a lifelong commitment, and want to be sure that they're marrying the right person. However, the majority of men will have had some kind of sexual experience before tying the knot, while most young women haven't.

Despite the negative attitude towards sex outside marriage, men can always pay for sex. Prostitution was banned in 1949 and is officially illegal, but it goes on in disguise. A surprising proportion of karaoke rooms are used for prostitution; so much so that a recent law was passed requiring the doors to karaoke rooms to have clear glass panels and no locks. Plenty of 'foot massage' parlours offer stimulation of more than just your feet. Stay in a hotel, even a five-star establishment, and you may find a business card or flyer in your room offering 'massage' services, or notice good-looking girls trawling the reception area.

Sex with a prostitute is viewed by many wives as less of a betrayal than having an affair. Some married men pay for sex, but most are faithful to their wives, at least emotionally. In many ways, the Chinese are rather 'old fashioned' about marital fidelity. There's a well-known saying, *Hong qi bu dao, tai qi piao piao,* which literally means 'the red flag (of China) blows firmly out into the wind, but the brightly-coloured other flags flutter loosely in the breeze' – this is a roundabout way of saying that your wife will stick by you through thick and thin, but a pretty girl who catches your eye will just as easily flutter away. With both partners working, and sharing the support of their child and probably one or two elderly relatives, sex may be quite low down on their list of priorities. However, when couples are parted, with each working in a different city and only seeing each other during Chinese New Year – quite a common occurrence – this puts a strain on their relationship, and may cause them to look elsewhere for satisfaction.

Modern Concubines

There's a trend among wealthier men, particularly government officials, to have one or more girlfriends on the side to demonstrate their 'manliness'. These girls, the modern-day equivalent of an emperor's concubines, are called *bao er ni* ('wrapped second woman') in reference to the fact that most are hidden away in apartments and only occasionally brought out for show. It isn't an easy life for the girls, who usually get the blame for the man's shortcomings. When a government official is caught accepting bribes, as frequently happens, he often claims pathetically that he had to take the money to satisfy the demands of his 'girlfriend'.

Women

Chinese girls are rarely coquettish or provocative in their dress, and are much less likely to flaunt their sexuality than women in the West. They invariably dress neatly and modestly, without over-exposing their bodies. For most of the year, women (young and old) wear trousers, and even on hot summer days those wearing skirts are in the minority. They may dress conservatively, but young Chinese women are increasingly independent. Most have a job and, other than in politics, the glass ceiling is set higher than in most countries. Several women have been highly successful in business in recent years, and women can be found at all levels in local government, many professions and in industry.

Women's independence looks set to increase in the future as the pressure of an unbalanced male/female ratio, an unforeseen side effect of the one-child policy, starts to affect the way men feel towards women and vice versa. The most recent statistics indicate that in China as a whole, the ratio of men to women is 120:100, while in rural areas and outlying provinces such as Xinjiang it's as high as 140:100. This can only lead to a situation where a large proportion of Chinese men will never find a partner and where women can afford to be choosy about whom they marry.

Despite this, most women have an old-fashioned approach to marriage and sex. Like men, they want marriage to be a lifelong contract and, while they like the idea of a romantic marriage, they're fairly hard-headed. They don't necessarily want their future husband to be rich, but he must have the potential to become rich, and they prefer it if he earns more than they do. So if the woman has a Bachelor's degree, they want their future husband to have a Master's degree. They want to look up to him, and not just in mental ability; they also prefer him to be taller and preferably two or three years older as well.

Marriage with Foreigners

Some Chinese women are attracted to Western men and, although less frequently, Chinese men to foreign women. Chinese girls like the fact that Westerners are often tall, and are happy to have a Western man with them as 'eye candy'; although when it comes to marriage they're more cautious. Some Chinese men express a preference for foreign women, because they're more open about their views and attitudes, and less materialistic. Many feel that they cannot ask a Chinese girl to marry them if they cannot provide her with a home and a car, whereas Western women are less demanding.

There are no obstacles to a Chinese-foreigner marriage. The bureaucracy is minimal and many inter-racial marriages take place. However, never forget that marriage between two cultures takes a great deal of commitment and flexibility on both sides.

Harassment & Abuse of Women

The kidnap of women (and children) to sell as brides and workers in rural areas has gone on for many years, but the Chinese authorities are trying to deal with the problem and offenders face the death penalty if caught. For the average woman, China is a secure and respectful society. The attitude between men and women is one of mutual respect, there are laws protecting women in the workplace, and they're safer on

the streets than they would be in many Western countries.

> If a man makes unwanted advances, you can deter him by saying, loudly, the Chinese word for no (*bu*). It's pronounced like the English word 'boo!' and should have the desired effect.

Homosexuality

Most Chinese deny that there are homosexuals in their country, and many genuinely believe this. Homosexuality is looked upon by most people as an unfortunate and perverse condition that is prevalent in the West but doesn't exist in China. It was only decriminalised in the late '90s – although it was still classified as a 'mental illness' until 2001 – and the police can still act roughly towards anyone they suspect of being gay. Of course, there are homosexuals in China – some estimates put the figure at 30m – but they keep quiet about it, and you never hear of anyone 'coming out' publicly.

As attitudes towards homosexuality soften (slightly), there are a limited number of 'gay' bars in the major cities where homosexuals are welcome, but most keep a low profile. You won't see openly-gay couples or transvestites on the streets, and a gay foreigner living in China would be wise to keep his sexuality to himself – or live elsewhere!

MEETING PEOPLE

In such a crowded country, you would think it easy to meet people and make new friends, but cultural differences and the Chinese predilection for privacy in their personal lives make this more difficult than you might expect. The language barrier is another obstacle, and if you want to socialise with Chinese people you must make learning their language a priority. The Chinese are naturally curious about foreigners, and can be warm and welcoming once you conquer the communication issues. There can, however, be downsides to 'friendship': there are stories about Chinese women befriending foreign men with one eye on obtaining a visa, or students buttering up their teachers in the hope of sponsorship to study abroad. However, it's possible to make good and lasting friendships, and there are many places to start:

- **At work:** The workplace is probably the easiest place to strike up a friendship, as many Chinese people socialise with people from work. If you teach at a school or university, there will be sports days and outings and these are well worth going on. Joining in the fun makes you seem more approachable to your students and colleagues. Much the same applies at businesses and companies, where intra-company competitions are sometimes organised by the personnel department, or employers arrange 'banquets' for people joining or leaving an organisation or to celebrate a successful project. Make yourself available, even if you aren't keen on going. If you fail to attend, you may gain a reputation for lacking 'co-operation' – a deadly sin in the eyes of many Chinese.

- **Clubs & groups:** The Chinese have a surprising number of private clubs. If you're invited to one, take it as a compliment, as such clubs are often very exclusive. Without exception, membership is expensive, with the main facilities being a private restaurant and perhaps a pool. You will rarely see another foreigner there. For more information on clubs, including those for expatriates, see page 107.

- **Language classes:** These are an excellent way to meet other foreigners grappling with Chinese as well as Chinese people learning English. Offering to help teach English will win you many friends.

- **Expatriate organisations:** There are expat groups and clubs in China, especially in Shanghai and Beijing, which are good places to make contacts, although you shouldn't take everyone at face value. Some embassies and consulates maintain a list of local expatriate groups.

- **Church:** A surprising number of Chinese people are Christians, and many like-minded people meet at church.

- **Agencies & websites:** The Chinese often use dating agencies to find a partner, and there are dozens of websites offering chat, friendship and the chance to find romance. A similar service is offered via ads in some expat magazines. But be careful: many websites and advertisements are targeted at those seeking a quick thrill rather than a lasting relationship.

Where & When to Meet

The Chinese have a slow and steady approach to friendships and relationships, and most socialising takes place in public, with trips to the cinema, shopping expeditions and evenings spent in a restaurant or bar. Most large cities have an exhibition hall and art galleries, and a couple may visit an exhibition that interests both of them. Don't expect to be invited in for a coffee or to meet the family, at least until you've developed a deep friendship or your partner wants the relationship to progress much further. If you're a woman and a Chinese man asks you home, it's odds on that he wants his mother to meet you because he's contemplating popping the question. If a girl in the office were to ask a man home, it would be to see whether her family approved of him. Even then, she would probably take her intended to a relative's home (rather than her parents' house) or meet a relative at a restaurant, which allowed her to obtain the opinion of a less important family member before seeking the approval of her parents.

Paying the Bill

There's a strict protocol for deciding who pays the bill. Generally, the host pays for everyone. If a person senior to you has invited you to join him for a meal, he expects to pay. You can offer to pay, but your offer is likely to be refused politely. Never sneak across to the waiter and pay in secret as this will cause great offence and loss of face to your host. If a business contact asks you to join him for dinner, you can expect him to pay, but if you ask a colleague to join you for lunch, even casually, he'll think that you're offering to buy him a meal. The same applies if you ask a member of the opposite sex – man or woman – out on a date. If a group of equals go out together, it's considered an honour to pay for a meal, and people can go to quite devious lengths to collect the bill before any of their colleagues realise.

The Western system of 'going Dutch', whereby each person pays their own share of the bill, is highly unusual in China. Almost the only people who do it are students eating together, when they call it the 'AA system'.

INVITATIONS

Receiving Invitations

If you're invited to a formal event, such as a dinner arranged by a government organisation or an invitation to a garden party at your embassy, you'll receive a printed invitation and should respond to let your hosts know that you'll attend. However, usually you'll be invited by phone or in person. Again, it's polite to let your hosts know whether you'll be attending.

Dress Code

This depends on the circumstances. At a formal dinner, a smart suit and tie or cocktail dress are expected, but at a more casual event it's OK to wear smart-casual clothes – however, no shorts, vests or tatty jeans! Women should avoid revealing too much flesh. A low-cut top and short skirt are not appreciated by the conservative Chinese.

Gifts

If you're invited to a family gathering, it's fine to bring along a bottle of wine or a bottle of local alcohol such as *baijiu* for everyone to share. However, such is the honour of being invited to a Chinese family's home that you can be sure your hosts really want you there, and a gift isn't expected.

> There are some gifts which are associated with death, e.g. a clock, while giving someone a box of handkerchiefs suggests that they'll soon be in tears. Try to avoid blue or white wrapping paper, as these colours are linked to mourning. Red is a safe colour.

Greetings

When invited to join group of people at a social occasion, whether business associates or a colleague's family, you should always greet the eldest people first – see **Greetings** on page 122.

The Meal

Whether business or social, most invitations in China are for a meal in a restaurant. If you're lucky enough to

to drink whenever you feel like it. You must wait for your host to raise his glass and propose a toast at which everyone rises and drinks, sometimes clinking glasses together. Toasts are frequent, and can result in a boozy evening as you're expected to drain your glass each time (see **Toasts** on page 178.

When the last food has been served and the last toast made, the host will rise to his feet, say *zou ba* ('let's go') and that's it, everyone leaves. There's no leisurely sitting over coffee or brandy as there is in the West – you just cut and run. If there's any food left over, it's permissible to ask for a 'doggie bag' and take it home.

You may be faced with some unfamiliar and even unpalatable foods, and it's impolite to refuse them. Always take a little bit of everything that's offered. This doesn't mean you actually have to eat it all – the Chinese know that Westerners aren't partial to fishes' lips – but accepting it on your plate shows you're at least willing to try.

be invited to someone's home, you can expect to be served an elaborate meal – the Chinese don't invite honoured guests just for drinks and nibbles.

If you're the guest of honour, you're expected to sit beside your host. The food is often served on a Lazy Susan – a rotating turntable – and as each new dish arrives, your host may pick a tasty morsel with his chopsticks and put it on your plate. Many Westerners find this unhygienic but it's impolite to refuse, particularly if the person passing your food is older than you, your prospective father-in-law or your boss! A whole fish often forms the centrepiece of the meal, and the Lazy Susan will be turned with the head pointing at the guest of honour, who's then expected to take the first serving.

Drinks, usually wine or beer, are generally poured by one of the waitresses. You shouldn't top up your glass yourself, and you aren't expected

Making Invitations

You are expected to reciprocate invitations, and your guests will expect you to invite them to a restaurant and host the meal with great attention to detail. Bear in mind that it's your task to ensure that they enjoy it, by serving them the best food and providing sufficient alcohol for the many toasts.

Don't be afraid to invite Chinese people to your home. They are fascinated by foreigners' lives, and will jump at the chance to see how you live. Be prepared to conduct a guided tour of each room, explaining every ornament and picture on the wall. If you have a photograph of yourself with anyone famous, you'll be held in even greater esteem.

You cannot invite guests for just tea and cakes; they'll expect a full meal, and at least some of it should be food from your home country. The Chinese are willing to try anyone else's cuisine; although you should take any religious customs into account if any of your guests are Muslim or Buddhist. Don't be surprised if your guests jump up and leave as soon as the meal is over, just as they would at a restaurant.

RESPECTING PRIVACY

A Chinese man's home is his castle, and the drawbridge is usually up. It's rare that a stranger – foreign or otherwise – is invited across the threshold. Unlike in some Mediterranean countries, people won't appreciate you knocking on their door when you're 'just passing'. They probably won't answer or, if they do, they'll be acutely embarrassed. Chinese people are unlikely to turn up on your doorstep unannounced unless your house is on fire!

TABOOS

The Chinese accept that many foreigners find their culture very different, and they expect people to make mistakes. However, there are a few blunders and taboo subjects which you should try to avoid.

Conversation

The Chinese talk quite openly to strangers about subjects which you probably wouldn't discuss at home. People in the West rarely talk about money – aside from the value of their house – but the Chinese happily discuss and compare salaries, the cost of a meal that they've just hosted, and how much they paid for their shoes. Nothing is sacred on the money front. The same is true of health. People really want to know the ins and outs of any health problem you have, and will be full of ideas for cures, most of which involve eating some particular food. The Chinese are downright inquisitive and you must be prepared for this, but some subjects aren't open for discussion and they include the following:

● **Religion:** most employment contracts given to foreigners specifically state that you must not attempt to persuade Chinese citizens to take up your religion. It's not so long ago that the practice of religion was outlawed in China, and it's still a touchy subject with many Chinese. Never mention Falun Gong, a quasi-religious group which

Temple door, Tibet

has been effectively banned by the government.

- **Politics:** tread carefully. Conversation is infinitely more open than it was only a few years ago and, under Hu Jintao (General Secretary and leader of the CPC), the Communist Party has acknowledged that mistakes have been made in the past, but as a guest in China it isn't good to criticise your host. This includes passing comment on the current government, the late Chairman Mao or the events in Tian'anmen Square in 1989. Beware, too, of verbal faux-pas such as 'Red China', or referring to Taiwan as the Republic of China.

- **Sex:** this is a very personal subject for most people and isn't discussed in public.

> The Chinese don't wear shoes in the house, and you should always remove your shoes on entering someone's home. Many people have a small shoe cupboard by the front door, and hand guests towelling slippers to wear indoors.

EXPATRIATE COMMUNITY

There's a sizeable expatriate community in China, much of it concentrated in the four major cities: Beijing, Shanghai, Guangzhou and Shenzhen. Wherever there are expats, there are expat bars where local foreigners meet. Many are single and working in China, and some bars are magnets for lonely foreigners or heavy drinkers and can be more seedy than welcoming. Fortunately there are also a large number of specialist clubs and associations – including everything from bowling and rugby to women's groups – so if you live in an area popular with expats, you should have no problem finding people to socialise with.

Be wary of relying too much on expatriates. Many are a valuable source of information and support, who have been through similar situations and can show you the ropes; but there are always moaners who offer nothing but criticism of China, and will quickly dampen your spirits if you're feeling homesick. If they're people you wouldn't socialise with in your home country, ask yourself why you're spending time with them in China when you could be getting to know the Chinese.

CONFRONTATION

It seldom pays to get into a confrontational situation with a Chinese person. They'll end up losing face and so will you. If you must reprimand someone, do it when there are just the two of you present and be as diplomatic as possible.

Despite the low standard of driving and frequent bumps and shunts, road rage is rare. The two drivers involved may argue loudly with each other while they wait for a traffic policeman to arrive and sort out the blame, and they may well argue with him, too, but such incidents rarely end in physical violence. Caught in a traffic jam, drivers will sound their horn a couple of times, but they won't get out of their car and confront other drivers or the person causing the jam.

The Chinese react to being shouted at by smiling. This is called a 'bitter smile' and it signifies embarrassment, both for themselves and for the person who's berating them. If you see a foreigner angrily confronting a hotel receptionist, the angrier he becomes the more she smiles although this only makes him even more angry. It's a common sight, but don't let it happen to you. Patience and a genuine smile will always get you closer to sorting out a problem in China.

DEALING WITH OFFICIALS

Police

You're most likely to encounter the Chinese police (*jing cha*) when driving, or at the Public Security Bureau (PSB) while seeking the renewal or change of your visa.

The traffic police don't speak English, and if your Chinese isn't fluent it's better to pretend that it's very limited. Police are trained to deal more carefully with someone who's foreign and a guest of their country, and if you cannot understand them it makes their job even more complicated. Show them your driving licence and your registration book, plus your obligatory third party insurance certificate, but say as little as possible. You may be issued with a ticket for some offence but it's more likely, unless you've done something serious, that he'll just send you on your way. This saves him, and you, a lot of hassle.

Never argue with traffic police, just be polite and co-operative. If you're asked to take a breath test – more likely now that China is upping the pressure on drink-drivers – it's best to comply on the spot. It's an offence to have a reading of over 20mg per 100ml of alcohol, and the penalties are severe;

therefore if you're driving, it's better to drink no alcohol at all.

At the PSB, foreigners are assisted by the Foreign Affairs staff. They are ordinary police and usually well-educated, as they're in contact with people from many nationalities and most can speak some English; but remember that it isn't their native tongue, so you'll need to be patient with them.

Most visits to the PSB are on visa business, e.g. renewing your visa or changing it to a 'Z' visa which allows you to work. You're expected to provide the correct documents, including photocopies of the documents you provided to obtain your original visa, plus proof of registration at your address and, if you're seeking a 'Z' visa, a letter from your employer or a copy of your contract of employment. Photograph requirements are subject to frequent change, therefore if the PSB officer is unhappy with the photo you supply, you may have go to a second office and have a new photo taken in the approved style. It's a complicated process and some foreigners find it frustrating, so be prepared and don't expect to get it all settled in five minutes.

Generally, the PSB Foreign Affairs police are polite and helpful, but they cannot bend the rules for you. Should you have overstayed your visa, you'll be fined 500 RMB for each day that you've overstayed, and no amount of sweet talking will get the PSB to waive this. It isn't within their powers to do so.

You may also need to visit the PSB to report a theft or a loss. This takes place at their general office, as opposed to the Foreign Affairs section, and your statement will be noted in both English and Chinese (the police provide someone to translate it). You must sign the statement, so ensure that you're happy with its contents. Keep a note of the date and number of the statement, as you'll need it if you make an insurance claim.

Government Officials

If you're in business, you may need to visit government offices on occasion. As anywhere in China, it pays to be smartly dressed. It also helps to know someone in the office; even if he's not the person that you need to see, he can point you in the right direction. Business with government officials is carried out in much the same way as it is the world over, and politeness pays dividends. Unless the official asks otherwise, always refer to him as Mr (*Xiansheng*) together with his family name, and wait until you're asked before sitting down.

Teachers

Teachers in China live differently from teachers in the West. Most have accommodation on campus with their families, even at day schools – there are few boarding schools – and living in such a close community means that teachers end up being not just colleagues but also neighbours and friends. Unlike in many Western schools, teachers are respected by their pupils and pupils want to learn; education is seen as the key to a good job and a happy future. Certain state schools are classified by the local education authority as 'key' schools; they have the best facilities and attract the best teachers and the most promising pupils, and there's intense competition between parents to secure a place in a 'key' school for their child. Teachers aren't just respected, they're also loved. Many former pupils stay in contact with their teachers for years after leaving school, and there's even a national Teachers' Day in September, when pupils bring little gifts to their teachers.

Keep this background in mind when meeting teachers. Their position in society is similar to that of a doctor in the West, and they expect to be taken seriously. They don't expect to be blamed by complaining parents whose child makes little effort in school.

If you're employed as a teacher in China, you're expected to live up to your elevated social position; you certainly don't want to be spotted by parents staggering out of a bar! You'll receive respect not just from pupils but also from your fellow Chinese teachers, who may consult you for advice on the use of English or quietly join your class, not to spy on you but to see how you arrange your lessons and to learn from you.

Chinese bamboo slips

5.
THE LANGUAGE BARRIER

Some knowledge of the Chinese language, even a rudimentary acquaintance with spoken Chinese, should be an early priority for anyone planning to spend some time in China. The ability to communicate with the Chinese and know what to say and do when you meet them is essential. By taking some lessons before you go, you'll be saved the embarrassment of having to point at things you want, or dumbly nod and shake your head; and once there, a quick course in the basics will help you to cope with many everyday situations. Learning a foreign language is never easy and is full of potential pitfalls – most expats have stories to tell of when they said the wrong thing, often with embarrassing consequences. To help you to keep your collection of anecdotes as small as possible, this chapter offers tips on learning Chinese, some useful expressions, explanations of body language, forms of address and greetings.

> 'Learning is a treasure that will follow its owner everywhere.'
> Chinese proverb

There are a great many languages used in China, but the majority of people speak Mandarin Chinese. When learning Chinese, make sure that what you learn is Mandarin, as this is the official spoken language for the whole of China and is, by far, the most widely spoken form of Chinese. If you live in an area where people speak another language, e.g. Guangzhou, where many people also speak Cantonese, it's useful to know some words but isn't essential; however, without Mandarin Chinese, you'll struggle. This book also presents Chinese words in pinyin, which is the most familiar form of transliteration from Chinese script to the Latin (Roman) alphabet. All translations in this book are given in pinyin.

LEARNING CHINESE

Mandarin Chinese (*Putonghua*) is the official language of the People's Republic of China, and in offices and schools throughout China you'll see notices exhorting the people working or studying there to use *Putonghua* at all times. The word Mandarin is used throughout this book to describe standard Chinese because this is the term that Westerners use, but it's important to note that the Chinese call it *Putonghua* and many will be mystified if you talk to them about Mandarin.

It's the most widely-spoken language in the world, with some 850m people speaking it as their first language, more than all native English and Spanish speakers combined. One of the Sino-Tibetan languages, it's spoken across much of Asia and among Chinese communities the world over, from Australia to the US. However, it's completely and utterly different from Western languages, and one of the most challenging for a Westerner to learn.

The most difficult aspect for foreigners to grasp is Chinese writing which, while beautiful in its execution, is quite alien to anyone brought up with the Latin or Roman alphabet. Almost before you leave the airport, you'll struggle to understand signs and notices. Street signs generally include a translation in pinyin, but even in Beijing and Shanghai, where foreigners aren't uncommon, the majority of shop fronts display their name only in Chinese characters.

Restaurant menus are, almost invariably, printed or written in Chinese. More modern or upmarket hotels and restaurants in larger cities may have a description of dishes in English or a picture, but they're unlikely to include the names of the dishes in pinyin, so you cannot ask for a dish in Chinese. The English description may well be in Chinglish (see box below), but at least it will give you some idea of what to expect. Fast-food outlets such as Kentucky Fried Chicken and McDonald's display their offerings in Chinese characters on their wall menus, although there are illustrations and it's easy enough to count down the menu to highlight which item you want. However, if you want to eat **real** Chinese food in neighbourhood restaurants, you'll have to learn Chinese.

You may be able to get away without writing Chinese, but not being able to read it is a handicap and not speaking it makes communication much more difficult. Although English is officially China's second language and has been taught to children from an early age in the last 30 years, the emphasis has been almost entirely on teaching children to read and write, therefore people's speaking and listening skills are often poor. Relatively few Chinese can speak English well, and even fewer can understand you properly if you speak to them in English.

Fortunately, learning to speak Chinese is much easier than learning to read or write it, not least because you can pick up the basics in pinyin. The language nowadays contains quite a number of familiar words with roots in English, such as *kafei* (coffee) and *youmo* (humour) in much the same way that English contains some words based on Chinese such as typhoon (from *tai feng* meaning big wind) and kowtow from *koutou,* which literally means 'knock head' and refers to a low bow signifying deep

Chinese calligraphy

respect. Like many people across Asia, the Chinese call tea *cha* which sounds similar to 'char', the slang word for a cuppa in English.

The Chinese aren't precious about their language, and welcome foreigners' attempts to speak it. People will be surprised at first and then genuinely pleased that you can address them in Chinese and, no matter how badly you mangle the pronunciation, they'll tell you how brilliantly you can speak it. Enjoy this, but don't believe them and keep practising.

Chinglish

This is the name given to Chinese that has been translated incorrectly into English – by mistake rather than by design. A typical instance may be a sign saying 'Deformed Men's Toilet' rather than 'Disabled Men's Toilet' while a wine list in an expensive hotel might advertise an excellent Chateau-bottled wine as 'French Home Made Wine'. These errors of translation make foreigners smile, although some take some puzzling out. An often-seen sign which warns 'Please Slip Carefully' actually means 'be careful, the floor is slippery'.

Is Chinese Essential?

If you're going to China to teach English at a school or university, you can probably get by with a few rudimentary words of Chinese, although you'll be limited to communicating with English-speaking colleagues and students. In all other situations, you must learn some Chinese. Learning the language makes life much easier and far more interesting. You understand better why the Chinese people do things the

way that they do and as you learn more, so China will open up to you; the more that you learn about this fascinating country, the more that you want to learn. There are other reasons which make some knowledge of Chinese vital:

- In an accident or emergency, your ability to communicate with the police, fire or medical services could save lives. It's very unlikely that you'll get through to an emergency services operator or find a doctor or police officer who speaks English.

- All forms are in Chinese. Officials are usually happy to explain them to you, but the explanation will most likely be in Chinese.

- If you can communicate simple instructions to tradesmen, cleaners or even your hairdresser, they'll feel more comfortable and you won't have to waste time or spend money on finding someone to translate for you.

- Neighbours, colleagues and, if you have them, Chinese in-laws will appreciate your efforts. And if you have a Chinese partner, speaking Chinese will bring you closer together.

- You will quickly widen your circle of friends and won't have to rely on expatriates for company.

Know Before You Go

Aim to start learning Chinese at least three and preferably six months before moving to China. It won't be easier to learn once you're there – so-called 'immersion' learning only works if you give it your full attention, and that isn't possible when you're juggling the demands of relocation. It's more beneficial to gain some knowledge of Chinese, however basic, before you arrive so you can exchange courtesies, ask for things in shops and count up to ten.

Many schools and colleges offer language courses, ranging from beginners' classes to those for business people. There are also a large number of online courses, many of which are free, but it's better to use one with an audio facility which aids pronunciation by allowing you to hear how words **should** sound. If you're pushed for time, you could hire a private tutor. Many advertise on community websites such as Gumtree (🖥 www.gumtree.com).

> '**If you talk to a man in a language he understands, that goes to his head. If you talk to him in his language, that goes to his heart.**'
>
> Nelson Mandela (South African political prisoner, president & statesman)

When in China

If you work as a teacher in a school or university, your employer may arrange lessons for you, often free of charge. Government organisations or private companies are less likely to have in-house teaching facilities, so you'll have to attend classes. Your employer can probably recommend a language school and may even be willing to foot the bill. Otherwise, you'll have to find your own language classes. Many courses are advertised in free expatriate magazines, which are found at all the expat haunts, as well as on the internet.

There are a great many language schools, and perhaps the best way to choose one is to obtain recommendations. Beijing's Chinese Language Education (🖥 www.chinaledu.com) claims to have a client base which includes several embassies, and fees start from US$800 for a four-week course comprising 20 hours a week, which works out at US$10 or around 65 RMB an hour. Attending classes can be fun, and is a good way of meeting people, but always ask for a free 'trial' lesson before committing yourself to paying for an entire course, and make sure that your knowledge of Chinese is assessed and that you're put in a class to suit your level.

Employing a private tutor allows you to learn at your convenience with lessons tailored to your ability, but fees can be high. One-to-one teaching in Beijing costs from 100 to 200 RMB an hour, although fees are lower away from the capital; for example, in Zhengzhou (Henan province), it costs between 80 and 150 RMB an hour. It may be possible to share a tutor with someone, which has the added advantage of giving you someone to practice with.

Tips on Learning Chinese

● **Focus on speaking and understanding:** Leave the complexities of written Chinese until you have a better understanding of the language.

● **Get to grips with the pinyin alphabet:** This will get you talking quickly. Practice pronouncing pinyin by reading street names and then saying them out loud, as this helps you to become more familiar with the language.

- **Use the language whenever you can:** Speak Chinese to market traders, your neighbours and work colleagues. The more you speak the language, the more comfortable you'll become speaking it.

- **Organise a language exchange:** Many Chinese want to improve their English, so find a willing 'student' and arrange to spend half the time speaking English and the other half talking in Chinese.

- **Ask for help:** If someone speaks too quickly, ask them to say it again. Say '*Wo ting bu dong*' (I don't understand).

- **Get stuck into soaps:** Watching television is a good way of tuning your ear to the language, and low-brow soaps and series are entertaining ways to pick up Chinese.

- **Never give up:** Some days you'll feel as if you're making no progress at all, but these will pass; keep practising, and you'll get through these 'plateaus' and keep honing your skills.

> Taxi drivers are good for practice; most are pleased to have a conversation with a foreigner, and they cannot escape! Start by learning a few typically Chinese questions, such as 'How old are you?' or 'Are you married?' and 'How many children have you got?' but make sure you also know how to say 'I don't understand'. You'll need this response when the taxi driver replies with rapid-fire Chinese in a local dialect.

Children

If you're moving to China with your family, your children will also need to learn Chinese. It will help them make friends and fit more comfortably into the culture of their new home. Younger children pick up languages easily – sometimes within a matter of months – but older children and teenagers may struggle. Like you, they'll need to attend language classes, and will benefit from lessons before leaving home.

All state education facilities teach in Chinese, and no allowance is made for children who cannot speak it. State schools aren't accustomed to foreign students, and if your children attend one, they'll be treated exactly the same as Chinese children and have to follow their lessons – apart from English – in an

alien language. For this reason, many parents choose to send their children to an international school, especially if they're at a crucial stage in their education.

> For safety's sake, make sure that your children can say their address and phone number in Chinese. It's a good idea for them to carry this information with them on a card in Chinese script.

WRITTEN CHINESE

Understanding written Chinese is, for Westerners, a major task. It isn't easy for the Chinese, either; they have to memorise characters from an early age, and many continue to study and practice writing them throughout their lives. A knowledge of the written language and an ability to write it artistically, as calligraphy, is the mark of a well-educated person.

There are said to be a little over 50,000 different characters, but a number of these are now obsolete or highly specialised and rarely used today. Most educated Chinese know only between 3,000 and 5,000 characters, and this number is sufficient in daily life. In order to read a newspaper properly you need to know about 3,000 characters, but you can grasp the gist of the content with around 1,500. Farmers in remote areas will know perhaps only around 400 characters, but even this is still a large number compared to the 26 letters of the alphabet and ten numerals that most Westerners learn.

Chinese is written in the same manner as English, i.e. from left to right, and consists of individual characters – more correctly called ideographs, pictographs or logograms – each of which represents a concept or idea. When the Chinese first put quill to parchment some 4,000 years ago, these characters were originally simple pictures or diagrams, and in a few cases they still represent a single idea. However, this logic has slowly been lost over the centuries, until today there's little that is directly pictorial about most of the characters, and sometimes there's also no link whatsoever between one character and another very similar one, although a few visual examples remain (see box).

To the Western eye, Chinese characters appear extraordinarily complicated compared to the Latin alphabet. However, as you become more accustomed to seeing these characters, you start to notice that there are not as many character forms as you had thought at first. Many of the same shapes keep appearing, either on their own or more often as part of a compound character, many of which are made up of two, three or even four basic characters. Characters may be tall and thin or short and fat, but all fit within a single square.

The Logic (or not) of Chinese Writing

Some Chinese characters are eminently logical. These include the character for good (*hao,* 好) which is made up of the character for woman (女) together with the character for child (子). The character which represents bright or brilliant (*ming,* 明) comprises the character for the sun (日) together with the character for the moon (月). And

Friendship Award Certificate

there's good logic for the character for a tear (*lei*, 泪) which combines the character for water (水) with the character for eye (目). Sadly, though, such rational examples are the exception rather than the rule.

In many cases a slip of the pen can totally change the meaning and the sound of a character. Take the word big (*da*, 大). Add an apostrophe and you get the word dog (*quan*, 犬) but add two apostrophes and you get head (*tou*, 头). Add a line to big and you get heaven (*tian*, 天), but move that line and the resulting word is husband (*fu*, 夫).

There are some important characters which you see frequently, and must learn: these include the signs used for men (*nan*, 男) and women (*nu*, 女) on toilets – these usually carry the universal figures, but not always – and the signs for entrance (*ru kou*, 入口) and exit (*chu kou*, 出口). Beyond these and, perhaps, the characters for numerals, you'll find that learning Chinese characters is a lengthy business. Not surprisingly, few Westerners become genuinely proficient at reading or writing Chinese. You can

practise with the aid of a set of 'flash cards', which can be obtained from any Xinhua bookshop, but there's no quick way to absorb a system of writing which the average Chinese student spends at least 14 years learning.

To make matters a little more complicated, a fair proportion of the more commonly used Chinese characters were changed to a simpler form some years ago in an effort to make learning easier. All Chinese script within mainland China is written using these simplified characters, although sometimes, if a company thinks that an old-style character would make their letterhead or shop front look better, they use it.

> **'Life is a foreign language; all men mispronounce it.'**
>
> Christopher Morley (American writer)

CHINESE NUMBERS

Numbers are almost always written in the way that you're used to seeing them, i.e. the figures 1, 2, 3, etc., rather than in their Chinese characters. Characters sometimes replace numbers in company or street names, but rarely otherwise. You will never see a Chinese person adding up a column of Chinese numerals; Western numerals are the norm for all bills, accounts and receipts.

There's a series of ten different signals that people make with the fingers of their right hand to indicate the numbers one to nine, while they

(Mind your head)

cross over the forefingers of both hands to indicate ten. These gestures differ slightly according to where you are in China, but it's well worth learning the local variation, as they're widely understood and can help when asking for something or checking a price, or when indicating something to someone whose knowledge of the language is limited, such as a farmer.

PINYIN

To master Chinese at a basic but practical level, the first step is to learn the pronunciation of pinyin. Pinyin is the approved way of transliterating Chinese phonetically using the Latin or Roman alphabet, and replaces similar previous systems such as Wade-Giles (though you can still find this used in older books about China). Pinyin was first drawn up in the '30s with the assistance of the Russians, not just as a way of converting Chinese to Latin script but also as a first step towards discarding written Chinese. The latter proved so contentious that it was quietly dropped, but pinyin survived and was adopted by the Chinese government in the '50s around the same time as Mandarin was being promoted as the standard language throughout the nation. Although it can be read by relatively few Chinese, it's a boon to foreigners.

Pinyin transforms written Chinese into something that you can read easily. More than half the alphabet is pronounced in exactly the same way as in English and, while the pronunciation of some other letters and diphthongs is a bit different, there are really only two letters, c and r, that will give you any serious difficulty.

With pinyin it helps if you practice as much as possible, perhaps by trying to write down in pinyin short sentences that you hear spoken in Chinese. As your vocabulary increases, you'll find that brief sentences can be formed quite soon, as Chinese grammar is largely a simpler form of English grammar but with few plurals, no tenses and virtually no genders.

Many books on learning Chinese emphasise the importance of the four tones that are used in Mandarin (*Putonghua*) to create four different sounds from the same syllable (Mandarin isn't **so** bad – Cantonese has eight tones). The four tones are indicated by accents when Mandarin is transliterated into pinyin. If you ask a question out of context, e.g. asking for a street by name, it's important to get the tones correct if you want to be understood. Nevertheless, in most other cases, the listener should understand what you mean from the context of the sentence, and it's better to get to grips with speaking the language rather than fretting about achieving the correct tone – that can come later when you're more expert.

Pronunciation

Pinyin consists of 25 letters: 20 consonants and five vowels. Most consonants are pronounced as in English, but there are five exceptions as follows:

c – sounds like the **ts** in cats;

q – sounds like the **ch** in cheap. There's no need to follow q with a u.

r – sounds like the **r** in the French word *bourgeois*;

x – sounds like the **sh** in shin;

z – sounds like the **ds** in suds.

There is no v in Chinese.

Vowels are pronounced as follows:

a   as in father;

e   as in her. You **always** pronounce an e which appears at the end of a word, e.g. *xuande* should be pronounced *xuande**r***.

i   as in see. But when i follows c, ch, r, s, sh, z or zh it's pronounced like **er** in butter. This is the one main irregularity in pinyin.

o   as in sore;

u   as in the French word *tu*. There are some inconsistencies such as the word *lu* (road) which rhymes with flu.

Once you feel fairly satisfied with your ability to pronounce words written in pinyin in a way that can be understood by native Chinese speakers, you can start to memorise words and short, commonly-used sentences. Then you'll start gradually to be able to both speak and understand Chinese. Don't just memorise words or sentences, but try to remember how they sound; this way you'll sound like a local and not like a foreigner speaking Chinese.

Don't expect to become fluent quickly. It takes a lot of time and diligence, but the satisfaction that you get when you're able to ask someone something, or understand something

---

Common Sounds in Pinyin

The most common diphthongs and paired consonants are pronounced as follows:

ai as in fly	**er** as in fur	**ua** as in suave
ao as in how	**ia** as in yak	**uai** as in why
an as in fun	**ian** as in yen	**ue** as you air
ang as in hung	**ie** as in yeah	**ui** as way
ch as in cheese	**iou** as in yeoman	**uo** as war
ei as in pay	**ou** as in coat	**zh** as ja
eng as in hung	**sh** as in show	

said to you in Chinese, is reward enough. Much the same is true when you find yourself understanding a number of Chinese characters and then working out what a notice says. Neither is easy, but the number of expatriates who speak fluent Chinese shows that it isn't impossible. You probably won't end up as skilful as Dashan, the Canadian expert that you see on television but, like completing a marathon as a fun runner, the satisfaction of achieving even some small measure of ability in Chinese is tremendous.

Make sure when buying an English-Chinese dictionary that you get one which includes entries in English, Chinese **and** pinyin. Most dictionaries sold in China only have English and Chinese, which is fine for the locals but utterly useless if you cannot read written Chinese.

Chinese Tongue Twisters

If Chinese doesn't twist your tongue sufficiently in the first place, try these linguistic riddles which most Chinese children learn around the age of nine:

Si shi si, shi shi shi, shi si shi shi si, si shi shi si shi. (Four is four, ten is ten, fourteen is fourteen, forty is forty.)

Chi putao, bu tu putao pi, bu chi putao, dao tu putao pi. (If you eat grapes, don't spit out the skins. If you don't eat grapes, you don't need to spit out the skins.) This is a roundabout way of saying that if you cannot do something one way, there may be another way of doing it.

OTHER LANGUAGES & DIALECTS

Although it's the official language, used in all government departments and schools and across the Chinese media, Mandarin is by no means the only language spoken in China. There are a huge number of languages and dialects, some widespread and others spoken by just a handful of people.

Official figures state that there are seven principal languages used in China. They are known as Sinitic languages, part of the Sino-Tibetan language family, and are shown in the table opposite.

This accounts for 1,158m of the 1.3bn plus people living in China. The remainder, particularly people living in the autonomous regions, speak their own indigenous languages such as Mongolian, Tibetan and Uyghur, and there are a number of foreign languages

Chinese Languages	
Language	**Spoken By**
Mandarin (*Putonghua*)	850m Chinese, and understood across most of the country, even by people for whom it isn't their first language. It's sometimes called *Guanhua* which means 'official language'.
Wu	87m people in Shanghai, Jiangsu and Zhejiang;
Min	68m in Fujian;
Cantonese (*Yue*)	66m in Guangdong (and Hong Kong);
Xiang	36m in Hunan;
Hakka (*Kejia*)	30m in southern China;
Gan	21m in Jiangxi.

also spoken in China, including Korean and Russian.

Although the Sinitic languages are related, they're often mutually unintelligible, so that a Cantonese speaker from Guangdong will find it almost impossible to explain something to a Mandarin speaker from Beijing unless he reverts to Mandarin. As well as its abundance of languages, China also has a great many local dialects which further complicate communication between different inhabitants of this vast country. Mandarin itself has eight different dialects and a multitude of sub-dialects. Dialects can alter the way that people speak to a large degree, in much the same way as a British Geordie or a native of Louisiana in the US sound utterly different when speaking the same language. The Beijing dialect is the basis for standard Mandarin; it is, if you like, China's version of the Queen's English.

As a foreigner, the choice is easy: learn Mandarin and you'll be able to communicate with the vast majority of Chinese people.

SLANG & SWEARING

Every language has its share of slang words and Chinese is no exception. Using local slang helps convince people that you can speak Chinese fluently – provided you say it in the right context. Swear words are different. The Chinese use them a lot, women as well as men. The Chinese version of the 'F' word is *ta ma de*, which is a less-than-polite way of telling someone to go away, and is often used by outspoken women to get rid of a persistent (annoying) admirer. They may follow it up with *san shi ba* which directly translates as '38' but is a Chinese way of casting aspersions on the morality of someone's mother. A lot of slang and curses employ numbers (see box).

Many Chinese swear words include references to body parts and bodily functions, although foreigners find them amusing rather than offensive: telling someone that they have mentally-defective testicles would enrage a Chinese but make a Westerner laugh.

As well as derogatory remarks about ancestors and a great many allusions to dogs, among the most wounding insults are the old-fashioned turtle curses. Saying that someone is the grandson of a turtle or a turtle's egg sounds fairly innocuous to most foreigners, but it's a deadly insult to the Chinese.

With all this in mind, it's unwise to swear in China unless you're fluent in the language and completely sure of your audience!

> There's one curious profanity, *er bai wu*, which is used frequently to imply that someone is slow or stupid. It's a fairly low-level insult, and people often say it with a grin. *Er bai wu* translates as '250', and is related to an ancient story from the Qin dynasty some 2,000 years ago. In this era, coins were kept in groups of 500, thus *er bai wu* suggests you only have half the required amount and are, therefore, a halfwit.

BODY LANGUAGE & GESTURES

The Chinese don't have a great vocabulary of body language, and the few gestures they employ should be familiar to foreigners. They nod for 'yes' and shake their heads for 'no'; they point and clap and scratch their heads in much the same way as people in the West, and it all means the same things. Most people understand what a 'thumbs up' means, but are less conversant with a 'thumbs down' and have no idea what thumbing a lift is.

The 'V' sign is popular, particularly among youngsters who love to stand next to a friend when a photo is being taken, drape an arm behind their friend and display a 'V' sign over their head. Unfortunately, they don't known that the 'V' sign can mean something other than victory if the hand is reversed, with the palm facing away from the camera, and they often make this error.

There are few common gestures, other than those used to indicate numbers (see page 117). Children use a hand signal to indicate that they want to go to the toilet: they raise their right hand with the thumb and forefinger bent towards each other to create a letter 'C' and splay their other three fingers to make the 'W'.

Most Chinese people find winking difficult, and are fascinated by the ease with which foreigners wink, even if they don't understand what it means. Teaching a recalcitrant child to wink could make him a friend for life.

GREETINGS

By far the most common greeting is '*ni hao*' which means 'you good?' The response is exactly the same. You can say *ni hao* to anyone, including strangers, just as you might say 'hello' or 'hi' in your home country. If you know the person you're greeting, it's more usual to say '*ni hao ma*' ('how are you?') or, more formally, '*zao shang hao*' which means 'good morning'. If greeting people that you know, even vaguely, around mealtimes, it's common to ask if they've eaten ('*chi fan le ma*?'), but be careful or they may think that you're inviting them to eat with you.

When meeting someone new, of either sex, don't stand too close; with China being such a crowded country, most people like to maintain a certain amount of personal space. If meeting you on a formal basis, men may offer to shake hands – this is an increasingly well-known practice, and many Chinese regard it as a modern thing to do – but if they don't, it's simply because it's a gesture that they aren't accustomed to and you shouldn't read anything into it. No one will take offence if you offer your hand in a friendly way. Don't attempt to greet women with a peck on the cheek. Kissing strangers is never done! A small inclination of the head – a sort of mini bow – or an offer to shake their hand is more appropriate. Chinese men, and sometimes women, often greet each other with a hug, but they're unlikely to offer a hug to you, unless they know you very well.

To welcome someone, the Chinese say '*huan ying*', which is a standard salutation from the gorgeous girls who greet you at restaurants. If you thank someone for something, such as a waiter, they reply '*bu yong xie*' ('you're welcome'), and your response is '*xie xie*' ('thank you'). On leaving, people say '*zaijian,*' which means 'goodbye' – although nowadays they often say 'bye-bye' in English. There are comparatively few Chinese surnames but a great many given (first) names. According to government statistics, the population shares about 100 surnames, with the most common being Wang, Li and Zhang – there are over 93m people with the surname Wang in China. Among the thousands of first names, Wei (a male name meaning 'great') and Ying (a female name meaning 'beautiful' or 'elegant') are frequently used.

NAMES, TITLES & FORMS OF ADDRESS

To a Westerner, Chinese names appear back to front. The surname or family name comes first, followed by the given or first name, so that a man with the surname Li and given name Yang is called Li Yang but would be known as Yang Li in the West. It follows that John Smith becomes Smith John in China.

The Chinese are quite formal when addressing each other and the use of given names between colleagues and acquaintances – or between anyone not closely related – is uncommon. They refer to each other by surname or by surname and title, so Li Yang should be addressed as *Xiansheng* Li (Mr Li) and never *Xiansheng* Yang. Women are always referred to as Miss (*Nushi*), whether or not they're married. A woman married to a Mr Wang used to be called Mrs Wang, but this practice was discontinued in 1949 and married women retain their original family name after they're married. Since married women don't wear wedding rings, it isn't easy to tell whether or not a woman is married.

Titles can also refer to someone's rank or occupation. If Mr Wang is a government minister, his title is *Buzhang* Wang; if he's a university professor, he's *Jiaoshou* Wang. This occupational title also covers doctors (*Yisheng*), teachers (*Laoshi*), engineers (*Gong*) and managers (*Zong*), although top managers such as a company's CEO are usually referred to as *Guozong*.

Use of people's given names isn't common, even within families, where people use names to denote each person's position in the family hierarchy: husband, sister-in-law, son's child and so forth. For example, the oldest brother is called *da ge ge*, usually shortened to *ge*, while the youngest daughter is known as *xiao mei mei* or *xiao mei*. Mother and father are *ma* and *ba*.

Many Chinese people have nicknames which are used in place of their first name, and some can be quite vulgar. While at school, teachers often give another, English name to each child as part of their immersion into learning English. This is a comparatively recent thing, but it means that younger people are quite likely to ask you to use that name, e.g. 'please call me William', and will appreciate it if you do. Some 'English' names are quite old-fashioned or not particularly appropriate as given names, such as Grannie for an 18-year-old girl student; but don't point this out, just accept what they have told you, and use that name when addressing them.

It's a good idea to ask a good Chinese speaker to translate your name into Chinese – it won't sound exactly as you're used to hearing it, but it will be close enough. You can use this as your 'Chinese name', and have the characters printed on one side of your business card.

Children

Western children are often on first-name terms with adults, but this is frowned upon in China, where all elders should be addressed as *Xiansheng* if they're male or *Nushi* if they're female; a woman who's a public figure might also be addressed as *Xiansheng*. Teachers should be addressed as *Laoshi*.

TELEPHONE, LETTERS & EMAIL

The Chinese still send letters, particularly business letters, but the use of letters is decreasing as it is the world over and, among the young especially, more people use email and text messaging to stay in touch. Email and text etiquette is no different from

中国邮政 CHINA 3.70元

Panthera tigris altaica

2000 - 3   东北虎   (10 - 9) T

that used in the West, but there are some things you should know about using the phone or writing a letter.

Telephone

Mobile phone use is ubiquitous in China, and mobiles are answered anywhere and everywhere, usually in a loud voice. All phone calls are normally answered '*wei*'. This directly translates as 'hello', but is a word that's reserved for the phone. On greeting someone in person, you say '*ni hao*' instead.

Letters

Starting

Business letters should begin with the words '*Jin ai de*', which is the Chinese equivalent of 'Dear Sir' or 'Dear Madam'. You begin a letter to a loved one with the words '*Qin ai de*' ('Darling' or 'Dearest'), followed by the addressee's first name, e.g. '*Qin ai de* Ying'.

Addresses

In Chinese, addresses are always written in the opposite way to the manner that they're written in the West. This follows the Chinese idea that the largest, least specific things are listed first, down to the smallest, most precise. So, the country comes first, then the province and postcode, then the street, the house number and finally the name of the recipient. Postcodes are a six-figure number, and most standard envelopes feature a printed box in which to write them.

The address can be written in pinyin, although it's better to write it in Chinese characters where possible. Major post offices always have someone who can write the Chinese characters on the envelope if it has been addressed in either pinyin or English.

Date

If written in an English-language letter, the date is usually written day/month/year, as in the UK. However, if the letter is typed in Chinese characters, it should be written exactly the opposite: year/month/day.

Signing Off

Business letters usually end with '*zheng chen*' ('faithfully'), although another sign-off phrase, sometimes used sarcastically, is '*Xie xie ni de he zuo*' ('Thank you for your co-operation'). A letter to a loved one

---

Chinese Addresses

Country	*China*
Province and postcode	*Beijing 100600*
Street	*Ritan Dong Lu* (Ritan Dong Road)
House or building number	*70 hao lou* (building number 70)
Flat number	*3 dan yuan* (apartment number 3)
Name of recipient	*Li Yang.*

6.
THE CHINESE AT WORK

Working in China is different from working in your home country, although not as much as you might expect. Despite the language and cultural differences, there are many similarities in the way people work, and as China looks increasingly westward it's adopting more Western working practices. The differences are most pronounced if you're working for a Chinese employer and less noticeable if you're employed by a foreign multi-national or joint venture.

> 'Choose a job you love and you will never have to work a day in your life.'
>
> Confucius (Chinese philosopher)

A large proportion of the jobs available to Westerners involve teaching – usually teaching English to Chinese students – and much of the information in this chapter focuses on opportunities and conditions within the teaching sector. It also explains the Chinese work ethic and factors affecting employment (such as obtaining the necessary permits), and provides tips on finding a job and what to expect once you start working. Last but not least, it contains information about starting a business and business etiquette.

WORK ETHIC

In a country where wages are low and there are few holidays and little legal protection for most employees, gaining sufficient qualifications to enter a professional career is paramount. Most Chinese youth spend their teenage years with their noses in textbooks to achieve this aim. In spite of its seemingly unstoppable economic evolution, there's no real social security safety net in China; if you don't work, you don't eat. As a result, most Chinese take their work very seriously. They're diligent employees who rarely question their boss's or supervisor's instructions. If something needs to be done they do it, and if told to do a task in a particular way, they comply and continue to do so until told to stop, rather than looking for an alternative method or a short cut.

In many ways they're ideal workers, but there's a flip side. Almost every Chinese employee would prefer to be self-employed if only they could find a way to achieve it, and they're always looking for ways to work for

feel they have good working conditions and a reasonably well-paid job for life, provided they do nothing stupid. As a bonus, many officials have a certain amount of power over ordinary people which they aren't averse to wielding. Power alone is enough for many, but they also have opportunities thrust before them daily – maybe a bribe, or the first choice of a cut-price property on a new housing estate – and these open up the possibility of making money on the side. Many succumb to temptation, and surprisingly few are caught.

Unemployment

China's true level of unemployment is difficult to gauge. Government figures for autumn 2010 put the urban unemployment rate at just over 4 per cent, but this

themselves. If they see a process at their workplace that's productive and profitable, they'll put a great deal of energy into studying, perfecting and even copying it. If successful, they're off like a shot, setting up in direct competition with their employer and undercutting him ruthlessly.

Even if they aren't planning their own enterprise, Chinese employees aren't particularly loyal to their employers – perhaps because employers show remarkably little loyalty to their staff – so if another organisation is looking for employees with their skills and offers a higher salary, they don't hang around.

People working for government departments are the exception. Most

doesn't take into account the millions of migrant workers who move from area to area in search of work, or the farmers who live off their land. The market for jobs is extremely flexible and fragile, and China's fledgling economy is easily affected by changes in world finances. When the export markets for Chinese goods evaporated at the start of the global recession in September 2008, many factories laid off their workforces. However, rather than joining the ranks of the unemployed, the workers returned to their farms and laboured there, albeit for a far lower wage – there's no such thing in China as redundancy pay or unemployment benefit – so despite losing their jobs, they weren't technically unemployed. A year later, the tide had turned and many migrant workers returned to the factories which had re-focused from the overseas market to the domestic market. China's labour market is unusual in that the division between unskilled and semi-skilled labour is blurred, and people switch between the two to suit demand.

China has the largest labour force in the world – some 813m people are available for work – but there's a shortage of skilled labour and experienced supervisors. There's no system of technical schools and apprenticeships, and so-called craftsmen such as carpenters or plumbers are invariably self-taught and rarely expert in their trades. This 'learn as you go' attitude has filtered through to the more technical skills needed in industry. As a result, the shortage of skilled and educated workers is a major problem in fast-developing areas, such as Shenzhen, and someone with suitable qualifications and experience should have little problem in finding a well-paid job.

> **'Be not afraid of going slowly; be afraid only of standing still.'**
>
> Chinese proverb

Discrimination

Chinese people genuinely believe that there's no discrimination in China, and it's true that age discrimination doesn't exist. Women officially retire at 55 and men at 60, but there's no pressure to get rid of people simply because of their age. On the contrary, older people are considered to have valuable experience, and the elderly are regularly consulted in the workplace so that others can benefit from their experience. However, some foreigners do face racial discrimination. The average Chinese person expects a foreigner to be white with fair hair and blue eyes, and if you fit this image you may be treated with an almost embarrassing level of respect – certainly, you should find it easier to gain employment. If you're Asian or black, your appearance may work against you; Asian people from nearby countries, and particularly some indigenous people from Africa, face far more problems in China.

WORK & BUSINESS VISAS

There are strict regulations governing who may work in China, and the system is policed by the Public Security Bureau (PSB). In brief, the only people who can legally work are the following:

- Chinese citizens normally resident in China;

- Citizens of the Special Administrative Regions (SARs) of Hong Kong and Macau, provided they hold a Mainland Travel Permit;

- Citizens of foreign countries who hold a Foreigners' Residence Card (valid in Shanghai) or a Foreigners' Permanent Residence Card (valid throughout China).

All of the above people may work without further documentation. Anyone else who wishes to work in China must obtain the appropriate visa. This is usually a Z type visa, although an F visa allows business people to work in China for up to three months – but it can be extended – while a J visa is issued to journalists on an assignment. In order to obtain a Z visa, you must have a job offer and proof in writing such as a letter from the employer or, better still, a signed contract. In a few cases, your employer may offer to obtain your (Z) visa for you, but most people obtain their own. If you're planning to conduct business in China, you need written confirmation from your employer. If it's your own business, the onus is on you to prove that it's viable and that you have the funds to establish and operate it. The best tactic may be to apply for an F visa initially, and then try to change it to a Z visa once in China. If you have funding and a good business plan, and can persuade someone at the PSB that you know what you're doing, you may well succeed.

Foreigners in possession of a Z type visa must also obtain a Work Permit for Foreign Experts (also called a Foreign Expert's Certificate). This is issued by the Foreign Affairs department at your local PSB office, and is usually valid for one year and must be renewed annually. The permit is usually retained by your employer as proof that you're legally employable, but goes with you if you change jobs. If you're recruited from overseas, generally your employer pays for the cost of your visa and any renewals necessary. If you take up employment while already in China, you must fund your own Z visa, although your employer may be willing to pay for renewals.

Visas can be renewed at the PSB and, provided all the necessary supporting documents are furnished and up to date, this takes around five working days. Make sure that you prepare the necessary paperwork well in advance of your visa's expiry date. You can also change your visa, e.g. from a student (X) visa or tourist (L) visa to a Z visa, provided you have written support from a prospective or current employer.

For a foreign citizen to work in China without the correct papers is a serious offence and can lead to deportation.

> If you have visions of going to China to study, and paying for your trip by working in your spare time, perhaps by teaching English, be careful. There are many opportunities, but if you don't have a Z visa and are caught working illegally, you may be summarily deported and your passport noted, which will make it difficult to return. Your prospective employer – provided it's a proper language school or university, rather than a private citizen – should be able to arrange the correct paperwork. If they cannot, it's better to decline the job.

FINDING A JOB

Until recently, most people seeking work in China were travellers or backpackers who wanted to subsidise their stay by working. Any other foreign workers had either been sent there by an overseas employer or had secured a job before arriving, and opportunities for casual work or self-employment were limited.

This has changed and now, although most foreigners working in China arrive with a secure job offer, there are an increasing number of expatriates who travel to China on spec in the hope of finding work. In many cases

they're successful. Unlike many other countries, such as the UK and US, it's possible to travel to China as a tourist, find work and convert your visa to a work visa without having to return to your home country first.

The main sources of work for foreigners in China are as follows:

- **Language schools and universities:** Teaching provides by far the most work opportunities, and most jobs involve teaching English. Employers prefer teachers to be aged between 21 and 65, but age limits aren't strictly enforced.

- **Chinese-foreign joint ventures:** It may be easier to research vacancies at a business in your home country, or a multi-national company that works in partnership with the Chinese.

- **Foreign embassies and non-governmental organisations (NGOs):** Start with your home

country's missions based in China, and check the websites of organisations such as the Red Cross.

- **Chinese businesses and organisations:** Those that have considerable contact with overseas companies, such as China Central Television, provide the best opportunities for foreigners.

- **Self-employment** – Entrepreneurs have an increasing chance of success in China, but need a good idea, careful planning and not a little luck.

- **Friends & acquaintances:** In China, with its culture of *guanxi*, who you know is as important as what you know, and many people secure work through their connections. Cultivate as many contacts as possible to increase your chances of finding a good job.

When looking for work in China, it pays to be persistent and proactive. If you're already in the country, you could try visiting prospective employers on spec with a copy of your CV (resumé), but ensure that you look presentable. Staff will often take your CV and offer to ring you back, and many an expat has got a job this way. You can also apply direct to schools and universities. Another option is to contact the various chambers of commerce and business organisations linked to your home country. Most have a website and these quite often list vacancies with major overseas employers, within their local joint venture organisation, which are sometimes quite senior positions. Many embassies have a link on their website labelled 'jobs', 'careers' or 'employment opportunities'. Jobs are also listed in free expatriate publications in China.

Overseas Business Organisations

The following organisations can assist foreigners in finding work or setting up a business. All are useful for meeting with other business people and for learning of changes in the laws affecting business. Full contact details are listed in **Appendix C**.

● **Australia:** The China-Australian Chamber of Commerce has offices in Beijing, Shanghai and Guangzhou. Another useful organisation is the Australian Trade Commission (Austrade) which has local offices in a number of Chinese cities including Beijing, Chengdu, Guangzhou, Kunming, Shanghai and Wuhan.

● **Canada:** The Canadian Chamber of Commerce of South China is based in Guangzhou. In addition, the Canadian-China Business Council (CCBC) has offices in Beijing, Chengdu, Nanjing, Qingdao, Shanghai and Shenyang.

● **European Union:** The EU Chamber of Commerce represents all the EU countries, including Ireland, and has offices in Beijing, Chengdu, Guangzhou, Nanjing, Shanghai, Shenyang and Tianjin.

● **New Zealand:** The New Zealand Chamber of Commerce is based in Guangzhou (☎ 020-8667 0253). Elsewhere in China it collaborates with the China-Australian Chamber of Commerce.

● **UK:** There are British Chambers of Commerce in Beijing, Guangzhou and Shanghai. It's also worth contacting the China-Britain Business Council which has offices in several UK locations, including London, Manchester, Glasgow and Leeds, and offices in Beijing, Chengdu, Hangzhou, Nanjing, Qingdao, Shanghai, Shenzhen and Wuhan.

● **USA:** The USA-China Chamber of Commerce, called Amcham for short, has offices in Beijing, Guangzhou, Ningbo and Shanghai.

Speaking Chinese

Whether or not you need to speak Chinese varies from job to job. Many teachers can get by with limited or even no language skills, as they're cushioned by a largely English-speaking academic environment; but in almost any other jobs, some Chinese knowledge is an asset, and if you're working for a Chinese organisation it's essential.

Skills & Qualifications

Chinese employers expect you to have qualifications and want to see proof. In most cases, teachers must possess a Bachelor's degree from a recognised university, although it doesn't need to be a degree in English – any degree will do. Some previous experience of teaching is preferred but isn't essential. If you also have a certificate in teaching English as a foreign language, e.g. TEFL (see below), so much the better, but it isn't mandatory. Bring all certificates with you, along with several copies; the same applies to any qualifications which are listed on your CV.

You may be able to secure a teaching job with just a TEFL certificate or with no qualifications at all! If the head of a school or university likes you, he can apply to the provincial PSB's Foreign Affairs department and say that he has tried, but failed, to find a suitable candidate with a degree and, as a result, wishes to employ you. In many cases, the PSB will agree to your employment.

If you want to teach a subject other than English and have an appropriate degree, you must be able to teach this subject in either English or Chinese. Even if you aim to teach another foreign language, an ability to explain things in English is expected. English is now very much the second language in China.

There is also a demand for teachers to act as examiners for the two major foreign examinations in English: TOEFL (Test of English in a Foreign Language) and IELTS (International English Language Testing System). For these jobs, you must have a first in your degree and a TEFL (Teaching English as a Foreign Language) or TESOL (Teaching English to Speakers of Other Languages) qualification from an accredited school, such as Trinity or Cambridge, and have taught English to adult learners for at least three years. For more information, contact the British Embassy's Cultural and Education Section in Beijing (☎ 010-6590 6903, 🖳 www.britishcouncil.org.cn/en/china.htm).

Employment Agencies

There are a number of Chinese employment agencies, with the widest choice in the four major cities of Beijing, Guangzhou, Shanghai and Shenzhen, although many of the positions on offer are for English teachers. If you're looking for a different line of work, some international agencies such as Manpower, Adecco and Kelly Services have branches in China and you can search for jobs on their websites.

ChinaJob holds job fairs each year in Beijing and Shanghai, specifically aimed at expatriates. It primarily acts as a recruitment agency for jobs in teaching but has other positions – its website (💻 www.chinajob.com) is well worth a look.

Of all the agencies, one of the most enterprising is BMU Consulting (💻 www.bmuconsulting.com) which has offices in both Beijing (☎ 010-6641 1471) and Shanghai (☎ 021-5133 6646).

> If you use an agency to find you a teaching job, check the working conditions carefully. There have been some recent advertisements for jobs requiring teachers to work excessively long hours. There's no need to accept such poor working conditions as there are plenty of jobs to be had.

Employment Websites

There are a great many online agencies listing jobs in China – a few are mentioned in **Appendix C**. All feature the inevitable teaching jobs, alongside other vacancies. Dedicated websites for would-be English teachers include English First (💻 www.englishfirst.com/trt/teaching-english-in-china.html), China Teaching Web (💻 www.teachabroadchina.com/) and TEFL.com (💻 www.tefl.com).

Applications

Apply for as many jobs as you can. Your CV should be brief and to the point and it's worth mentioning any experience of travel, particularly in China. As well as your CV, include a covering letter explaining why you're interested in working in China. Schools and universities are specifically interested in native-born English speakers. If you're applying by post, reckon on ten days for mail to travel to and from China.

Selection Process

The Chinese don't generally go in for aptitude tests or ask for references. You may have to complete an application form, particularly if you're applying from overseas, but more often the employer bases his decision based on a short interview. At an interview, it's important to look business-like – a suit is ideal, with a white shirt and tie for men, while women should avoid low-cut tops or short skirts – and act in a polite and formal manner, e.g. don't sit down until you're invited to do so.

Salaries

Chinese wages vary enormously depending on the size of the employer, the location and the industry sector. Some workers earn surprisingly low salaries: a nurse in Kunming earns about 1,000 RMB a month, while a low-level government official in Shenyang earns just twice that amount. Wages are higher in major cities, and an office manager in a medium-sized private company in Beijing earns some 5,000 RMB a month.

Foreigners almost always earn considerably more than the Chinese. Overseas companies occasionally regard China as a 'hardship' posting, therefore an employee's salary is higher than it would be for the same position in his home country, sometimes with the addition of a 'local allowance' to cover costs he wouldn't incur at home, such as local travel and foreign phone calls. Someone already based in China joining an overseas organisation's joint venture may earn less than existing staff who've been

seconded from head office, and no local allowance is paid as you're already settled in the country. If you join a Chinese company your salary will be lower still, and teachers get the lowest pay although they do have some excellent perks.

The following is an example of salaries for foreigners doing some typical jobs:

● A foreman on a construction site seconded from the UK – 25,000 RMB a month, plus a local allowance of 5,000 RMB a month.

● An entry clearance officer at a foreign embassy, recruited in China – 18,500 RMB a month.

● An announcer on Chinese Central Television (CCTV) – between 10,000 and 12,000 RMB a month.

● A teacher with a bachelor's degree teaching English at a school or university – around 4,000 RMB a month in a third-level city such as

Zhengzhou. Salaries are higher in the major cities and at more prestigious universities, and if you possess a PhD you could earn up to 6,000 RMB at a top Beijing university. In contrast, Chinese teachers in most cities earn around 1,800 RMB a month, but they often get subsidised accommodation.

If your employer has no objection to you moonlighting, and not all employers agree to this, you can earn a great deal more. Some workaholics put in 40 or more hours a week teaching at multiple locations, and earn up to 20,000 RMB a month.

Salary Payments

Most people are paid monthly, and some of your salary may be paid into an account in your home country. You don't usually receive a pay slip unless you pay tax, and it's quite normal to be handed a wad of notes. If you earn enough to pay tax, this is shown on a pay slip. Social security isn't an issue as it doesn't, as yet, apply to foreigners.

Voluntary & Unpaid Work

The idea of hiring an intern as an unsalaried employee so they can learn the ropes is largely unknown in China, where people work to live rather than live to work. The only employers likely to offer places for interns are joint venture companies or, possibly, NGOs. There are openings for voluntary work in China, but many of those advertised overseas, such as helping on a giant panda conservation project, require you to make a hefty contribution towards your accommodation and food. Note that a voluntary position won't secure you a work (Z) visa.

CONTRACTS

Most Chinese employees receive a written contract, and foreign workers almost always do. Chinese entities employing foreigners, such as schools, universities and organisations such as China Central Television, usually base theirs on a standard format drawn up by the State Administration for Foreign Experts' Affairs (SAEFA). This consists of two pages in English, with a counterpart in Chinese, setting out the conditions of employment and the responsibilities and duties of both the employer and the employee. The contract is signed by both parties and each retains a copy.

Contracts include a clause requiring you to respect the government's attitude towards religion, and not attempt to convert Chinese co-workers to your faith. Another clause requires you not to moonlight for another employer without your employer's express permission. The point behind this second clause is that your employer may well be providing your accommodation and other expensive extras, therefore they expect you to provide a good service and not turn up tired, for example, after teaching private students in your spare time. If you're thinking of supplementing your basic salary with other work, discuss this in general terms before signing the contract. Many teachers do work a few hours a week at private schools or kindergartens, with or without permission, to earn a few extra RMB. Some employers may agree to you taking on additional work, although they may not approve of it, provided your ability to do your main job doesn't suffer as a result.

Joint ventures tend to have their own forms of contract, but they, too, usually contain the clause about religion and require employees to obey all local laws and behave in a moral manner.

> All contracts are normally conditional on you undertaking a medical examination at a hospital nominated by the employer; this is repeated each year or every six months. If an examination reveals that you have a serious sexually transmitted disease or are HIV positive, your employer will be obliged to inform the PSB and you can expect to lose both your job and your right to live in China.

WORKING CONDITIONS

Labour laws are limited in China where there's no automatic entitlement to sick pay, maternity leave or other benefits which are taken for granted in the West. Working conditions vary according to the type of job, the employer and where you were recruited, although it's likely that both the conditions and salaries will be better than those enjoyed by the majority of Chinese. Most foreigners work as teachers or for a foreign company or joint venture, while a few are employed by a Chinese organisation. The following information explains the type of working conditions that you can expect in two typical areas of employment.

Working for a Multinational Company

If you've been recruited or seconded from abroad to work for a multinational company, NGO or government organisation, your employer arranges and pays for any necessary medical checks and vaccinations as well as flights to China for your family. You're met at the airport and transported to your accommodation, and can expect a guided tour of your new workplace, while a colleague will probably show you how to use public transport to get to work. Your new apartment – and all its furnishings and contents which can range from plain to luxurious, depending on your occupation and rank in the organisation – is your employer's property and you're expected to treat it with respect. You're usually liable for the cost of utilities and telephone calls.

Very few offices have a canteen and, in most cases, you're expected to pay for your own food out of your local allowance; the main exception is large construction sites, where international contractors provide a free canteen for their staff, many of whom do shift work.

Your salary is usually paid on the same day as it is at home, but in two separate parts. Your base salary is paid into your nominated bank account and you may be obliged to pay your home country's income tax on it, while the local allowance is paid in China and you're liable to Chinese income tax on it if it exceeds 5,000 RMB a month or 60,000 RMB a year. It's worth obtaining professional advice regarding your tax situation, as it may be worthwhile opening an offshore bank account for your salary payments. If you work for an embassy, you're deemed, for tax purposes, to be working on home soil.

Your holiday allowance varies, but single people are usually entitled to a three-week trip home by economy air every six months, while those who travel to China with their family get a six-week break with tickets for all the family after one year's service. Your local allowance isn't usually paid during home leave periods. You should also receive paid time off on Chinese public holidays and, sometimes, also on those of your home country.

If you become ill, there will be clauses in your contract detailing what the employer will provide in the way of reimbursement of medical expenses, time off in the case of serious illness or accident, and even repatriation home in the worse cases.

All of the above applies to employees either transferred from or recruited in their home country. Employees engaged from within China are deemed to have less need for support and may not be granted accommodation or paid a local allowance. There are no free trips

Cormorant fisherman

back to your home country either, and you may not receive any paid holiday time other than Chinese public holidays – it's up to you to negotiate the best deal that you can. Any perks in your package largely depend on the skills you're bringing to the organisation, and how keen it is to employ you.

Working as a Teacher

In addition to your salary, most employment packages for state schools and universities – and some private educational establishments – include free accommodation, paid holidays and often a cash allowance for travel within China during your time off. Depending on the length of your contract, you may also qualify for a return flight to China at your employer's expense. Always check these points carefully before signing a contract, particularly if it's with a private employer.

Many teachers are recruited from abroad. If you're already living in China, you may be offered part-time employment, which is better paid – many private schools pay around 100 RMB an hour – although you're expected to provide your own accommodation.

Schools don't have to seek permission to employ you part-time, therefore you won't receive a contract. In order to work legally you must have a work (Z) visa, and to obtain one you need a letter from someone saying that you're an employee. There are people willing to do this – for a small fee. If you don't have a work visa you can be in serious trouble with the PSB.

The majority of Chinese teachers and lecturers at state schools and universities live on campus, and foreign teachers are usually provided with their own apartment on campus. Quality varies, depending on when the apartment was built, but most are adequate and include all furnishings and most utilities (see page 78). There are canteens and restaurants on campus providing cheap food, but usually only Chinese fare. Many teachers cater for themselves or eat out at restaurants.

Most schools or universities expect you to teach for between 14 and 16 hours a week; Chinese teachers put in fewer hours, but most receive only half the salary that foreigners are paid. Each lesson lasts about one hour and 50 minutes, with a ten-minute break halfway through – and foreign teachers are expected to teach seven or eight lessons each week, all on weekdays. It doesn't sound a lot, but it demands a good deal of preparation and concentration. The educational year runs from September to June, and is divided into two terms (semesters), each lasting 14 or 15 weeks and broken up by the Chinese New Year holiday. Teachers put in about 200 hours of teaching, each term; but in addition, there

are examinations at the end of each term, and teachers are expected to prepare, supervise and mark examination papers for the courses they teach.

University classes usually consist of 30 to 35 students, but schools may pack 70 or more students into a classroom. You'll rarely, if ever, have someone visit your classroom to monitor your work, but you'll be scrutinised by the students and management will quickly learn if you aren't doing a reasonable job.

Most teaching contracts are usually only for one or two terms. If you join a university in September, and sign a contract for two terms, you're paid during Spring Festival holiday; but teachers on a single semester contract receive no such benefit, although all teachers are offered a paid day off on Thanksgiving and Christmas Day. If you take time off for sickness without providing a doctor's certificate, or miss classes, it usually results in a pro-rata deduction from your salary.

In addition to their salary, some teachers receive a travel allowance. This usually takes the form of a lump sum for travel within China, and is paid just before holiday periods. Most teaching establishments will also provide economy airline tickets for travel between your home country and China: a return ticket for those signing a two-semester contract, and a one-way ticket to China for those who only sign up for one term.

STARTING OR BUYING A BUSINESS

Modern China feels a little like the Wild West, with fortunes being made and seemingly few regulations to hold you back. Foreign direct investment is actively encouraged, and the CIA World Factbook has estimated that by 2009, over US$576bn had been poured into China, making it the eighth most popular country for investors. This pioneering spirit, and the opportunity to make large amounts of money in a short amount of time, has tempted a flood of would-be entrepreneurs to come knocking loudly on China's door. However, many have had a rude awakening on discovering that the Chinese are pretty smart when it comes to business, and quite a few people have had their fingers burned.

Five rules for doing business in China:

1. **Think small – focus on one region at a time.**

2. **Skip the manager, talk to the clerk.**

3. **Study the side streets.**

4. **Get the goods to market.**

5. **Above all, be flexible.**

New York Times Magazine

The most popular sectors for foreign investors are manufacturing and export. The majority of investors come from Taiwan and Hong Kong, but the number of European investors is growing, particularly from the UK and Germany. The marketplace is already quite crowded. While most big business in China is government owned, there are an incredible number of small private businesses. Research has shown that most have a lifespan of around 12 years, and for each one that opens, another fails.

To make a success out of doing business in China, you need to research your market carefully, write a good business plan and, most importantly, make an effort to understand the people you'll be working with. Without some knowledge and appreciation of Chinese culture, you'll struggle to succeed.

China's bureaucracy dates back for thousands of years, and prospective investors must be prepared to negotiate a considerable amount of red tape. A foreigner wanting to start up a business in China has two alternative routes:

● A joint venture with a Chinese partner.

● A wholly-owned foreign enterprise.

Both must be registered with the relevant authorities and, depending on the scale of the proposed operation and the industry sector, the entire process usually takes between four and six months. The World Bank's Doing Business survey for 2010 ranks China 78th out of 183 countries for ease (or not) of doing business, but 149th for starting a business and a lowly 180th for dealing with construction permits. If you're going the joint-venture route, and your Chinese partner has *guanxi* (connections), it's possible to fulfil all the requirements in around eight weeks.

The key stages are as follows;

● Formally register with the Ministry of Commerce through the local Industry and Commerce Bureau;

● Register with the State Taxation Bureau;

● Register with the Provincial Taxation Bureau;

● Register your company seal with the Foreign Affairs office of the PSB;

● Open a Chinese/foreign currency bank account and deposit funds;

● Register at the local Foreign Exchange Administration Bureau and obtain a Foreign Currency Certificate;

● Register all expatriate staff and their families and their place of residence with the PSB;

● Register with the local Customs office.

Complying with these requirements is time-consuming but relatively inexpensive; average start-up costs are between 1,000 and 2,000 RMB. However, investors are required to deposit a substantial amount of operating capital in a Chinese bank. The amount varies according to the industry, but a wholesale or manufacturing business is required to deposit at least 500,000 RMB, a retailer about 300,000 RMB, a consultancy 100,000 RMB and a foreign language centre a little under 100,000 RMB; if you plan to operate in just one city or province, rather than nationwide, you may be able to deposit a smaller amount. Even your company name has a bearing on costs. You pay more if you want to include the name of the city where the business is established, more still if the name of the province is included and yet more if you use the words 'China' or 'Chinese'. You don't have to pay this directly, but must have sufficient funds on deposit to cover the cost.

> If you don't want to set up a new business, it's possible to buy an existing one; but this is risky, and you need to do your homework thoroughly to ensure that the business is fully licensed and as profitable as the vendor claims it is. Take particular care before entering into a partnership with the Chinese. If you fall out with your partner and end up in court, the law will almost always favour the Chinese national.

Loans & Grants

There are no government grants for setting up a business although a grant may, under certain circumstances, be forthcoming from an organisation in your home country. For example, UK citizens can check out the government's Business Link website (🖥 www.businesslink.gov.uk) for the latest situation. If a really major development is proposed, then either the Asian Development Bank or even the World Bank may lend support. Starting up in a city other than Beijing, Guangzhou, Shanghai or Shenzhen may lead to lower costs and possibly provincial government incentives, as China seeks to promote investment in other provinces, such as Sichuan and Yunnan in the west and Heilongjiang in the northeast.

There are no investment funds as such, and loans are generally only obtainable from banks. Most banks demand security in the form of land or property, although some are more flexible and may accept a particularly valuable antique as security.

Premises

Most business premises are rented, at least in the short term, and in many areas local governments and developers erect factory units for rent on new industrial estates. Renting commercial property is much the same as renting a house or apartment, and usually involves two fees: a payment to the agency which secures the property and a refundable deposit against damages. Each is roughly equal to a month's rent. If you're buying business premises, due diligence is required to ensure that you can operate your business there and that there are no local restrictions – don't take the vendor's word for it. Also bear in mind that, as with residential property, you'll only 'own' it for 70 years.

Working from Home

Depending on your business you can work from home, provided you don't disturb or otherwise inconvenience your neighbours, but you must still register your business officially.

Self-employment

It's possible, although not easy, to be self-employed in China. You must have a work (Z) visa to work anywhere in China, and you won't be granted one on the basis of being self-employed unless you can demonstrate that you can earn a viable income. There's little chance of being granted a work visa to operate as a plumber, mobile hairdresser or private tutor, as there are plenty of qualified Chinese willing and able to offer these services; but if you have run a successful bookshop in your home country and wish to open one in China, you're more likely to be looked upon favourably by the authorities. Most foreign-owned ventures operate as small businesses rather than sole traders. Expatriates have opened shops, schools and restaurants, started advertising agencies, architectural practices and import/export businesses, and even run small tourist hotels or tourist facilities such as riding stables. Many started off as employees, and built up their business on the side.

Professional Advice

Whatever your business venture, you'll need professional help: an accountant to help you unravel the taxation system, a friendly financial advisor, a lawyer to ensure you have the right contracts and a translator to ensure you understand them. A good place to start is the Chamber of Commerce from your home country. It also helps to have as many useful contacts as possible, preferably with good *guanxi*, and you should start cultivating connections as soon as possible after arriving in China.

Marketing

All the usual facilities are available in China, such as advertising using local radio (television is expensive), newspapers, flyers and leaflets in newspapers. Many companies promote themselves using text messages to mobile phones. Possibly the best marketing is through word of mouth, so don't neglect the personal touch. A banquet for prospective clients may pay more dividends than any amount of flashy brochures.

BLACK ECONOMY

China is a cash-based economy, therefore it's inevitable that much income goes undeclared and untaxed. Most part-time workers – Chinese or foreign – are paid in cash, and don't declare it to the tax authorities. As a foreigner, you can earn up to 5,000 RMB a month before you're liable to pay tax, but if you earn more than this and the tax authorities find out, you run the risk of being sent to prison.

WORKING WOMEN

China's women have more equality than women in many parts of the world, at least in urban China. You see them working in almost every occupation, including those which would be considered 'man's work' in many Western countries. Thus there are female street cleaners, municipal gardeners, bus drivers, car mechanics, taxi drivers and labourers – women even drive heavy construction equipment such as Caterpillar bulldozers. At the other end of the scale, there are many female managers and supervisors, and women hold positions as directors and chairs of public companies. Women are paid the same wages as men for doing the same job, and there appears to be little of the 'glass ceiling' for women, other than in politics, and this is due more to a lack of interest in politics than through discrimination.

In many families, both partners work – a surprising number of husbands and wives work in different cities, and only see each other at holiday times – while their child is brought up by the grandparents. The availability of a full-time family babysitter allows women to pursue further education and progress their careers, although at a cost to their family life. Even in China, it seems, women cannot 'have it all'.

BUSINESS ETIQUETTE

Most business in China is conducted much as it is in the West, although there are some important cultural differences that you should be aware of. Matters are discussed more cautiously and less directly, the overall objective being to get your point across without causing anyone to lose face, particularly in front of their superiors. This also applies when supervising junior staff. Before asking someone to perform a task, ensure that they're able to do it. If they lack the training or cannot manage it, they'll stay quiet and even hide from you rather than admit that they cannot carry out your instructions. They're likely to feel embarrassed by their failure and would prefer you not to know about it. Similarly, if an employee doesn't want or know how to do something, they're unlikely to refuse outright. If they demur by saying, obliquely, how difficult it will be, or suggest that you mustn't expect a good result, the task is probably beyond their capabilities and you should find someone else for the job.

First Day at the Office

This is your first opportunity to meet Chinese colleagues and make friends. On entering the office, greet your colleagues with a cheerful '*ni hao*'. There's no need to shake everyone's hand, as happens in some European offices. Use the same greeting if you meet someone in the corridor. Find out the routine for getting a cup of tea, and whether this is brought to you by a 'tea lady' or whether you should fetch it for yourself. Ask someone to show you where everything is, from the printer room to the toilets. You're unlikely to have a company car – which are rare in China – but if you do, make sure that you know where to park and how to get in and out of the car park. The same applies if you commute on a bicycle or electric bike.

Chinese offices can be quite formal. Junior employees treat their bosses with respect, standing up and addressing them as Mr (*Xiansheng*). Use of first names is rare except among expatriate colleagues.

Appointments

It's rarely necessary to make an appointment to visit a government department or business, unless you plan to meet someone high up in the hierarchy, in which case it's courteous to do so. Always be punctual!

Business Cards

Business cards are essential. All Chinese people in government, business or education carry business cards, and they also expect you to have them. Always carry plenty of cards, as some meetings involve many people and they'll each want one. It's best to have a simple white card with your name and business address printed on one side in English and on the other in Chinese. When offering your card to someone, always hold it with both hands. When receiving a card in return, place it neatly face up on the table in front of you. Never stuff it into the back pocket of your trousers; this suggests that you think so little of the giver that you're prepared to sit on him! There are neat little boxes which hold up to 50 cards, and most Chinese businessmen carry one.

Business Gifts

Gifts can be misconstrued as bribery. If you want to give a gift, ensure it's something promotional, such as a T-shirt with your company's logo on it, and hand it over openly in front of other people to avoid any accusation of malpractice. Chinese law is vague on what constitutes a 'state secret', and if you give something of value you risk being accused of obtaining state secrets from the recipient.

Business Hours

Working hours in most offices are between 8am and 6.30pm, five days a week, although not everyone works all those hours, and lunches can be long. Banks open at 9am, although staff are there an hour earlier, and close at 5pm. Most office workers put in a five-day week, with both Saturday and Sunday free, but if employees are asked to come in on Saturdays they don't usually get paid.

Business Lunches

Business lunches are quite common, although some people prefer to entertain clients over dinner in the evening.

Dress

Dress smartly but conservatively. For men this should be a dark suit, white shirt, a tie, dark socks and polished shoes; for women, something neat and simple and not too much make up. Chinese girls frequently wear no cosmetics or just a little lipstick, although their hair is usually immaculate. Some bosses allow their staff to wear more casual clothes, but it's better to dress up rather than down until you know what's expected. You may see some office workers wearing an extra sleeve over the lower part of their shirt sleeve. This is a means of keeping their cuffs clean, and used to be popular in draughtsmen's offices in Europe a century or so ago.

what you say. Above all, avoid putting someone on the spot and causing them to lose face in front of the assembled group. If someone has done something wrong, keep your temper and keep your complaint oblique; they'll appreciate your thoughtfulness and be more likely to help you in the future.

Meetings

Most meetings are well organised and take place on time. Chinese businessmen gather around huge conference tables, and you'll probably find everyone's place laid out with a pad, pencil and cup of tea (rather than water). Look for the place card bearing your name.

If applicable, the leaders of both parties start the meeting, but once introductions are complete and the agenda rolled out, they're happy to sit back and let their subordinates do the talking. The aim is to put forward both sides' point of view and their respective objectives, but it's rare that a final decision will be made at the meeting. This is usually reached at a one-to-one private meeting between the bosses at a later date. The Chinese prefer to leave the meeting first, and you should stay in the room until all the visitors have departed.

Meeting etiquette doesn't preclude smoking or answering your mobile phone, and you can expect at least some of the attendees to puff away at the conference table and to be interrupted regularly by mobile phones. However, politeness is paramount, so be careful

Language

Although younger Chinese have studied English since primary school, most have little experience of listening to and speaking English and you must anticipate this. Older people are less likely to know any English at all, and many cannot read pinyin either. If you cannot speak Chinese, it's best to take an interpreter to important meetings.

For more information about languages, see **Chapter 5**.

> Shaking hands doesn't always signify sealing an agreement, as it does in the West.

Negotiating

There are some important points which you should be aware of when negotiating any kind of business deal with the Chinese:

● Relationships are important, and you may spend a lot of time getting to know your business partners before anyone gets around to discussing the

matter in hand. Don't rush this; it gives you a chance to earn their trust.

- Chinese people don't like being pressured, so don't over-emphasise your deadlines.

- Chinese thought processes are different from a Westerner's. Rather than deciding between A and B, they may try to find a way of merging both options.

- Negotiations can move at a snail's pace, and the other party may attempt to drag out the process to frustrate you or they may conclude at breakneck speed.

- The Chinese aren't above sneaky tactics, such as a large banquet the night before the meeting to put you off your guard.

- Chinese people work through the wording of a contract in fine detail, but never forget that their version is written in Chinese, and Chinese is nowhere near as definitive as,

say, English or French; thus their understanding of a clause may be different from yours. This isn't necessarily evasiveness on their part, but due to the lack of precision of the Chinese language on technical matters.

- Even after laboriously agreeing to the final wording of a contract and signing it, don't imagine that it's binding, at least on the Chinese side. They may well stuff it in a drawer, and carry out the work in the way they always have.

Regional Differences

There are cultural differences between people from different parts of China, and these can have a bearing on how they behave in business. Beijing people enjoy cultural activities such as the theatre or art galleries, but they often act as if they're superior to people from the rest of the country – it's the seat of government, after all. They have a tendency to show off. Shanghai folk are more switched on about current trends, and knowledgeable about the economy, fashion and food. They firmly believe that Shanghai women are the most beautiful in China. Guangzhou people are born traders. For centuries, foreigners have traded with them – Guangzhou is a key transportation hub for China's export trade – and the local people know how to make a deal.

Timekeeping

The Chinese aren't usually obsessive timekeepers, but nor are they as relaxed as some Mediterranean people. Traffic can be bad in the cities, and everyone accepts that there are unavoidable delays, but you should never turn up late to make a point and should always advise people if you're likely to be delayed.

EMPLOYING PEOPLE

If you need employees there will be plenty of applicants, but most Chinese workers are only as loyal as their next pay packet. If they see the opportunity to make more money somewhere else, they'll leave without a backward glance; or they'll learn all that they can from you and then set up, across the road, in direct competition. There's little you can do about this, and it can be discouraging; but with their country going through so many changes, the Chinese are focused on looking after their own interests first.

The minimum wage varies according to where you are in China – in 2010 it was about 600 RMB in Henan province, 960 RMB in Beijing, and as high as 1,030 RMB in parts of Guangdong province – but many smaller businesses pay considerably less.

Contracts

All employees must be provided with a contract setting out their terms of employment and the responsibilities and duties of both the employer and the employee.

Domestic Help

If you employ a cleaner, gardener or nanny they'll expect to be paid cash in hand. Provided they're part-time workers this shouldn't be a problem, but you're legally responsible for them and should ensure that they're covered by workplace insurance. Many domestic staff are not Chinese but Filipino, and even Chinese employers prefer them as they're more hard-working than the Chinese.

Social Security

On top of each employee's wage, the employer is required, by law, to pay:

● medical insurance;

● social insurance;

● endowment insurance, which pays a lump sum on death to the insured's family;

● subsistence allowance, if an employee is living away from home.

These only amount to a small percentage of the employee's wage.

Tax

Employers are required to deduct income tax (if applicable) from the wages or salaries of all employees. For Chinese citizens, any earnings in excess of 2,000 RMB per month are subject to tax; for foreign employees, the starting point is 5,000 RMB per month.

TRADE UNIONS

China has strong trade union representation, with around a quarter of the workforce belonging to a union. The All-China Federation of Trade Unions has over 190m members and is keen to attract more. An umbrella organisation representing a number of smaller unions, the ACFTU has close links to the Chinese government, which has recently insisted that all foreign joint ventures must allow union membership, including companies such as Wal-Mart which has successfully resisted unions elsewhere in the world.

However, Chinese unions are considerably less vociferous than those of the more developed countries. They act as a conduit between employer and employee, and spend much of their time reducing, rather than aggravating, friction between the two and attempting to resolve individual grievances. They appear to work on the principal that if there's good co-operation between workers and management, then both parties are likely to be more satisfied and the result will be a happier workplace.

It's very unlikely that a foreign worker would be asked or required to join a Chinese union.

WORKING WEEK

There's no national standard working week, and hours vary from job to job. Most office workers put in a 40-hour week. Hours are longer in the construction and engineering industries, where people may work six days a week, starting at 6.30am or 7am and finishing at around 7pm; it's generally accepted that in summer, when the temperature exceeds 40°C (104°F), workers down tools on full pay until it cools down again. Agricultural workers put in similar hours during the

summer months. Teaching hours vary; lessons start at around 8am and may continue until 9pm.

Lunch Breaks

Although many Chinese business practices mirror those of Europe and the US, there's one major difference: lunch. Around midday, some of the working population stops for as long as three hours. This doesn't apply in factories or shops, banks or post offices, but it's the norm in government organisations, state schools and universities. Even some private offices take a longer break than you would expect in the UK or US.

You need to work around the lunchtime hiatus, and avoid planning meetings or appointments or making important calls during this time. If you try to phone someone at another office between 12 and 3pm, you may find no one able (or willing) to accept your call. If you're travelling, you may find yourself battling not two but four distinct rush hours: at 8am, midday, 3pm and 6pm.

Coffee/Tea Breaks

There are no designated breaks, and you take your refreshments on the run.

Holidays

An entitlement to holidays is a fairly recent concept in China. Until 2008, many employees took only one holiday: a four-day break at Chinese New Year. The Spring Festival now lasts for 14 or 15 days, and there are also various other public holidays (see table below).Most employees are paid during public or annual holidays. If they're asked to work during a public holiday, the employer is required by law to pay penalty rates, e.g. time and a half, on those days.

> Holiday allowances are more generous if you work for a multi-national, joint venture or foreign employer, and teachers may receive a travel allowance which they can put towards surviving the long summer break.

People who work for government departments may get no holidays at all, apart from public holidays, until they have completed five years of employment, after which they're allowed one day for each year that they have worked, i.e. five days after five years, and an extra day for each additional year. This is the price they pay for having a job for life!

Public Holidays

China has seven public holidays of varying duration. The biggest is Chinese New Year and its accompanying Spring Festival. This is a 14 or 15-day break, depending on which day it begins. The other public holidays are either political or cultural in context. May Day (also known as Labour Day or Workers' Day) is a one-day holiday. National Day, which celebrates the founding of the People's Republic of China in 1949, takes place on 1st October and is celebrated with parades and firework displays. It's sometimes extended to provide a seven-day break. Three new public holidays were introduced in 2008: Tomb Sweeping Day, the Dragon Boat Festival and the Mid-Autumn Festival.

During public holidays, workplaces, schools and universities close, but most shops, banks and post offices remain open; while airlines, trains and buses operate increased services. People often work during weekends in the run up to public holidays so that they can build up free time to coincide with the holiday and take a longer break.

The duration of the National Day and May Day holidays has been subject to change in recent years. Both were originally one-day holidays, but in 2004 the government decided to increase their length to a full week to give workers the chance to travel home to their families and to boost domestic consumption. Known as 'golden weeks', these were a resounding success, so much so that trains and long-distance buses were crammed, while tourist spots and shops were crowded. As a result, the government decided to cut both holidays back to a single day, and introduce three further one-day national holidays. In 2009, the National Day holiday was lengthened again to eight days to celebrate the 60th anniversary of the Republic.

Other Special Days

Some specific groups of people have their own designated day, e.g. teachers and the armed forces; but while these days are usually celebrated with parades and festive activities, some of which are broadcast on television, they aren't public holidays and everyone else goes to work as usual.

Christmas & Easter

Christmas Day is acknowledged in the major cities, and seems to get more popular each year; local governments put up coloured lanterns in the main streets,

National Public Holidays

Date	Holiday
1st January	New Year's Day (*Yuan Dan*)
January/February	*Chinese New Year and the Spring Festival (*Chun Jie*)
8th March	Women's Day
5th April	Tomb Sweeping Day (*Qing Ming Jie*)
1st May	Labour Day
1st June	Children's Day
June/July	*Dragon Boat Festival (*Duanwu Jie*)
1st July	Chinese Communist Party Day – celebrates the party's founding in 1921
1st August	Army Day – takes place on the date of the Nanchang Uprising in 1927
15th September	Teachers' Day (*Zhaoshi Jie*)
September/October	*Mid-Autumn Festival (*Zhongqiu Jie*)
1st October	National Day (*Guoqing Jie*)

* indicates that the timing of the holiday is dependent on the lunar calendar.

Jingle Bells plays in department stores and shop assistants wear Santa hats. It's a retail opportunity rather than a religious occasion, although Chinese Christians celebrate it in church. Other international holidays are largely ignored, except for Valentine's Day which is an excuse to sell overpriced roses. Schools and universities employing foreign teachers frequently offer them a day off on Christmas Day and Thanksgiving Day, as well as on Teachers' Day, and embassy staff get time off on their own national holidays as well as on Chinese holidays. Boxing Day and Easter aren't acknowledged in China.

Local Holidays

There are some more localised celebrations, although even if you live in the area where they take place it doesn't follow that you'll get time off work. For example, in Yunnan province, people celebrate Water Splashing Day in mid-April, while the people of Shandong mark the birthday of Confucius on 28th September. One of the largest local celebrations is Inner Mongolia's *naadam*, a festival featuring local sports such as horse-riding skills and wrestling. Depending on when the grass is at its greenest, these are held at sites throughout Inner Mongolia between 15th July and 15th August, often on different dates in different cities and towns.

Leave

Employees' benefits are limited in China. The generosity of employers varies, and as a foreign employee you should ensure that your entitlement to certain types of leave, in particular sick leave, is fully detailed in your contract.

Li-river, Yangshuo (Guilin)

Shanghai at night

7.
ON THE MOVE

For most foreigners, driving in China isn't the default option. Many visitors, when they first see the local driving habits, perhaps in a taxi from the airport driven by someone who they suspect may have escaped from an asylum, decide it's too risky to drive. Moreover, rumours abound that large parts of the country are forbidden to foreign drivers. Both are incorrect and this chapter tells you of the ways that you can enjoy driving in mainland China. However, if you don't want to drive yourself, or the time you'll be spending in China is too limited to justify getting a car, it explains the other options, from cycling to public transport.

> 'Where so ever you go, go with all your heart.'
> Confucius (Chinese philosopher)

DRIVING

It **is** dangerous to drive in China, but it's even more dangerous to ride a bicycle or walk. Motorists are involved in a lot of minor and low-speed accidents in the often unpredictable driving conditions in cities, but relatively few drivers die in high-speed collisions on the open road. Overwhelmingly, the people who are killed or injured are pedestrians and cyclists.

The road accident statistics in the box here indicate the number of deaths and injuries in China in 2008 compared with the UK and US. It's important to compare not only the number of deaths and injuries, but also the number of vehicles on the roads of each country.

The table of accident figures reveals that despite its relatively small number of vehicles, the number of fatal accidents in China is very high compared to Britain or the US, which have much smaller populations but a much higher ratio of car ownership and a higher proportion of accidents resulting in injury. This is because the Chinese, both drivers and other road

Road Accident Statistics				
Accident Statistics Comparison				
Country	Population	Vehicles	Deaths	Injuries
China	1,330m	65m	73,000	305,000
UK	61m	34m	3,000	245,000
US	304m	470m	43,000	2.9m

users, are inexperienced. Most Chinese grew up in a society where cars and trucks were rare; just ten years ago there were virtually no private vehicles on the roads. As a result, people who live outside cities – over half of the population – are still unused to vehicles and unaware of how dangerous they can be.

However bad the statistics, they don't mean that you cannot drive safely in China, but that you must expect the unexpected and drive defensively. As a general rule, traffic travels far slower than it does in the West, other than the on the expressways. Driving can be enjoyable as it allows you to see a lot more of China's countryside, which is beautiful and far more representative of the country than the cities. However, driving at night is seriously unpleasant and dangerous. Outside city centres, street lighting is minimal, if it exists at all, and there are the additional hazards of oblivious pedestrians in dark clothing walking in the middle of the road and vehicles without lights. Most bicycles have no lights, while the riders of electric bicycles switch off their lights to save their batteries; farm vehicles and trucks carrying bricks have no lights either, and a considerable number of mini-vans and buses drive without their lights switched on. Stopping at red lights at night is also treated as optional rather than mandatory, particularly in the suburbs and countryside, the theory being that the faster you go across a red light, the less chance there is of you being in a collision.

Driving Licence & Driving Test

As a foreigner, you may drive on a full overseas driving licence from your home country initially, although you must take a local driving test and obtain a Chinese driving licence as quickly as you can, certainly within three months of arrival.

Licences are issued separately for drivers of cars, motorcycles and trucks, with different tests for each type. Riders of electric scooters don't need a licence, but petrol-powered scooters may only be ridden if you have a motorbike licence. The test for a driver's licence is made up of a 45-minute multiple choice test on a computer and a fairly brief road test.

The computerised test is based upon China's 'highway code' and you must study a copy of the reference manual, which contains questions and answers and is available in English and several other languages (the price is around 150 RMB). The test may be available in English; if not, you can ask for an interpreter to sit alongside you. You must pass the theory test before you can take the road test and the pass score is 90 per cent; if you fail you may take it again a week later. You also need to pass a medical examination, which includes an eye test and a test for colour-blindness. In addition, you must provide a copy of your overseas driving licence and at least five photographs, which must have a white background and be 2.5 x 2.5cm (1 x 1in) in size, i.e. smaller than a passport photograph.

> **The best advice for most foreigners regarding driving in China is – don't even think about it!**

The actual road test is a fairly straightforward drive through local streets, and it's unlikely you'll be asked

Chinese 'smart' car

to make any complicated manoeuvres. Assuming you pass, a driving licence costs 70 RMB and comes in a black, credit-card sized booklet. It's valid for up to six years, but you must undergo a medical examination each year and evidence of this must be stamped into the licence annually. You must be over 18 to apply for a driving licence and at the age of 70 it will be taken away! Women should note that some police aren't keen to issue you with your first driving licence if you're aged over 45. You must carry your driving licence with you at all times. If you're stopped by the police, your licence, along with your car's registration booklet, is the first thing that the officer will examine.

Possession of a Chinese driving licence doesn't mean that the owner has passed a driving test or knows anything about road rules. If you know the right person, it's possible to get a licence without taking a test. In 2009, a government official who was involved in a collision was found to have no licence. Investigation of the local government department he worked for revealed other officials with licences who had never taken a test. When told that they would all have to take a test

to have their licences renewed or lose them, they protested bitterly on the grounds that they already had licences and without them they couldn't do their jobs. There are websites which offer to 'sell' foreigners a Chinese driving licence for around 2,000 RMB, but it would be foolhardy, never mind illegal, to drive on Chinese roads without some sort of national qualification.

The situation with an International Driving Permit (IDP) is anomalous. China isn't a signatory to this scheme so, in theory, such a permit has no validity in China, but it contains one page of explanation written in Chinese, and if you rent a car in China the rental company may insist that you have an IDP.

Chinese Drivers

Chinese drivers aren't particularly aggressive or impatient but they're often inept. Many lack the experience of living in a motorised society, so are neither skilled nor conversant with the rules of the road. They don't like to flag up their own or other drivers' mistakes, and the result is a country where drivers cruise along in their own private world, with little regard for other road users.

Chinese regulations state that drivers must sound their horn when passing a cyclist or a pedestrian. A sensible rule in the countryside, but one which is impossible to apply in the cities which overflow with cyclists and which often have local bylaws forbidding the use of a horn except in emergencies. Despite this, horns are still used far more frequently than in the West, not just as a warning but more often to demand that other road users get out of the way. It's easier to press the horn than the brake pedal.

> Drive through the Chinese countryside at harvest time and you encounter an unusual hazard. Farmers use the road for drying sesame and sweetcorn, often occupying half the width of the road. This is relatively easy to avoid; however, many farmers believe that cars and trucks make good threshing machines so they pile cut wheat or barley across the entire road up to over half a metre high, and expect you to drive your vehicle through this, crushing the wheat and shaking loose the grain. It doesn't hurt the car, but be careful of pitchforks left lying around!

The overriding 'rule of the road' in China, day or night, is that the bigger your vehicle the more rights you have (might is right!). But there are exceptions. The armed police (*Wu Jin*) and the Chinese Army give way to no one, and both break traffic rules continuously. Their vehicles, and the cars used by drivers of government officials who consider themselves important, have special horns, reminiscent of a flatulent duck. If one of these starts quacking behind you, you're expected to pull over and let them pass as quickly as possible.

Many people drive in a rather pleasant and sedate manner, although many have dangerous habits, such as failing to indicate, ignoring their rear-view mirror – many are not accustomed to mirrors, as bicycles don't have them – and cutting into your lane right in front of you. You must be constantly on the lookout for the unusual, such as a car driving towards you in your lane because it's a short cut to wherever the driver wants to go, or someone driving along on the pavement to get to the front of a queue of traffic.

Parking skills are often abysmal with cars dumped anywhere there's room, blocking pavements, doorways and other drivers.

Chinese Roads

Contrary to popular opinion, there are few restrictions on where you may drive in China, even as a foreigner. Some areas, such as military installations and airfields, are restricted for security reasons, but it's possible, though not desirable, to drive the almost entire length of the country, which stretches over 5,000km (3,000mi) from west to east. If you do this, you'll encounter an astonishing array of roads, varying from dreadful, pot-holed earth tracks to fine expressways.

China's network of expressways has increased substantially since 2000, and there are over 65,000km (40,000mi) of expressways linking major cities with the best connections in the south and east of the country. In recent years, China has built as much new expressway, every year, as the UK, for example, has in total, and it has the second-largest network in the world after the US.

Some roads have just two lanes in each direction, but most now have four or five lanes each way, with a central reservation complete with hedges and barriers. On hills there are often additional lanes for slow-moving trucks. The police patrol these roads

Road junction, Hangzhou

gear and gently move off. Police control of traffic is different from what you may expect; during rush hours, you'll see police at every city junction, not trying to stop drivers but actually urging the traffic on.

As the volume of traffic has increased, so the incidence of traffic jams has multiplied. These occur daily on the inner ring roads of Beijing, but resolve themselves relatively quickly. Elsewhere, road works can lead to traffic jams and delays and, during 2010, there have been reports of quite monumental traffic jams caused by a combination of too many trucks and extensive road works, leading to some truck drivers being delayed for days rather than hours. But, to date, other than within the cities, such problems are unusual, although the continuing rapid increase in the number of vehicles in China doesn't bode well for the future.

extensively, but often ignore speeding drivers. Their main concern seems to be to keep the traffic flowing and they're assisted in this by numerous CCTV cameras, dotted along the central reservation and powered by solar panels, projecting images back to a central control room from where reports of traffic congestion are sent to the patrol vehicles.

Using Chinese roads usually involves paying road tolls. Almost every city has a toll gate on its approach road which charges 10 RMB for every car; additionally, all expressways are toll roads, as are many bridges, and the cost can soon add up: a 200km (125mi) road trip can cost around 60 RMB in tolls, all of which must be paid in cash.

Unlike Chinese driving standards, traffic control is much better than in some developed countries. In the cities, many traffic lights have large illuminated signs showing the directions in which you're allowed to turn and the number of seconds before the light will change. In the West, a countdown like this would probably lead to a Grand Prix-like start every time a light went green, but in China people just wait until the light changes, leisurely engage

In summer 2010, a combination of road maintenance work and congestion led to a monster traffic jam on a highway from Beijing to Inner Mongolia. The jam, which stretched for some 95km (60mi), trapped drivers for over a week.

(Reported in the UK's *Daily Mail* newspaper)

Road Rules

China's road traffic safety laws were introduced in 2004 to tackle the alarmingly high accident rate. Not all drivers adhere to them, but so that you know what you should be doing, some of the most important points are listed below:

- The Chinese drive on the right and, in theory, give way to traffic approaching from the right. However, a 'first is right' mentality means that the first driver to reach a gap in the traffic, whether merging with other traffic, changing lanes or turning left, claims right of way – and so you should always leave plenty of space and yield to all other drivers, regardless of which direction they're coming from!

- Speed limits are 30kph (19mph) on city roads, 40kph (25mph) on single carriageways and up to 80kph (50mph) on dual carriageways. On expressways the limit is 120kph (75mph), and there's a minimum speed limit of 50kph (30mph). Slow-moving vehicles such as tractors and motorcycles aren't allowed to use them. Traffic police don't, as a rule, target speeding drivers, but if you exceed the posted limit by over 50 per cent the official penalty is a 2,000 RMB fine.

- All cars in China are fitted with seat belts to the front seats only. You're obliged by law to wear one, but many drivers don't and can be seen hurriedly draping the belt over themselves as they pull up at a toll station where there are often attendant police.

> Roundabout rules are the same as in other countries, but if a roundabout is blocked many drivers will go round it the wrong way just to get past!

- If you're involved in an accident, even a minor one, you're required by law to leave your car where it is, even if it blocks the traffic, until a police officer arrives at the scene. The officer questions those involved and often allocates responsibility there and then. **Note that where an accident involves a car and a pedestrian or cyclist, the driver usually gets the blame.**

- Drink-driving laws are strict. It's an offence to drive with just 20mg per 100ml of alcohol on your breath and you can be put in a cell for the night if caught; if it's more than 80mg, you may be charged with 'drunken driving' and spend a month in prison. It's also an offence to get into a car with a driver who you know has been drinking.

During 2009 there were four cases of drunken drivers ploughing into people on pedestrian crossings and causing multiple deaths. In one case a young driver was engaged in a race with a friend. The culprits were all caught and either imprisoned or, in two cases, sentenced to death for 'endangering public security' (one had his sentence reduced to life imprisonment on appeal). These cases have highlighted the problem and raised the subject of the excessive toasting with alcohol that so is often a part of Chinese 'banqueting'. A limit of 20mg means you shouldn't drink at all when driving in China.

Traffic Fines

There are a limited number of speed cameras in China, mainly on the roads leading to Beijing and Shanghai airports. More common are cameras on traffic lights to catch the many motorists

coloured tourist boards advertising local places of interest. However, on minor roads the road signs are in Chinese only, therefore you should memorise (or draw) the Chinese characters for your destination before setting off.

Most Chinese maps aren't printed to scale and are extraordinarily difficult to follow. One reason for this is that the military regard maps as a way to leak potentially sensitive information, and view cartographers with suspicion. Satellite navigation systems have also been slow to catch on in China, possibly for the same reason.

who drive through red lights. If you're caught doing this, you won't receive a penalty notice; instead, a record is kept of your offence and if you're stopped by the police for any reason, they'll check if you have any outstanding offences and issue you with a notice for a 200 RMB fine for **each time** you've run a red light.

A retired teacher from Lanzhou became famous in 2009 for his one-man campaign against drivers who routinely ignored red lights at a crossing near his home. According to a report in the *China Daily*, he threw rocks at the cars and damaged 30 before the police arrived to stop him. In an online poll, 80 per cent of respondents supported his actions.

Finding your Way

Expressways and major routes through the countryside have good signposting, with destinations indicated in both Chinese and pinyin, with distances in kms; there are also road signs on brown-

Motorcyclists & Electric Bicycles

There's a saying that there are no old motorcyclists in China, and there's some truth in this. Motorcyclists are given no consideration by drivers of cars, buses and trucks and it's a dangerous way to get around. Almost all motorcycles have a 250cc engine or less (the majority are no more than 150cc). Although there are a few old 750cc locally-made sidecar outfits and larger-capacity imported machines – including some Harley Davidsons, which are strictly for posers – most motorcycles are quite slow. For this reason, they're banned from expressways, so you can only ride one on rustic byways or city streets, and some city centres have also banned them.

A popular alternative is the electric bicycle. Because these two-wheelers are classified as a bicycle, anyone can ride one provided they can see over the handlebars – there's no age limit and they're ridden by children as young as 12 – and there's no requirement to wear a helmet, have insurance, pass a driving test or pay road tax. They can carry two adults and are cheap to run, easy to ride and can be parked alongside regular bicycles. The downside is that riders are extremely vulnerable, and often behave as if they're driving a truck and not riding a flimsy two-wheeler.

If you're brave enough to try an electric bike, there are two types; one looks like an oversized lady's bicycle and costs between 1,200 and 1,800 RMB, while the other resembles a scooter, with all enveloping bodywork, and costs 2,300 to 3,500 RMB. The latter 'cooler' option is more popular with younger Chinese. Both are operated by a battery which powers an electric motor forming the rear hub of the machine, and can travel at up to 40kph (25mph) for up to 50km (31mi) on a single battery charge. A single charge takes several hours, but they can be charged at home – just plug them in

to your mains electricity – and you can pedal them if the charge runs out.

The Chinese have honed the avoidance of eye contact to a fine art. Cars pull out of side turnings with no regard for traffic already on the road, and they do this by deliberately looking anywhere but at the traffic rapidly approaching them, so that cars on the main road have no alternative but to stop to let them out. They don't just edge out but come out at speed. If you see a car in a side turning, on either side of the road, you must be prepared for them to pull out straight in front of you, all the time pretending that they cannot see you. Electric bicycles and cyclists do this, too, and it's a major cause of accidents and often fatal injuries among electric-bicycle riders.

Cyclists & Pedestrians

The bicycle may be a Chinese icon, but cyclists are at the bottom of the heap on Chinese roads, just one step above the lowly pedestrian. No one stops for either on a pedestrian crossing, where the only way to cross is to wait for a group of pedestrians and cyclists to reach critical mass, forcing the cars and buses to stop by the sheer weight of numbers. On major roads, cyclists are often waved onto the footpaths to give cars more room, but on country roads where there are no paths, both cyclists and pedestrians must take their chances in the road.

Cycling may look dangerous – **it is dangerous** – but if you go with the flow, surrounded by other cyclists,

you'll find it a great way to get around, cheaper than driving and without the hassle of parking.

A new single-speed bicycle can be bought for around 300 RMB from specialist shops and supermarkets, and comes complete with front basket, rear rack, prop stand and lock – but no lights. Mountain bikes are available from 500 RMB, and beautiful racing bikes for several thousand RMB.

The Chinese are loath to sell their bikes because they consider them so useful; therefore, while some large cities have secondhand bicycle markets, many of the bikes have been stolen. Bicycle theft is rampant in China, so most people keep their bike looking dirty and always lock it, even if they're just slipping into a shop for a packet of cigarettes. **Fail to lock your bike, even in the guarded office car park or the foyer of your apartment, and you'll lose it.** Most shopping areas have cycle parks where it costs just two *jiao* (0.2 RMB) to leave it under the eagle-eyed stare of a very sharp-tongued lady.

a series of separate strips, each one lane wide and more manageable. The drivers are used to this manoeuvre, and the cars flow past on either side.

Walking can be a good way to get around, but beware of Chinese city maps; the scale can be deceptive and what looks like an easy stroll on a map can turn out to be a hike. Many Chinese prefer not to walk and will often exaggerate distances involved, encouraging you to take a bus or a cab. If you jog, be prepared for some strange looks, particularly in the countryside. The average Chinese farmer firmly believes that a second-class ride is better than a first-class walk. Walking is usually perfectly safe, but it's sensible to avoid walking along unlit city streets or through parks at night, and in the countryside it's a good idea to have a companion. Don't forget that most rural people assume that as a foreigner you must be rich, and by their standards you probably are.

> Punctures are a regular hazard, but fixing them is cheap: just 2 RMB for a bicycle or 5 RMB for an electric bike.

Pedestrians have devised their own strategy for surviving the city streets. If you need to cross a road in heavy traffic, watch how the locals do it. They wait until there's a gap in the nearest row of traffic and immediately walk out on the pedestrian crossing to the first lane line and stop, facing the oncoming traffic. Then as a gap appears, they walk briskly to the next lane line and so on. In this way they divide the road up into

Fuel & Servicing

Petrol is sold by the litre in three grades – 90, 93 (the most commonly used) and 97 octane – and costs around 6 RMB a litre. If a pump says E93 it means the petrol contains 10 per cent ethanol; in theory, cars should be converted to run on this fuel, but no one bothers and it works perfectly well. Diesel cars are rare. Taxis often run on liquid petroleum gas (LPG) and a few service stations sell only LPG; you can spot them by the long queue of taxis waiting to fill up.

Petrol stations are huge, but usually the only amenity is a particularly unpleasant toilet; there are no shops. Oil is available but not air (for tyres), for which you must visit a tyre repair shop or car wash. Self-service isn't encouraged, and attendants fill up your car; although one of the largest fuel companies, Sinopec, provides customers with a card which slots into the petrol pump, allowing you to fill up and pay later. The Chinese tend to buy petrol by value rather than volume, e.g. 200 RMB worth. The car manufacturer BYD has led the way with electrically-powered cars in China, and is working on a system for filling stations that will provide rapid battery charging.

Car servicing is fast and efficient. In every city, major manufacturers run their own garages, each with numerous work bays and every spare imaginable. There's usually no need to book, and you'll be guided to a work bay where the service will take place immediately; it usually takes less than an hour and costs around 150 RMB, which you pay in cash. If an item needs replacing, such as brake pads, and you don't have enough cash on you, the garage will let you drive off to get more cash, provided you leave your car registration certificate with them as security.

Car washing is big business; cars are washed by hand and the interiors cleaned and vacuumed by a team of youths. It takes around 20 minutes and costs about 20 RMB.

> In hot weather, rural car washes do more than just wash cars. They also spray trucks carrying livestock, such as pigs or chickens, giving the animals a nice cooling shower on their journey.

Parking

Parking is no problem in villages and rural areas, but in major cities finding somewhere to leave your car can be a nightmare – another reason many Chinese rides bikes. Multi-storey car parks don't exist, and most parking is on the street or footpath, but it's better to park in a guarded area if possible. These are used by cyclists and drivers, but while it costs just two *jiao* to park your bicycle, a car costs at least 4 RMB. Many new housing estates have underground car parking with card-operated security gates, and most villas have garages; however, you may find that, even though you own an apartment, you must pay to park your car there. To date, parking fines are rare,

although this may change as the number of cars on the roads increases.

PUBLIC TRANSPORT

Chinese public transport is extensive, reliable and reasonably priced, and makes a more sensible option than a car in the larger cities. It also gives you a much better insight into the country and its culture than you experience from the insulated bubble of your car. However, it can also be crowded and tickets can be difficult to obtain in the run up to holiday periods. The main public transport options are described below.

> Despite the addiction many Chinese have to smoking, it's banned on most public transport, with the exception of slower trains.

Air Travel

China is vast, and travelling by plane is often the most sensible way of travelling the long distances between cities. The three largest airlines are Air China, China Eastern and China Southern. All are government owned and as well as domestic routes, they also serve a number of international destinations – Air China, the national carrier, has the largest number of overseas flights. In addition to the big three, there are a number of local airlines such as Shanghai Air, Hainan Air or Xiamen Air, which are generally owned by the province or city in which they're based. Of these, Shanghai Air is the largest and most efficient. Since 2006, some privately owned low-cost carriers such as Spring Airlines have entered the market.

Flying is probably the most expensive travel option in China, and an economy class seat between Beijing and Shanghai costs about 800 RMB each way, although there are frequently discounts available (up to 40 per cent in some cases) if a flight is at an unpopular time. Low-cost airlines offer significant savings.

You can book tickets from either China's Civil Aviation Authority (CAAC, 🖳 www.caac.gov.cn) or the state tourism agency, the Chinese International Travel Service (CITS, 🖳 www.cits.com.cn), or from the airline's own office or a travel agent, many of whom have offices in the larger hotels. You can also buy tickets online from airlines' websites, although the smaller airlines may not have an English-language option. Many tickets are now issued as electronic e-tickets.

Here are a few things you should know about air travel in China:

● Airport terminals are typically modern and well run. The larger airports with international connections have facilities for changing money, together with shops and restaurants; and even special areas with softer seats reserved for mothers with young children, the disabled and the elderly. Your flight is called, first in Chinese and then in English. Airport signage and departure boards usually feature an English translation, although English-speaking staff are few and far between.

- Check-in for domestic flights is one hour before departure. The desk closes 30 minutes before take-off and any remaining seats – including yours if you turn up late – may be sold to stand-by passengers. Flights are generally on time.

- Economy-class passengers are officially allowed 20kg of luggage and one cabin bag, but many passengers bring a number of carrier bags as well, so the overhead lockers fill up quickly.

> Until recently, passengers were charged an airport construction tax of 50 RMB before each domestic flight, and you weren't allowed into the departure lounge without showing proof of payment. Since 2006, the tax has been incorporated into the ticket price; however, at some airports, you may be accosted by a person selling 'airport construction tax receipts' who will insist that you still need one. This is a scam.

- Many airports have machines that wrap stiff binding tape around your bag for protection. These machines are usually located at the end of the check-in counters, and the service costs around 10 RMB.

- Booklets and plastic membership cards are offered to travellers in departure lounges by teams of young ladies in official-looking uniforms. These handouts are worth having, as they offer excellent discounts on hotel bookings, so collect as many different ones as you can.

Airports

All the major cities have airports, but the main international hubs are Beijing's Capital, Guangzhou's Baiyun and the two airports in Shanghai: Pudong and Hongqiao. Facilities in these airports are on a par with those in the West. Some airports have airport buses or even a train service into the city, but buses can sometimes deliver you to inconvenient places, such as Air China offices which are often far from the town centre. Until you learn your way around, a taxi is usually the most convenient option and – compared to West countries – a relatively inexpensive one.

In Shanghai, most international flights use Pudong airport (PVG) to the north east of the city, whereas most domestic flights are routed through Hongqiao (SHA) which is west of the city; there's an express coach which links them, departing every 15 minutes, but you should allow at least an hour for the journey. Pudong also has an exceptionally fast magnetic levitation (Maglev) train which can whisk you into the city centre in less than ten minutes, and the government is considering extending this service to Hongqiao.

Although both Beijing and Guangzhou have separate terminals for domestic and international flights, they aren't far apart and transferring between them isn't a problem. Both have fast connections by rail, which link the terminals to the cities' subway systems.

Trains

China's huge but generally efficient train service is probably the safest and most reliable way of getting around the country, but it can take a long time to reach your destination. A flight between Beijing and Shanghai takes two hours and ten minutes; to make the journey by train can take 13 hours plus, although the latest high-speed trains have cut the journey time to five hours (see below).

The government views the railways as not only a means of transportation for people and freight, but also as a way of linking this enormous country. It spends a lot of money on maintaining, modernising and extending the network which comprises some 86,000km (53,438mi) of track and runs over 36,000 trains a day. Since 2005, a completely new line been built,

under difficult geological conditions, connecting Lhasa in Tibet with the main railway network, while many established lines have been upgraded to allow the introduction of new high-speed trains. The bulk of the Chinese rail system is concentrated in the east and southeast of the country. There are few lines serving the far western provinces, and to travel there you may need to take a bus or fly.

The state operator is China Railways, which oversees a number of smaller railway companies. There are five types of train operating in China. The slowest, stopping at every wayside halt, are called *Putong che* and these are identified by a number only. Then there are the faster *Kuai* 'inter-city' trains which have a 'K' prefix, followed by the express trains (*Tekuai*) which carry a 'T' or 'Z' prefix and can reach up to 200kph (125mph).

The most luxurious options are the 250kph (155mph) bullet trains, introduced in 2007, which have a 'D' for *Dongche* in front of their number, and the even faster *Gaosu* or 'G' trains, introduced in 2010; the latter travel at speeds of up to 350kph (217mph). These trains are more like planes, with aircraft-style seats, all facing forwards, and aircraft-style (clean!) lavatories. However, a seat costs about twice as much as a ticket on one of the *Tekuai* trains. For example, to make the five-hour journey from Beijing to Zhengzhou (the capital of central China's Henan province) by bullet train costs at least 213 RMB for a one-way ticket. A Soft Seat

CRH high-speed train

(see below) on a *Tekuai* train costs 94 RMB, but the journey takes one and a half hours longer. In comparison, one-way travel by air between the same destinations costs around 600 RMB and takes one hour and ten minutes.

There are also four classes of tickets to choose from, depending on the distance you're travelling and the level of comfort you require:

● **Soft Sleeper (*Ruanwo*):** this costs almost as much as an airline ticket, but you get a bed in a four-berth cabin with a fan, radio (which can be switched off), a soft mattress (as the name suggests), somewhere to stow your suitcase and a flask of hot water. You may also get a choice of Chinese or Western-style lavatories at the end of the corridor. If your journey is overnight, this is the most comfortable option.

● **Hard Sleeper (*Yingwo*):** the price is about two-thirds of the cost of the Soft Sleeper option, and berths are arranged in three tiers in an open-fronted compartment. You get a surprisingly comfortable, yet firm, mattress and the inevitable flask of hot water for tea making, but your luggage has to stay in the rack in the corridor and you would be wise to secure it with a chain. Each tier is priced a little differently, with the lowest tier the most expensive; but if you want to read, get a top berth close to the overhead lights (which are switched off at around 11pm). There are two fold-up seats in the corridor opposite each compartment, but people tend to use the bottom tier as seating during daylight hours.

> Passengers in sleeper compartments frequently aren't allocated by gender, so you can get any combination of men and women in a compartment. The lavatories in Hard Sleeper carriages are usually of Chinese style, and you should never think of using them in the middle of the night without putting your shoes on first.

● **Soft Seat (*Ruanzuo*):** well-padded seats, with a table between them and lots of leg room. If your journey is during the day these seats are fine,

● **Hard Seats (*Yingzuo*):** the cheapest option of all, although 'hard' is a misnomer nowadays. The seats are every bit as comfortable as those on Western commuter trains and there's enough room to get up and walk around. This option isn't recommended, however, when the train is full, such as during a public holiday.

Maglev train, Shanghai

Note that if you're in a sleeper, the attendant takes your ticket and gives you a metal tag in return. In the morning, the process is reversed and you're given your ticket, which you need to exit the station at your destination.

One feature of all China's trains is the availability of food, perhaps in the form of pre-packed meals in Styrofoam boxes or instant noodles, plus fruit, chocolate and drinks brought round on trolleys. There may also be a dining car next to the Soft Sleeper compartment. Not only do you get trolleys bringing round refreshments, but often other vendors bring magazines and sometimes toys or oddities, such as 'socks that you cannot wear out'!

Tickets & Timetables

Reading Chinese rail timetables isn't easy, and they don't seem to be available in English. There are a number of websites which attempt to unravel the confusing array of timetables, routes and ticket prices, although they may not be up to date. Try China Train Guide (⌨ www.chinatrainguide.com) and Seat 61 (⌨ www.seat61.com/china.htm). Johomaps also has a good online train map of China (⌨ www.johomaps.com/as/china/chinarail.html).

By far the easiest way to buy tickets is to go to a travel agent, tell them where you want to go and when. They'll charge a small booking fee, perhaps 10-20 RMB, but it will save you a lot of trouble. If you speak some Chinese and are feeling adventurous, you can visit a China Railways advance purchase office in the city centre, or the booking office at the railway station. Neither is particularly easy to use. If you change your mind after the clerk has printed your ticket and want a refund, you'll only get back between half and three quarters of the ticket price!

> You cannot buy tickets online from China Railways. If you buy them from a travel agency website and the tickets are priced in US dollars, you'll probably be paying much more than the regular fare.

Tickets are sold as one-way and, if you want a return, you'll receive two tickets, one for each journey. Very often you'll be told that you can have a ticket to your destination but must buy the return ticket when you arrive, therefore you set off not knowing for certain that you can get a train back! There's no discount for buying a return ticket. In fact, other than discounts at less busy times of the year and concessions for children which are based on height rather than age – children under 1.4m (4ft7in) pay half fare unless they're occupying a sleeper, while children under 1.1m (3ft7in) travel free but don't get a seat – there are few price reductions. Daily commuting by train is rare, so there's little demand for season tickets, although monthly frequent-user tickets are available on city subways.

Your ticket will show you the train number, the departure time, your carriage and the seat number – all seats are reserved on Chinese trains, except for slow local trains. On arrival at the station, you must queue to have your ticket examined and your suitcase x-rayed before you can enter, where a board tells you the departure time and which waiting room to go to. If you've booked a Soft Seat or a sleeper ticket, there's often a special waiting room provided with overstuffed armchairs and hot tea.

Holiday Travel

The worst time to travel by train – or travel, full stop – is during public holidays, particularly the period before, during and after Chinese New Year, when it appears as if the entire population is going home for the holidays. This period of travel, known as *Chunyun*, has been described as the 'largest annual migration in the world', and while all public transport is affected, the majority of travellers go by train. In 2008, during this period, there were 2.26bn passenger journeys; this equates to the entire number of rail journeys undertaken on the UK's rail service in a year.

Tickets are almost impossible to come by at this time; the rail authorities won't sell them more than ten days in advance, and as soon as they go on sale they're snapped up by touts (known as 'yellow cows') who sell them on at inflated prices. Even if you can get a ticket, it's wise to avoid travelling by train if at all possible, as trains carry twice their normal passenger capacity, and it's standing room only on many trains, while football-stadium-sized crowds mill around outside the stations. The pressure is exacerbated by the fact that many people are travelling in the same direction – usually east to west – and then reversing their journey at the end of the holiday.

Buses

There is every size of bus imaginable in China. At the top end of the spectrum are the long-distance coaches, such as those made by Yutong – a joint venture

with Germany's MAN – which have comfortable recliner seats, on-board movies, lavatories and air-conditioning; at the other extreme are the tiny 800cc minibuses (*xiao mian bao che*) into which people are crammed like sardines.

Buses are a little cheaper than trains and don't have such a good safety record, but they provide a way of reaching places that aren't served by the rail network, particularly in western China. Long-distance express buses (*kuai che*) are the best option. They are comfortable, and offer all the above amenities, while your luggage is stowed under the floor in a locked compartment. For very long trips, there are sleeper buses (*wopu che*) with simple bunk beds. These allow you a more restful journey, and if you reach your final destination during the night, the bus will park and let you sleep on. However, if you're taller than 5ft7in (1.7m) or well built, you may find the bunks uncomfortably cramped.

Local Transport

A number of cities in mainland China have subway (metro) or light rail systems. These include Beijing, Guangzhou, Nanjing, Shanghai, Shenzhen and Tianjin, with another due to open in Kunming in the near future and many more in the pipeline. All these systems are relatively recently constructed, reliable and clean. They are a cheap and convenient way of travelling, typically costing between 2 and 5 RMB to travel anywhere within the system, and as a result, they're crowded during peak hours when passengers try to force their way onto trains as other passengers try to

disembark. It takes a lot of physical effort to board or get off during rush hour.

Tickets are available from ticket offices and automatic machines. Some cities sell cards that can be used on either the subway or buses, but make sure that you have a ticket, as there's a sizeable fine for not having one. As you approach each station, its name is announced in carriages by loudspeaker.

All cities and large towns have commuter buses. These vary enormously in quality but, as a general rule, buses operating in and around city centres are in better condition than those in the suburbs and country towns, partly because the roads are in better condition.

Cities usually have two kinds of bus: ordinary buses with basic seating and no air-conditioning or heating, which stop at every bus stop and charge a set fare of 1 RMB for any length of journey, and express commuter buses, with air-conditioning and heating, which make a limited number of stops. They usually cost 2 RMB, and are less crowded. You can identify them by the K (for *kuai*) in front of the bus service number.

With commuter buses, you either pay on entry or buy a season ticket from a kiosk, valid for either a week or a month. You invariably enter a bus via the front door, put your money into the box by the driver, and exit via the central door. Like metro stations, bus stops can be a real scrum.

There are also mini-buses (*xiao mian bao che*, which translates as 'little bread loaf-shaped bus') which often serve tourist attractions. Most of these don't run to a timetable, but simply wait until the bus is full before leaving.

Taxis

You can flag down any taxi displaying a lighted 'taxi' sign in its windscreen by simply holding out your hand. Taxis are usually safe, even if the driver's skills are nerve-wracking – many cabbies display some of the worst habits of Chinese drivers! If you really feel that your life is at risk, ask him to stop and get out. Cars are maintained in good order, and fares are reasonable: usually a flat fare for the initial 2km (1mi) of between 5 and 10 RMB, and then a further 2 to 3 RMB for each additional km. **Always insist that taxi drivers switch on the meter.** You should pay exactly what it says on the meter, plus any tolls the taxi has had to pass through, and nothing more. There's no need to tip, but you can round up the fare if the driver has been particularly careful and courteous.

Passengers are expected to sit in the back. If you want to wear a seatbelt you must sit in the front, although this seat is traditionally reserved for women. Wherever you sit, a steel mesh divides you from the driver.

There are a lot of pirate taxis, but genuine ones will almost always have a meter. They should also display a photo of the driver, together with his name (in Chinese) and his driver number, should you wish to report him for reckless driving. All licensed taxis are required by law to display their rates in a rear window.

Other Public Transport

Apart from the ordinary cars used as taxis, there are lots of other smaller and cheaper ways to get around. If you can put wheels on anything, the Chinese have done so. Some transport options look like the front half of a motorcycle attached to a box at the back with seats for two (or three or four, if you don't mind sitting on someone's lap). They're known locally as 'tuk tuks', and they're fine for short trips. And then there are pedicabs, which resemble a bicycle-powered rickshaw, although most now have an electric motor. They're a fun way to travel, although the drivers have a reputation for over-charging foreigners. A popular trick is agreeing a fare in RMB and then demanding the same number of dollars! Some cities have motorcycle taxis, which transport passengers riding pillion on a truly hair-raising journey, and are best avoided if you want to reach a ripe old age.

At airports, you'll be approached by touts offering taxis without queuing. Don't use them. Most have no meters and will rip you off. It's better to go to the official queue which is well organised and moves along quickly.

Blue rice terraces, Yuanyang (Yunnan)

8.
THE CHINESE AT PLAY

For many Chinese the most popular entertainment is a meal, usually dinner at a restaurant. The scope and excellence of Chinese food, from fine dining to street fare, will amaze you, but there's a tremendous variety of other leisure activities, ranging from Chinese opera to table tennis. This chapter highlights the most interesting and important, and explains why they're special to the Chinese.

'*Chi zai Guangdong; chuan zai Shanghai*' (**Eat in Guangdong and get your clothing in Shanghai'**).

Popular Chinese saying

Becoming socially adept in a different culture is one of the greatest challenges you face in your bid to fit in, as you're more likely to do or say the wrong thing when in company. To help you avoid social gaffes, this chapter also provides guidance on how to dress and behave in social situations, from a formal dinner to family celebrations such as weddings, what to do (and not do) when dining out, and your options for eating, drinking and having fun. It also explains the most popular festivals, sports and pastimes, and provides a taste of Chinese popular culture and arts.

DRESS CODE

The Chinese dress to suit the seasons rather than the latest fashion. Depending on where you are in China, the climate ranges from bitter winters to blisteringly hot summers, and most people prefer casual clothing which suits the prevailing climate.

The Chinese take wrapping up for the winter very seriously, especially for children, partly because there's often no central heating in their homes, schools or workplaces. People keep warm in multi-layers of clothing; thermal underwear is essential, and people wear two or even three layers, one on top of the other. Over these go jeans or quilted trousers and a heavily-quilted or leather coat, topped off with a knitted wool or fur hat and accessorised with gloves, scarves and even special knee protectors. In spring and summer the layers are bundled away and replaced by t-shirts or polo shirts with jeans or twill trousers; women dress much the same as men although, as the weather heats up, a few girls and women swap to dresses, skirts and blouses, or shorts – a few brave teenagers wear extremely short shorts. In parts of central China and particularly Shanghai, the locals keep cool by going about their business and shopping wearing their smartest pyjamas.

Traditional clothes are rarely worn in modern China. Some smart ladies' clothes mirror traditional fashions with their high collars, wrap-over fronts and cloth buttons, but the only girls you see wearing a *qipao* (*cheongsam*) – a tight dress with a split skirt – are those standing at the doors of restaurants to welcome diners or modelling at car shows. The most traditional clothes are worn by ethnic minorities, ranging from the simple white hats that distinguish the Muslim Hui to the tiered headgear, ornate silver jewellery and colourful clothes of the Dai and the Miao tribes.

Home

Unexpected callers are rare, therefore the Chinese dress for comfort at home. This often means a pair of pyjamas – cotton or silk in summer and warm quilted ones in winter.

Social Occasions

For formal events such as dinners and weddings, people dress in their Sunday best: suits for the men and smart dresses or separates for the women. Very formal attire such as dinner jackets and tuxedos are rarely worn, unless requested for a special event, e.g. at an embassy.

Work

In the office, men wear dark suits, white shirts and ties, while women wear smart jackets with trousers or skirts – a few workplaces allow employees to wear more casual clothes. Employees in banks, department stores and supermarkets wear uniforms. The police change their uniforms with the seasons:

motorcycle police wear white crash helmets in the winter, primarily to keep their ears warm, and change to white topped peaked hats in summer.

Grooming

The Chinese visit the hairdressers regularly. Women usually have immaculate hair, and men are also fussy about their appearance and can take up to an hour having a haircut. Almost to a man, they begin colouring their hair as soon as the first glimmer of grey appears, and most continue to do so until their dying day.

Hairdressers advertise their shops with a striped pole, similar to a British barber, although not always in the barber-shop colours of red and white. Many hairdressers are unisex, with clients of both sexes being tended to by female hairdressers and male barbers. You can get a shampoo and haircut for about 20 RMB.

EATING

Not so long ago, the Chinese ate whatever they could just to stay alive. As recently as the mid-'90s, almost the only winter vegetable available, even in Beijing, was the humble cabbage and every apartment balcony would be heaped high with cabbages to last the family through the coldest months. Nowadays, the Chinese can eat almost anything, including a surprising amount of imported food, at any time of the year, provided they can afford it. However, most prefer Chinese cuisine to that of other countries.

Regional Cuisine

China possesses one of the world's great cuisines and is far more varied than you'd guess from the menus in Chinese restaurants in the West. There, the dishes are usually based on Cantonese recipes from southern China and are frequently adapted to suit local tastes, sometimes to the degree that they're almost unrecognisable to the Chinese.

The Chinese identify eight different cooking styles, but for foreigners it's only necessary to appreciate the differences between the four main regions:

- **North:** The standard is Beijing or Shandong cookery, where wheat or millet is used to make noodles or steamed bread, pancakes and dumplings, and there's an emphasis on cabbage, onions, garlic and soy sauce. Compared with other parts of China, the food tends to be heavier and well suited to the cold winter months.

- **South:** Southern cooks can choose from a far wider choice of fresh ingredients and the quality is the highest in the country. Cooking styles are more adventurous and dishes are often presented looking like a work of art – *dim sum*, small portions of food designed to appeal to the eye as well as the palate, has its roots in Cantonese cooking. Flavours are more subtle than elsewhere, relying on the flavours of the food rather than additions such as garlic and ginger.

- **East:** This is epitomised by the Shanghai style of cooking which features many fish and shellfish dishes. Eastern food tends to be rather sweet and oily compared to northern fare; noodles and dumplings are often made with rice flour rather than wheat flour. Shanghai is also famous for its huge variety of street food, such as fried dumplings and tea eggs – chicken's eggs boiled in water containing herbs, tea and star anise, which taste much better than they look.

- **West:** The further you travel west, the more hot and humid the weather becomes. People need to sweat to cool down, and the food, as in India, is hot … **very** hot. In Sichuan and Hunan, people like their food chilli-hot. Sichuan pepper is used liberally to create an intensely spicy cuisine, and it's difficult to persuade a Sichuan chef to hold fire on the chillies, although the fact that there's an unusually high incidence of throat cancer in Sichuan suggests it may not be entirely good for you.

There's a saying that 'if it's got four legs and isn't a table or if it can fly and isn't an aeroplane, the Chinese will eat it' and that's not as far-fetched as it sounds. They are nothing if not adventurous in what they eat, and the people of Guangdong are the most daring of all. There are many strange and exotic dishes to be found on menus, particularly in the south. You can sample fried crickets, giant snails, bullfrogs, turtle, scorpions, fish stomachs (called fish maw) and crocodile, for example, and chefs work wonders with parts of the pig that Western diners would decline, such as its intestines, ears or even its genitalia!

The severe acute respiratory syndrome (SARS) epidemic in 2003 wiped many of these items off the menu after government research suggested that it may have been spread by the breeding and eating of civet cats. This was followed by a crackdown on the sale and consumption of many wild creatures that had previously been a feature of many restaurant menus, and you may be disappointed, for example, if you want to try snake.

Meals

Breakfast

Breakfast is eaten early, usually before 8am, and many people eat at one of the innumerable small shops serving breakfast dishes or at a worker's restaurant, similar to a British 'caff' or an American diner. A traditional Chinese breakfast usually consists of oil sticks (deep-fried bread, twisted like a rope), soya bean milk, tea eggs followed by rice porridge (*congee*) and steamed bread with pickles. In some places, there may be noodles and a green vegetable rather than the oil sticks. This is a far cry from a typical Western breakfast, but try it; other than the oil sticks, which are tastier than they sound, it's a healthy start to the day. Eat breakfast in a hotel and you may find that one of the chefs is doing a brisk line in fried eggs to order; they may even be able to produce some sachets of Nescafé, pre-blended with powdered milk and sugar.

> **Don't expect toast, bacon or cereals anywhere, except perhaps in a four- or five-star hotel catering to foreigners.**

The ingredients for a traditional English or American breakfast are available in the larger cities, where supermarkets such as Carrefour and expat-run delicatessens stock foreign-made breakfast cereals, German muesli and other staples. You can buy gadgets such as toasters and coffee makers quite cheaply. Finding sliced bread and fresh coffee can be more of a challenge, although if you live in Yunnan province, where coffee is grown and produced, you can buy coffee beans in supermarkets. Chinese coffee shops sell a decent cup of freshly ground coffee..

Lunch

Lunchtime starts at around 11.30am and most people have eaten by 2pm. At home, they tuck into something simple such as fried noodles or rice, while workers eat at a local restaurant. Lone diners are rare in China, where most restaurants are organised to serve groups of people eating at large tables and sharing dishes in the traditional way; however, single diners can always grab a quick lunch of a bowl of noodles in a worker's restaurant. There are no sandwich or salad bars, but there are a number of fast-food joints, both imported and Chinese. If you just want a quick bite, street vendors sell hot snacks.

Schools rarely have canteens; children have a three-hour lunch break, and are expected to go home to eat or to buy something from a vendor close to the school. Universities all have dining halls, and many workplaces and offices have canteens or a lunchtime food service.

Dinner

This is the main meal of the day, eaten at any time from 6 to 9pm. At a restaurant, the diners don't choose individual dishes from a menu but rather share a selection of dishes. It's usually the host, his guest or the most senior family member who makes the choice, selecting a combination of hot and cold dishes, some sweet and some sour, some peppery and others bland, some dry and some wet, i.e. soup, some based on vegetables and others including meat and/or fish. It's quite a skill to order a meal which is balanced, varied, nutritious and attractive.

If there's a large group at the table, say 10 or 12, the tradition is to have eight cold dishes and eight hot dishes, and meals will start with small bowls of appetisers to nibble, followed by the cold dishes and then the hot. The next course is soup, and finally rice or noodles – curiously, this last course is called 'main food' while the earlier plates of food are called 'dishes'. There is never any bread on the table. When people have had enough, slices of watermelon are served to cleanse the palate and signal the end of the meal. A meal at home follows a similar pattern, featuring several platters of food – though not so many – from which everyone helps themselves.

Banquets

These are formal meals which take place either at lunchtime or in the evening. Formal banquets follow the same order as a restaurant meal, but at a function with many tables each guest is served with a portion of each dish, one at a time, similar to a gala dinner in the West. Banquets are about much more than just food, and many business negotiations are settled over a banquet while family celebrations often culminate at the banqueting table.

Seating

The host sits at the head of the table. Where possible, this is the seat furthest from and facing the door. If you're the guest of honour, you usually sit next to the host but should wait for him to indicate where to sit.

Table Settings

The table has a number of small bowls containing pickles or nuts to be nibbled before the meal arrives, and each place is set with a small bowl and a porcelain spoon, a saucer to use as a plate, a cup, possibly a glass or two, chopsticks and a packet of paper tissues in lieu of napkins. There's no knife and fork unless you specifically ask for them.

As soon as you're seated, a waitress fills your cup with hot tea, which is topped up throughout the meal. Restaurants generally offer tea 'on the house' unless you request a particularly expensive blend.

When to Start

Nobody starts to eat or even sips their drink until the host signals that it's time to start, perhaps by saying *'dao'* ('start') and taking the first portion of food.

Table Manners

These are similar to table etiquette in the West, although there are a few important points to remember:

- Don't fill your bowl to brimming; it's best to take one or two items of food at a time. Place the food on top of your rice rather than mixing it in.

- Always accept offerings of food, particularly if they're presented by your host or an older person. You don't have to eat them immediately – or at all, if it's something you cannot stomach. However, if you at least attempt to try the more unusual dishes, your efforts will be admired.

> You can earn extra points by politely refusing offers of food – smile and say *'bu yong! bu yong!'* (Oh, I don't need it!) – and then giving in politely. By not immediately accepting what's offered, you demonstrate modesty.

- Don't spin the Lazy Susan without checking whether someone else is taking food. If you have to lift a platter to serve yourself, it's polite to offer it to your neighbouring diners first.

- Don't finish all the food on the table; the host will feel that he hasn't ordered enough and worry that people are still hungry. If you empty your bowl of 'main food' (see above), a second bowlful is likely to arrive promptly.

- Never leave your chopsticks sticking upwards in a bowl of rice. This is said to resemble incense sticks, and has associations with death. Place them by the side of your plate to indicate that you've finished eating.

- Most tables are provided with tooth picks, which should be used politely with a hand covering most of your mouth.

Noises

Many Chinese make slurping noises when eating noodles and consider this perfectly acceptable. There's no need to copy them.

Toasts

Toasts are offered throughout the meal and you're expected to respond by standing up, touching glasses with the person making the toast, and drinking. At a large table it's usually acceptable to tap your glass on the edge of the Lazy Susan rather than lean across the table to acknowledge a toast. Toasts can be made using any type of alcohol: wine, beer or, more likely, the local spirit called *baijiu*. If you don't like the taste, and many foreigners don't, put your hand over the top of your tiny glass when the waiter brings the alcohol round and ask for a beer (*píjiǔ*).

Toasts are accompanied by the word '*ganbei!*' which means not 'cheers' but 'bottoms up'. The Chinese mean this quite literally and you're supposed to drain your glass. If there are a lot of toasts, and there usually are, you can end up drinking an awful lot and this, to the Chinese, is part of the fun.

If you aren't a big drinker or you're planning to drive home, you can avoid the punishing round after round of 'bottoms up' by saying '*bu, bu, peng bei*' which means 'no, no – cheers' and sipping from your glass instead. You can also explain that you're driving, and respond to toasts by drinking something non-alcoholic such as tea. People won't like this but they'll accept it. Following a series of widely reported cases of drunken-driving resulting in multiple deaths, the Chinese are more aware of the importance of driving sober.

Conversation

Meals are a chance to get to know your hosts and fellow diners. Unless it's a business meal, it's probably best not to discuss work but stick to safer subjects such as the weather, your travels and experiences in China and (good)

impressions of the country, and avoid contentious subjects such as politics and religion (see **Taboos** on page 106). You'll be bombarded with questions by the curious Chinese.

The End of the Meal

The meal is over when the host calls for the bill by saying '*mai dan*', and settles the bill. Don't be surprised if other guests ask how much it cost or if the host tells them.

DRINKING & SMOKING

The ability to hold your liquor is admired by many Chinese. Teetotallers are sometimes looked upon as spoilsports, especially in the *ganbei* atmosphere of a banquet, where people can be bullied into drinking more than they want to and some guests end up seriously drunk. Many Chinese believe that the reason foreigners sip their wine is not because they want to savour the taste of it, but because they cannot afford a second bottle. They themselves quaff wine at the same speed as beer. Despite their love of alcohol, few Chinese men visit bars, and most only drink as an accompaniment to a restaurant meal. It's rare to see a drunk in the street; if someone is suffering the consequences of one too many toasts, his friends smuggle him home quietly.

Spirits, wine and beer can all be purchased in the numerous liquor shops or in supermarkets. China's 'national' spirit is *baijiu*, a potent brew made from rice, sorghum or millet, which far outsells foreign spirits such as whisky or gin. The best-known brands are Maotai and Wuliangye.

Beer is the second most popular drink in China. The first major brewery was opened by the Germans in 1903 in their concession in Qingdao, Shandong province. Sold as Tsingtao beer, this is now China's best-selling brew, available at nearly every bar and restaurant, and is a pleasant, lager-type beer, best drunk cold. Many world major brewers now produce their own brands in China, and if you want to try something different, the German brewer Paulaner has an excellent restaurant in Beijing, with its own mini in-house brewery. There are also a lot of Chinese-brewed beers and some are good, but avoid any which claim to be brewed from bitter melon; they're alleged to have medical benefits but taste unpleasant.

Wine is a definite third choice after *baijiu* and beer, but is growing in popularity. You can buy wine from all the world's major wine-growing countries, and some locally-made wine is also very drinkable. The Dragon Seal label, produced by a Chinese/French joint venture with an Australian winemaker, takes some beating.

> **The legal age for purchasing or drinking alcohol in China is 18. There's no legal age for smoking, and children can buy cigarettes.**

If you don't drink alcohol, there are many soft drinks to choose from. Street sellers wire their refrigerator to a lamppost, and offer bottles of water, iced tea and lemonade, and the inevitable cola, plus local ice creams. A bottle of water costs about 1.5 RMB, or it's around 2.5 RMB for a cola. Shops and supermarkets have a far wider range of soft drinks, including fruit juices and some canned drinks unique to China, made from ingredients such as lotus roots and apricot stones. Some are delicious. Try a Lu Lu made from almond stones, or the local tinned coconut juice.

Smoking

One-third of all the world's cigarettes are smoked in China. The majority of men smoke, although few women do – it's seen as something that 'girls in bars' do. Cigarettes are very cheap by Western standards: some brands sell for as little as 3 RMB for a packet of 20 (less than 30p). Well-known Western brands, such as Marlboro, are available everywhere, although many are copies of the real thing. Roll ups are rare, while pipes are generally the preserve of elderly farmers deep in the countryside – huge bamboo water-pipes are a feature of rural Yunnan. Cigar smoking is virtually non-existent.

Smoking is deeply embedded in Chinese culture. Mao Zedong and Deng Xiaoping were both heavy smokers, and it's estimated that half of all doctors smoke. Luxury-brand cigarettes such as Panda are given as gifts or to seal a business deal. Cigarettes are handed out at funerals to pacify the deceased's cravings, and at weddings to increase the bride's chances of having a baby. If a traffic policeman stops a car, it's odds on that the driver will offer him a cigarette.

The Chinese government is trying to curb the habit, which leads to some 1.2m deaths a year. Smoking is now banned on aircraft, express trains and buses, but everywhere else it's rampant, including in taxis, restaurants and even hospitals. Non-smokers will have a tough time of it in China.

BARS

Bars seem to proliferate in certain areas in the larger cities, where there are often entire streets lined with bar after bar. Most are relatively small, but some have live entertainment while others feature a vast television screen showing sporting events. There are no licensing hours; bars open as early as 10am and may not close until daybreak.

Businessmen visit bars to discuss a deal, although many bars are aimed at foreigners and you'll find the usual American sports bars and Irish 'pubs' in cities with an expatriate community. They can be smart or seedy – and some are the haunt of 'bar girls' who are adept at parting an unwary foreigner from his money at lightning speed. If you want to visit a bar, check out the free magazines for expats or ask for recommendations. Drinks aren't particularly cheap but some bars have happy hours.

Traditional teahouses are an alcohol-free alternative for a business meeting or romantic date, although many are little more than tourist traps and the prices are accordingly high. Although the Chinese drink tea by tradition, there are many Chinese coffee bars which offer a quiet haven from the crowded streets. The coffee is excellent; freshly ground and made to order, a cup costs between 30 and 38 RMB, while something to eat – both Chinese and 'Western' dishes are available – will set you back about 40 RMB. Chinese coffee bars are cheaper and more authentic than the US chains. The latter are making inroads in China, although they're mainly patronised by foreigners and Chinese people who've picked up the coffee habit abroad.

RESTAURANTS & EATERIES

In China, you're rarely more than a few steps away from somewhere to eat. From street stalls to world-famous restaurants, the range and variety of eateries is immense and discovering them is one of the great pleasures for foreigners in China.

> **'Governing a great nation is like cooking a small fish – too much handling will spoil it.'**
>
> Lao Tse (Chinese philosopher)

Chinese Food

The most expensive places to eat are the dining rooms in upmarket hotels, where the prices are often on a par with similar fare in London or New York. Slightly cheaper are those in three- or four-star hotel chains, although most add a 15 per

cent surcharge (service charge) to your bill, without any explanation of what it's for. Hotels often have a choice of dining room, with the option of Chinese and perhaps Japanese, Thai or Western food. Their menus are usually available in English and some of the staff speak English.

Independent restaurants come in every style and quality, from 'greasy spoons' up to high-class establishments. Many are set over two or more storeys and consist of an enormous dining room, sometimes large enough to seat hundreds, plus a number of private rooms of varying sizes, some of which have televisions so you can entertain yourself with karaoke during the meal. Many restaurants are noisy, therefore if you're planning a romantic evening or a business lunch, private rooms offer a more peaceful alterative (apart from the karaoke). Wherever you choose, the menu is the same: an extensive list of dishes written in Chinese, although there may be pictures to help you choose. A good meal can cost anything from 30 to 80 RMB a head, excluding alcohol.

Workers' restaurants are simple places with hard chairs and plastic- or glass-topped tables, but if you want a quick meal they're ideal – a huge bowl of, say, beef noodles (*niu rou lamian*) costs just 3 to 6 RMB. There's no menu as such, but you can often just point at the dishes you want to eat. Everyone, from construction workers to soldiers and office staff in smart suits, patronises these cheap and classless eateries.

The cheapest food of all is sold by roadside vendors. You can choose from a wide variety of street snacks, such as cold noodles, hot dumplings, stuffed steamed bread, omelettes, tea eggs and pancakes, all for just a handful of small change.

Some aspects of dining out which you should be aware of include:

● **Opening hours:** Mealtimes are geared to a society traditionally tied to the countryside and the work pattern in the fields, therefore breakfast is available between 6am and 8am, lunch between 11.30am and 2pm and dinner between 6pm and 9pm. No one comes into a restaurant at 9pm and asks for a meal, except in a five-star hotel where they're more used to foreigners' strange eating habits, and many restaurants close even earlier. If you get peckish during the late evening or night, your choice is restricted to expensive hotels, bars and Chinese coffee houses, many of which serve a limited number of dishes, and street vendors.

Pagoda, Yuyuan Garden, Shanghai

- **Booking:** This is necessary in more popular restaurants, particularly if you want a private room.

- **Seating & service:** On arriving at a restaurant you may be greeted at the door by two or three tall girls, usually very good-looking and dressed in a *qipao*. It's their job to welcome you and show you to your table or private room. Waiting staff are predominantly female. The service is usually attentive without being annoying, and you rarely need to catch a waitress's eye.

- **Water:** The Chinese believe that drinking cold water is bad for the digestion, so most restaurants serve tea rather than water. If water is served, it will be boiled and served at the same temperature as tea. If you want bottled water (*kuang quan shui*) you must ask for it specifically.

- **Bill:** Ask for the bill by saying '*mai dan*'. A few upmarket establishments add a 10 or 15 per cent service charge to bills, but the majority of restaurants don't. Never tip in a restaurant. It isn't expected, and you'll just be causing problems for other customers.

International Food

In the larger cities there are restaurants serving foreign food. Italian is the most commonly available, followed by Korean and German food. You may also find French, Russian and Turkish restaurants, as well as Argentinian and Brazilian, but curry lovers may struggle to find Indian food. Some Chinese restaurants and coffee houses serve their own versions of Western food, which doesn't always taste authentic. Pizza and spaghetti are usually acceptable, but a decent steak is difficult to find, even in some famous hotels. Most Chinese chefs seem to believe that a steak should be beaten to death then overcooked, and the result is frequently something squashy and tasteless. And it will probably cost you more than a first-class steak in the West.

Fast Food

America's fast-food giants have made great inroads in China, and you can find Kentucky Fried Chicken (the first US chain to open in China and by far the most popular), McDonald's and Pizza Hut throughout the country, frequently in major department stores. The food tastes exactly the same as it does the world over, and is considerably cheaper than in, say, Europe. As a bonus, the toilets are usually spotless.

Their success has spawned a great deal of imitators. Among the best are Dicos, which sells burgers and chips, together with a limited range of Chinese dishes, and Mr Lee, which sells Chinese fast food such as noodles in bright and clean surroundings.

The 'flavour enhancer', mono-sodium glutamate (MSG), is used with great abandon by many Chinese chefs. In the West it has been blamed for a range of ailments, such as headaches and nausea – the so-called 'Chinese restaurant syndrome' – and some countries require it to be stated on food labels. Probably the only way to avoid it in China is to cook at home.

NIGHTLIFE

Dance Halls & Discotheques

Most cities have dance halls and clubs where people dress up to see and be seen. Clubs are located within upmarket hotels or in private premises, and play every kind of music, from techno to rock and roll. Most open around 8pm but don't get going until after 10pm and stay open until the early hours. Some clubs are sophisticated, but most are simply places where boy meets girl in a deafening and crowded atmosphere. There's usually an entrance fee of between 20-150 RMB, depending on the cachet of the place, which may include a free drink. On certain nights, girls may be allowed in free. Don't be surprised if you're pestered by 'working girls', and be aware that drugs are usually on offer. As a result, these places are routinely checked by plain-clothes police.

Dancing isn't just the preserve of the young and trendy. In the early mornings, any open space – under flyovers, in car parks, on wide footpaths or town squares – is filled with dozens of people dancing. The dancers are usually middle-aged or older, and the music is strictly slow tempo: waltzes, foxtrots and quicksteps, plus maybe a little Country & Western, to the accompaniment of a tape or CD player which one of the dancers brings along. It's spontaneous but also very decorous and anyone can join in. Some of the dancers know the tunes well and quietly sing as they dance. The dancing carries on until around 8am when the dancers drift away to their homes and offices. This phenomenon takes place throughout China, and far more people dance in this way than ever visit a nightclub.

Karaoke

Invented in Japan, karaoke is ubiquitous in China. There are buildings dedicated to this interactive singing game, consisting of several floors of separate, relatively sound-proofed rooms. If the thought of going to a room with a few friends and taking turns to sing to each other appals you, these aren't the places for you, but many people really enjoy the experience, particularly after a drink or two.

You're offered a 'menu' of songs, mainly Chinese but also some Western hits too, with the words displayed on a large television screen. In a restaurant's private room this may well be free, but in a karaoke parlour you pay by the hour. They open from about 10am and it's cheaper to visit during the day than in the evening, but you should expect to pay at least 25 RMB an hour.

> **Some karaoke bars offer more than the chance to make a fool of yourself with a microphone. If you notice a number of young girls hanging around, take care. They are known as** *san pei xiaojie* **or 'three accompaniment girls' which means that, for a fee, they'll accompany you in your singing, dancing or drinking. However, you may be offered rather more than just company, and your evening could end up costing you several thousand RMB.**

FAMILY CELEBRATIONS

The Chinese put family above anything else, and some of the most important events in China are family celebrations.

Birth

In China, some people are literally 'born lucky'. It's considered particularly auspicious to be born on a day containing a series of lucky numbers, e.g. 8th August 2008 – it's no coincidence that the Beijing Olympics began at 8.08am on that day – and certain years in the Chinese zodiac are also lucky, particularly the Year of the Tiger which most recently began on 14th February 2010 and continued until 2nd February 2011. A baby born on 10/10/10 would be considered very fortunate indeed!

A birth is often celebrated when the baby is 100 days old, when his parents and grandparents treat guests to a banquet at a restaurant. Guests often bring red envelopes containing money, known as *hong bao*, as a gift.

Birthdays

Children's birthday parties often take place in a KFC or McDonald's, although teenagers and adults are treated to a family banquet in an expensive restaurant. Guests may burst into a rendition of *Happy Birthday to You* (in Chinese), and enormous cakes made of sponge with masses of cream are divided up and slices passed around. However, no one sends birthday cards and only close family members give gifts.

> If you want to wish someone 'Happy Birthday', say '*Sheng ri kuai le*'.

Weddings

Chinese people don't get engaged. There's no stage between being single and getting married; no engagement rings and, for that matter, no wedding rings either. But getting married is still a big deal. The date, and even the time of the wedding are carefully considered so as to provide a favourable start to the marriage, and on particularly 'lucky' days there may be group weddings with many couples marrying at the same time. Unlike in the West, it's usually the bridegroom's family who arranges and pays for the wedding – perhaps a throwback to the days when marriages were arranged and they would have to pay a 'bride price' to secure their new daughter-in-law.

Many couples visit a wedding photographer in advance of their wedding to pose for their wedding photographs. Some are ferried around the local area in a minibus full of other couples, all in wedding outfits, to various local beauty spots and pose for pictures at each stop. The photographs are collected together in softly bound books which form the first family treasure. This is now an almost obligatory part of getting married.

Ceremony

If the couple are Christians, the wedding ceremony is conducted by a priest in a church or cathedral, much as it is in the West, complete with white dress, top hats and a long white limousine. There's a church just off Beijing's Tian'anmen Square where several such weddings take place each week. However, most couples marry in a register office. They supply a photograph of the pair of them – like a two-headed passport photo – the registrar's fee and a certificate from a nominated hospital stating that both are in good health. No witnesses are necessary. The registrar verifies the documents are in order, completes the wedding certificate (a nice padded red booklet) with the couples' details and photograph, after which the fee is paid and the couple are man and wife.

Invitations

Wedding invitations are always red and feature the Chinese characters for happiness (*xi*) in duplicate. This depiction of 'double happiness' is a central theme in Chinese weddings and is used in the hope that the couple will live 'happy ever after'. Foreigners are quite often invited to Chinese weddings, although the invitation will be to the banquet rather than the ceremony itself.

Gifts

Guests are expected to bring a gift for the happy couple. A *hong bao* or red envelope containing money is the most common gift, although a specific gift for

Hóng Bāo

their new home is perfectly acceptable. If you're giving money, you should include a 'lucky' amount, i.e. one which includes the numbers eight and nine, rather than the unlucky number four, and be aware that the amount may be announced to everyone at the wedding banquet.

Parents lavish as many gifts on the couple as they can afford, especially for the marriage of an only child (which is most children). Gifts often include a new bed and bedding in the hope that they'll becomes grandparents before too long. A rich family may even provide the couple with a new home.

Dress

It's traditional for the bride to wear Chinese dress for the wedding banquet. This is a red dress, often richly embroidered and sometimes with an ornate headpiece – the colour signifies happiness. The groom usually wears a light-coloured suit, and the guests all wear their smartest clothes.

Key Player

Apart from the bride and groom, a number of people have important roles at a wedding. There is usually a maid of honour to accompany the bride, while the groom has a best man. The best man, along with the bride and groom's fathers, makes a speech at the banquet. One of the most important key players is the Master of Ceremonies or MC, who orchestrates the entire event and ensures that speeches and toasts are made at the right times. Foreign guests often leave a Chinese wedding with their ears ringing from the MC's loud and continuous announcements.

> When greeting the happy couple, it's nice to say '*Xin hun yu kuai*' which translates as 'Congratulations, may you have a long and happy marriage'.

Procedure

The actual wedding is likely to be on a weekday, unless it's a church wedding, but the wedding party or banquet is usually held on the following weekend. It takes place at a local restaurant, and wealthy families take over an entire restaurant to entertain relatives and guests. This can be a huge and costly affair. In the cities, a table for ten (and there may be lots of tables) will probably cost about 2,000 RMB, which would pay for ten tables at a rural venue.

The guests line up to hand over their gifts or *hong bao* before the couple arrive together to the sound of firecrackers, and everyone tucks into a lengthy meal containing up to 12 courses. There are Western elements to the reception, such as dancing and possibly the cutting of a cake, but it may also include Chinese traditions such as a formal tea ceremony in which bride and groom serve tea to family and close friends.

FUNERALS

In the cities, funerals are simple family affairs and foreigners are unlikely to be invited. There are no church graveyards and, by law, all bodies must be cremated. The ashes are put into an urn which is stored at the crematorium for as long as the family continues to pay for shelf space. If payments cease, the crematorium disposes of the ashes. You may also ask to have your ashes scattered in a favourite place; former leader Deng Xiaoping had his strewn over the sea.

In the countryside, many farmers and their families prefer to be buried on their land and, irrespective of the fact that this is illegal – technically speaking, the state owns the land – many are still 'laid to rest' in their fields. Most of the village attends the funeral, and you may see a procession of the deceased's family and friends, all dressed in white, following the coffin to its last resting place. When the coffin is lowered into the grave, firecrackers are let off and imitation banknotes are burned to accompany the deceased on his travels. Cardboard replicas of essential items such as a house and car, and even kettles and DVDs players, are also burned to provide comforts in the afterlife.

Foreigners who die in China can expect to be cremated. If you wish to be buried, this is possible provided your family are wealthy (and well connected) enough to pay for it, or your body may need to be repatriated to your home country for burial.

Dress

The Chinese colour for death is white, so people wear white at funerals – if not white clothes then at least a white armband – and carry white flowers.

CLUBS

For such an egalitarian society, China has many private clubs, some of which are exclusive with high membership charges. They usually provide their members with a restaurant, swimming pool, perhaps a sauna and hot baths, a fitness room, table tennis and quiet rooms for conducting business. Many also have pleasant gardens and even a lake or a pond for fishing. Most are Chinese-owned and run. Foreigners can join, provided they can afford it, but would find themselves very much in the minority.

In major cities, you may find a number of expatriate clubs, such as the American Club and the Alliance Français. The Rotary Club has branches in China, and there are groups of Hash House Harriers in several cities. Clubs are frequently run in collaboration with a national Chamber of Commerce, and also act as forums for meetings and are clubs in themselves – you can obtain details from your home country's embassy in China. Local expatriate clubs also exist in areas with a large foreign population. Joining a club can be a lifeline for a new arrival, and a good way to meet new people.

POPULAR CULTURE

As the Chinese grow more prosperous, so there are more opportunities for leisure activities, and while the Western influence is strong (for example, in the number of fitness clubs which have sprung up across the country), many popular pastimes remain essentially Chinese. The Chinese like to enjoy themselves in public, as a group, rather than sitting indoors in front of a computer, and many activities take place in public places, such as communal dancing or the practice of martial arts such as *Taiji Quan* (also known in the West as *Tai chi*). Many pursuits are artistic or traditional, although the Chinese also do some quite oddball things to amuse themselves. For some reason, they particularly enjoy touring the furnished show houses in new developments, although this is more entertaining than it sounds.

Pastimes & Pursuits

Some of the most popular Chinese pastimes and pursuits are described below:

Calligraphy

The art of writing Chinese characters neatly and stylishly is performed at all levels of Chinese society, and books are available with pages divided into squares, into which each character is painstakingly scribed. Office workers practice at their desks during a quiet spell, and in parks you can see people practicing their calligraphy on paved areas, using metre-long brushes and a bucket of water.

Jianzi

A *jianzi* is a small metal disc with coloured feathers attached, similar in appearance to a shuttlecock. Children play *jianzi* by throwing the disc in the air, catching it with the heel of their shoe and kicking it back up again, the winner being the child who can keep the *jianzi* up in the air the longest without it hitting the ground – a bit like 'keepie uppie' with a football. Adults turn it into a serious game, not unlike volleyball played with your feet. There are two players on either side of a net, and the *jianzi* is kicked over the net and caught on the foot of an opponent who kicks it back. This requires a lot of skill.

Kite Flying

Practised by young and old and popular during a windy spring, kite flying is practiced everywhere; in the spring, Tian'anmen Square is transformed into a riot of fluttering colour by the multitude of airborne kites. You can buy a serviceable kite for 10 RMB, but the best cost 60 RMB or more.

Kongzhu

This is the Chinese version of the yo-yo, in which a reel-shaped disc is balanced on a cord and manipulated to perform tricks. The activity, which dates back some 2,000 years, is said to be a great all-round exercise, improving coordination, stamina and flexibility. Middle-aged men are particularly adept at it.

Mah-jong

A fiendishly complicated game played with 152 tiles featuring different Chinese characters. *Mah-jong*, in which the aim is to collect particular groups of tiles, was invented in China – some claim by Confucius – and is popular with all Chinese, especially middle-aged women. A great deal of money is wagered on *mah-jong*.

Martial Arts

A number of martial arts are performed in streets or parks during the early morning or evening. The Chinese like other people to see how accomplished they are in these arts, hence the public practice. *Taiji Quan* (*Tai Chi*) looks as if it's strictly for older people, as its elderly practitioners go through their movements slowly and deliberately... until you try it. This martial art requires extraordinary flexibility, and its skills take years to acquire.

Festivals

Christmas is acknowledged in the cities, but this is mainly for the benefit of the retail trade. Hotels hold expensive

Christmas dinners, and supermarkets play *Rudolph the Red-nosed Reindeer*, but the religious aspects of the holiday are only acknowledged by Chinese Christians. In expat communities there are celebrations of other major festivals, such as Easter and Thanksgiving, but the Chinese have many festivals of their own and these are well worth joining in.

Chinese Zodiac

The Chinese zodiac – or *sheng xiao* – has a 12-year cycle, with each year related to a different animal. People born in a particular year are said to have the attributes of that animal, both good and bad, so someone born in the Year of the Tiger is passionate but obstinate, while someone born in the Year of the Monkey is quick-witted but vain. If this sounds too simple, the months and even the hours are also allotted to one of the 12 animals so that anyone can have a menagerie of characteristics and influences.

Chinese New Year

The Chinese take time off on January 1st, but their year doesn't begin until a month later when the entire country celebrates Chinese New Year (*Chun Jie*) and the subsequent Spring Festival. Like many Chinese festivals, Chinese New Year is linked to the lunar cycle and the date changes each year, but it usually takes place in late January or February: in 2011 it fell on 3rd February. It's a 15-day celebration, and is on a par with Christmas in Christian countries, as the whole country joins in the biggest party of the year.

In the run-up to Chinese New Year, factories and building sites wind down as workers start heading home. It can take a migrant worker from Xinjiang nearly three days by train to reach his home from one of the booming east-coast cities, and most migrant workers are making similar journeys. The result is public transport chaos. As the holiday draws closer, there's a frenzy of cleaning – no one picks up a broom during the Spring Festival for fear of sweeping away good luck – and people buy new outfits. Lucky red signs are put up on front doors. On the eve of Chinese New Year the atmosphere is similar to Christmas Eve; people head out to restaurants and drink too much and then, at midnight, the streets go crazy with firecrackers. The deafening noise is designed to frighten away bad luck.

On the actual day, most shops are shut and the towns and cities become quiet as everyone prepares for a huge lunch with their parents to celebrate the New Year. Auspicious dishes include ravioli-like *jiaozi* dumplings which resemble purses full of money, noodles (for long life) and fish, because the Chinese word for fish (*yu*) sounds

Chinese New Year celebration

like the word for 'surplus'. There's no Chinese equivalent of Father Christmas, but children and young people receive gifts of money from older relatives.

Most of the temples open the following day and organise entertainment for the locals and, slowly, the retail trade comes back to life. Chinese New Year takes place in winter, and in many places it's bitterly cold, but that doesn't stop people taking the opportunity to explore the country. The Great Wall is crowded with tourists, while in Harbin there's a famous exhibition of ice sculptures. As lakes freeze over, people strap on skates and glide over the ice to the sound of stirring martial music relayed over loudspeakers; skates only cost a few RMB to hire, and it can be great fun to join in.

The festivities culminate in the Lantern Festival on the 15th day, during which people take their children out in the late evening, the youngsters clutching tiny home-made, paper lanterns with a candle inside. Seeing their excited faces is a highlight of the holiday.

New Year's Greetings

To wish someone a Happy New Year say '*Xin nian kuai le*'. An alternative salutation is '*Gong xi fa cai*' which means 'Congratulations, you will have a large fortune'. Either will be very much appreciated.

Other Important Festivals

- **Tomb Sweeping Day (*Qing Ming Jie*, 5th April):** The Chinese take this day seriously. People visit their ancestors' graves, to tidy up their tombs and leave offerings of food and flowers, rounding off the occasion with firecrackers. On the evening before, families gather on street corners, lighting little fires of imitation money and paper gifts as offerings to their ancestors.

- **Water Splashing Day (*Po Shui Jie*, mid-April):** In Yunnan province, people throw water on passers-by to wash away the unhappy events of the last year and give a fresh start to the new. It began in Xishuangbanna but has spread to other tourist spots in Yunnan. The rest of China may not be far behind.

- **Dragon Boat Festival (*Duanwu Jie*, mid-June):** This public holiday commemorates the demise of the poet Qu Yuan, who threw himself into a river as a protest against corruption in the Qin dynasty's government. People race dragon boats (long red canoes with a dragon's head on the front) across lakes and rivers and eat *zongzi*, dumplings of glutinous rice wrapped in bamboo leaves.

- **Mid-Autumn Festival (*Zhongqiu Jie*, September/October):** This national holiday takes place on the 15th day of the 8th month of the lunar calendar. It's a family day when people gather to celebrate the success of the harvest by eating moon cakes (*yue bing*), which are small pies with a variety of fillings.

- **Winter Solstice (*Dongzi*, December 21st):** The culinary centrepiece of this midwinter festival – filling and warming *tangyuan* dumplings – means that it's also commonly known as 'Dumpling Night'.

Gambling

Gambling is illegal in China, but this doesn't stop the Chinese being inveterate gamblers, and gambling addiction is increasingly common. It's been estimated that as much as one trillion RMB is staked annually on illegal gambling, from backstreet card games and 'private' mah-jong clubs to the many online gaming opportunities which can be accessed via the internet, and pop up as fast as the authorities can block access to them. Others gamble on the stock exchange – almost everyone is a day (or even hour) trader rather than an investor – while those with money to burn fly to the nearest legal casinos in Macau or to Hong Kong to gamble on horse racing. China has two state-run lotteries, the proceeds of which fund sports facilities and welfare programmes, but its revenue lags far behind the fortune wagered on illegal gambling.

Sport

Sport isn't high on most people's agenda. The Chinese are the complete opposite of, say, the Australians, and few people take part in sport once they're out of their teenage years. Many people, particularly rural folk, regard it as a waste of energy. Among the sports that they do play are badminton, croquet, golf and table tennis. Golf clubs are springing up around China, including the massive Mission Hills complex in Guangdong which has a dozen designer 18-hole courses, but a round of golf will set you back at least 1,200 RMB at an average golf course, and annual membership fees can easily be 100 to 200 times that. Golf is such a prestigious sport that tuition is included in the syllabus of some business schools.

Fitness clubs are a fairly recent introduction. There are gyms in many cities, but the Chinese prefer to exercise outdoors and even the smallest towns have a number of exercise facilities in local parks, featuring a range of equipment that's free to use; those in the park beside Beijing's Temple of Heaven are extensive. These are a great place to work out, as many people use them and a foreigner usually just fits in rather than being stared at. Jogging is catching on among city dwellers – though not in the countryside – and competitive marathons are organised in cities throughout north and central China. The largest is the Beijing Marathon which is run from Tian'anmen Square to the Workers' Stadium in October each year.

> **Many new housing estates incorporate sports facilities for residents, which may include a swimming pool, fitness room and/or outdoor fitness equipment, table tennis and even tennis courts. These are sometimes free to residents, but even if there's a charge it's much cheaper than a private club.**

The Chinese may not be a sporty nation, but the Beijing Olympics in 2008 and China's international success in a range of sports, from athletics to table tennis, have helped to focus people's interest in competitive sports, and many people watch sport, either live or on television. The main spectator sports are as follows:

● **Basketball:** This has captured the imagination of countless Chinese, no doubt boosted by the success of Yao Ming in the National Basketball Association (NBA). Most schools and universities have basketball courts, and more hours of basketball are shown on television's Channel 5 than any other sport.

- **Cycling:** Excerpts from the Tour de France and other international cycling events shown on Chinese TV have spurred an interest in cycling as a sport, rather than simply a way of getting from A to B. In recent years, the Chinese have staged a series of 'Tour'-type races, culminating in the Tour of Qinghai Lake in 2007. If you want to take part, most cities have cycling clubs with weekend runs, and there are expatriate cycling clubs in both Beijing and Shanghai.

- **Football:** Football (soccer) is the one foreign sport that China has really taken to its heart. There are Chinese players in the English Premier League, in Germany's Bundesliga and in several other European countries. The national Chinese Super League (CSL) is the top grouping, with two further leagues below it, and among the most successful clubs are Dalian Shide and Shandong Luneng. Chinese football mirrors the country's economic evolution. A top foreign striker in the CSL can earn US$400,000 a year, while a Chinese footballer can earn at least 1m and as much as 4m RMB.

  Football is shown regularly on television, and matches are well supported by fans, although ask a Chinese child which team he supports and he's more likely to say Real Madrid or Manchester United than Beijing Guo'an. China has had trouble competing on the world stage – the national team has failed to qualify for all recent World Cups with the exception of the 2002 competition, in which it failed to score a single goal – although it's been more successful in Asian tournaments. The beautiful game hasn't been helped in China by a not so beautiful succession of scandals involving rigged matches, bribed referees and gambling scams.

- **Motor Sport:** China has two major race tracks: the older Zhuhai track in Guangdong and the Shanghai International Circuit. Opened in 2004, the Shanghai track was designed to resemble the Chinese character for the 'Shang' in Shanghai, and is the venue for Formula One and Moto GP races and home to the Chinese Grand Prix. In addition to track races, China hosts a number of rallies, such as the Hong Kong-Beijing rally.

If you enjoy sport, the best place to find details of local clubs is in one of the free expatriate magazines. There are clubs dedicated to all manner of sports, from darts to rugby. Magazines also publish the dates of important sporting events, such as a visit by a well-known football team or a motor rally.

Kings of Ping Pong

Table tennis is China's national sport. The Chinese excel at it – they have long dominated the game at international level, and won four gold medals at the Beijing Olympics – and there are tables (sometimes even made in concrete) everywhere: in parks, in schools, in hotels and even in bars. A table in a sports club costs around 10-20 RMB an hour to hire, and you often have to wait for one to become free.

Out & About

China is a country with innumerable cliffs, gorges, mountains, rivers and lakes to tempt adventurous travellers; its wildlife is unique and its temples are fascinating. One of the best ways to see China is on foot: take a walk along Shanghai's Bund at dusk, explore the Fragrant Hills outside Beijing, or stroll around Guangzhou's Shamian Island with its wealth of colonial architecture. With such a treasure chest of attractions, the Chinese love to spend time in their great outdoors.

- **Boat trips:** Whether a cruise on the Yangtze River or a gentle journey up the River Li from Guilin to Yangshuo, boat cruises are a wonderful way of exploring China's stunning scenery and a popular pastime for Chinese tourists. Fares for the same trip on the same boat can vary wildly, depending upon where you buy your ticket; the cheapest tickets are sold by Chinese travel agents, but buy from an in-house travel agent at a five-star hotel and you could pay twice as much.

- **Parks & pleasure gardens:** As well as tree-lined paths, small lakes, flower beds, grassy slopes and massive show-pieces of rock, many parks also feature fairground attractions, such as bumper cars or a bungee jump. Many make a small entrance charge of around 1 RMB or less, but it's well worth it to experience a slice of real Chinese life: grandmothers herding their little charges, musicians and singers practicing their skills, orators spouting forth, couples dancing cheek to cheek, and groups of elderly people demonstrating their skills at martial arts. There are also amusement parks offering rides of various sorts, ranging from a gentle ride in a cart drawn by a dog or goat to a spin on a Ferris wheel. Negotiations have begun to open a Disneyland in Shanghai, but in the meantime there are several good theme parks, including one in Kunming which highlights the lifestyles of ethnic minorities in China.

- **Temples:** There are numerous interesting temples in China. Among the best are in Henan province: the Shaolin Temple where the monks perfected the martial art of *Gongfu* (Kung Fu) and the White Horse Temple outside Luoyang in Henan, which is considered to be the cradle of Chinese Buddhism. Many temples are sited atop sacred mountains,

Temple, Yunnan

and are accessed via designated routes equipped with steps, handrails and even ladders in some places, although the climb can be exhausting and take hours to complete. Visitors experience a real sense of achievement on reaching the summit, which is dampened somewhat by the sight of little old Chinese ladies who've already made the journey to sell their bottled water and biscuits.

● **Zoos:** Most of China's zoos are old and not particularly animal-friendly, but there are some excellent breeding research facilities dedicated to endangered species. The Wolong Nature Reserve in Sichuan is famous for its work with giant pandas, but sadly had to close due to damage sustained in the 2008 earthquake, in which both staff and animals were killed. However, the research centre in nearby Chengdu is excellent, as is the Siberian Tiger Park near Harbin.

THE ARTS

Cinema & Theatre

Chinese cinema has enjoyed international success in recent years with glossy epics such as *Crouching Tiger, Hidden Dragon* and *Hero*. The Chinese are loyal to their film industry, and there's a rule restricting the importation of foreign films to a small percentage of the total market, although most Western blockbusters make it to China, usually at the same time as they're released in the West, along with art films from France and Russia. If you go to watch a Chinese film, be prepared for a good cry; most end with all the principal characters either dead or dying.

There are theatres in all major cities, which are used for concerts, opera and ballet, as well as theatrical and acrobatic productions. *China Daily* lists performances in the major cities. Serious drama is uncommon in theatres – when the Chinese talk about theatre they generally mean Chinese opera (see below) – but musicals such as *Cats* or musical entertainments such as *Riverdance* are popular.

Another form of dramatic performance enjoyed by the Chinese is acrobatics. Many provinces have schools where budding acrobats learn their skills alongside academic subjects, and troupes of highly-skilled acrobats, some as young as six, tour all the major cities. The individual acts, which include complex juggling, trapeze work and even balancing up to 15 people on a single bicycle, are astounding. Some shows are billed as circuses, but the emphasis is on acrobatics, with limited animal acts.

When attending a performance, it's worth knowing the following:

- **Subtitles:** Virtually all films have Chinese dialogue, and even foreign films are dubbed into Chinese. In Beijing and Shanghai, enterprising expatriates run mini-cinemas showing films in English, French, Russian and Japanese. See free expatriate magazines for information.

- **Rules:** Smoking is forbidden, and people whose mobile phones ring are expected to exit rapidly or switch them off.

- **Comfort:** Cinemas vary widely from modern, multi-screen complexes with overstuffed sofas to '50s flea pits with seats that are uncomfortable if you're taller than around 5ft (1.52m).

- **Prices & discounts:** Tickets cost between 10 and 80 RMB, depending on the venue and how close you are to the action. Cinema tickets are up to 25 per cent cheaper at less popular times.

Music & Dance

Opera is sometimes seen as exclusive entertainment in the West, but in China it appeals to the masses. Chinese opera is enormously popular, particularly among middle-aged and older people, who know the stories in detail and can sing along to every word; at weekends, there are often spontaneous amateur performances in local parks. Foreigners tend to refer to Peking opera or Beijing opera, but each region of China has its own version, so there's Shanghai opera, Shaanxi opera and Cantonese opera (etc.), and fans can instantly tell the difference. Channel 11 on Chinese television shows nothing but Chinese opera and related news all day. It's worth going to see a performance at least once.

Even if you cannot understand the words, you'll marvel at some of the acrobatics and the way that one of the characters changes his face in a split second. Some Western opera is performed in the major theatres, and it's intriguing to see Chinese actors wearing period clothing and coloured wigs to sing their parts.

During the Cultural Revolution, Mao Zedong's wife Jiang Qing organised the production of a series of purely Chinese ballets to replace Western ballet, and these are still performed today. They are all heavy with political significance, pitting wicked landlords against heroic workers. The most popular is called *The Women Soldiers of Hainan*, and it makes a grand evening out: the dancing of the girl soldiers carrying little wooden rifles is spectacular, the music majestic and the rapturous clapping from the audience when the landlord gets his come-uppance is spontaneous.

China's musical heritage dates back to the beginning of its civilisation and warrants a book in itself. As well as opera, there are a great many regional and traditional forms of music, played on purely Chinese instruments, both haunting and uplifting, while the stirring military music of more recent times still has a willing audience. The Chinese also excel at Western classical music, and there are many orchestral performances, both Chinese and Western, at theatres or entertainment centres. Overseas orchestras, rock groups and artists visit China, with groups performing in sports stadiums to huge crowds and visiting orchestras given star treatment, with the very best playing in prestige venues such as the Great Hall of the People in Tian'anmen Square. By Chinese standards, prices aren't cheap but to Westerners they're a bargain.

Poetry

Poets have a special place in the hearts of the Chinese people who revere Du Fu and Li Bai, both from the Tang dynasty period, as two of their most accomplished poets. Mao Zedong, too, was regarded as a fine lyricist and, to this day, anyone over 30 can recite many of his poems. Children are taught poetry at school, and birthday greetings are often written in the form of a rhyme.

Museums & Art Galleries

Every city has at least one museum, and the Chinese visit them frequently. Most museums are collections of locally made or discovered artefacts such as bronze, embroidery, furniture, jade, porcelain and pottery, but there are some museums that commemorate historic events such as the Taiping

Forbidden City, Ming dynasty painting

Rebellion and the Nanjing Massacre. In Hunan province, there's one dedicated to the Flying Tigers, American airmen who flew with the Chinese Air Force during the Second World War.

The best-known museum is Beijing's Forbidden City. Also called the Palace Museum – it's the former seat of the Emperors – this huge complex takes a day to tour. Also in Beijing, the Natural History Museum is well worth a visit; Western visitors are amused by the section on birth control, where all the models are foreign. The National Aviation Museum just outside Beijing is situated on an old airfield, with the best exhibits housed in a hangar tunnelled into an adjacent hill, and the access road an ancient runway. Away from the capital, the Shanghai Museum has some magnificent collections,

China has a recorded history going back some 5,000 years, and much of the country

is an outdoors museum. Sadly, in the rush to modernise China, many fine old streets and buildings have been destroyed, but there are lovely places to visit in every province, including towns and villages where developers haven't yet had time to demolish historic buildings. Beijing's *hutongs*, a network of ancient alleyways, are a good example. The Chinese are beginning to restore and promote some of their heritage, and there are 40 UNESCO World Heritage sites in China, including the old town of Lijiang and ancient villages in the southern Anhui province. If your Chinese is up to it, bookshops stock a good range of travel guides.

> China is extraordinarily photogenic, but it's forbidden to photograph anything to do with the military or even anything that might be considered strategic, such as railway stations and bridges. Temples often ban photography inside shrines. Most people have no objection to being photographed, but it's only polite to ask first, by gestures if necessary.

The Great Wall of China is the country's largest 'museum', and the view of it snaking away into the distance, as far as the eye can see, is a wonderful sight. The Great Wall can be visited in a day from Beijing, although the most visited section at Badaling is best avoided. Instead, try Mutianyu where there are fewer crowds or vendors selling tatty souvenirs. You can take the chair lift up to the Wall and walk back down. Visitors can also access the Wall at Juyong Pass, Simatai, Jinshanling and, possibly best of all, the very natural section at Huanghua. Expect to pay about 20 RMB at any of these sites. And be careful: China isn't hot on health and safety, and it's possible to twist an ankle or fall along many sections of the Wall.

From ancient pottery to modern paintings, China has one of the fastest-growing art markets in the world, and many Chinese are avid collectors. It follows that there are many galleries to visit. As well as art and photography exhibits, some feature skills such as woodcut printing and paper cutting. Exhibits are sometimes for sale, but expect the prices to be high. If you fall for a piece of art, negotiate hard. All provincial capitals have exhibition halls where you can view presentations of local produce, bicycles, medical equipment and many other strange but interesting aspects of Chinese life. Entrance is usually free.

When visiting a museum or gallery, note the following:

- **Opening hours:** most museums and galleries are open from 9am to 5pm every day of the week.

- **Entrance fees:** The Palace Museum is one of the most expensive to visit, with tickets costing about 60 RMB, while it can cost as much as 90 RMB to view the Terracotta Army in Xi'an, but many Chinese museums are free. Where admission is charged, discounts are available for children or for the over 60s, and people aged 70 or over often get in free. Carry your passport as proof of your age.

- **Information & photography:** Labelling of exhibits varies, but many museums now provide information in English. Restrictions on taking photographs are rare.

Disabled Facilities

Stairs are a problem in many older venues but all the new sites have lifts, and disabled toilets are increasingly being provided.

Booking

Most cinemas, theatres, entertainment centres and museums have separate ticket offices – often tucked away in a corner and quite a way from the entrance. For most things, you pay and just go in. However, at entertainment centres and theatres, it's sometimes necessary to buy tickets in advance. For local spectaculars, you can often buy tickets at major department stores or at the travel offices in major hotels.

National Centre for the Performing Arts, Beijing

9.
RETAIL THERAPY

The Chinese enjoy shopping, even window shopping, although the Chinese retail experience is very different from pushing your trolley through supermarket aisles. Shopping in China is all about bargaining over prices – haggling is expected almost everywhere, and this brings a new element to most people's shopping expeditions. China is also cheap; finding asparagus at a fraction of the price it sells for in the UK, or a genuine, as opposed to copied, surf culture T-shirt for an eighth of its price in a US store brings a warm feeling to most people. Any disappointment lies in the lack of choice; for many simple, everyday items there's just one brand or version available, which is the same throughout the entire country.

> 'The Chinese do not draw any distinction between food and medicine.'
>
> Lin Yutang (Chinese author).

The Chinese aren't particularly loyal to Chinese brands. They buy them because they're cheaper, and if there are safety concerns – such as the recent scandal over baby milk manufacturers lacing their products with melamine – they're quick to buy imported products instead.

Most foreigners are fascinated by the unique and unusual items for sale in Chinese shops and markets, and this chapter tells you what to look out for. However, be warned, if you find something you like, and it seems to be the only one in the shop, haggle and buy it. If you wait until the following week, the chances are it will be gone and you'll never find another. China is notorious for one-off opportunities like this.

CUSTOMER SERVICE

In most shops service is quite good, although if you're from a customer-focused country like the US you may find it slow or frustrating. The Chinese hate to let a customer leave empty-handed. They also find it difficult to say 'no'. So if a shop doesn't have the precise thing you're looking for, the shopkeeper never says, 'but Wang's round the corner has one'; instead they'll try hard to persuade you to accept something different that they can supply.

Customer service takes many forms. In a meat market there's usually someone with an electric mincing machine who will mince the meat you have just bought, while in a cloth market there are a number of ladies in little booths with sewing machines ready to hem your curtains or make up pillow cases while you wait. Even department stores have someone available to trim and hem a pair of jeans you've just bought to suit your leg length – the work is done immediately and often at no extra cost.

If you buy a large item, such as furniture, the seller will organise the delivery. It's usually prompt and quite often it's free, but don't be surprised if something massive, like a three-piece suite, is delivered on a three-wheeled bicycle. Expect it to be carried up the stairs to your apartment and, if necessary, assembled on the spot. Buy a new ceiling lamp and the man delivering it will also install it. It's all part of the service!

> In food shops and markets, you're no longer offered a carrier bag and must remember to take your own. Mindful of their impact on the planet, the government has clamped down on the excessive use of plastic bags, particularly the thin ones that were regularly handed out in markets. In supermarkets, if you forget to bring your own bag or basket, they'll sell you a plastic bag for about 1 RMB.

OPENING HOURS

There are no official opening hours in China, where shopkeepers open at the times when people want to shop – which is late and often in most of the country! Virtually all retail stores open seven days a week, and while some small shopkeepers take a few days off during major holidays such as Chinese New Year, the large retailers stay open during public holidays so that they can sell to the holiday crowds. In some smaller towns and villages, some shopkeepers close for a few hours at lunchtime for a siesta.

Markets open earliest. Most are open by 7am and carry on trading until 3 or 4pm. Supermarket managers appear to be free to choose their own opening hours, which they adjust to suit local customers, so that there may be three Carrefour supermarkets in the same town all with different opening hours. You can generally find a supermarket open between 8am and 9pm.

Department stores often open later than supermarkets but, again, they adjust their hours to suit the local shopping culture. If there are several department stores in a city, they may all open and close at different times between 9am and 10pm. A 12-hour day, seven days a week, is quite normal.

QUEUING

In general, Chinese people don't queue, although Beijing has introduced 'queuing observance days' each month. In certain locations, such as ticket offices at railway stations, crush barriers are used to control people, at banks it's common to have a machine issuing numbered slips for people wishing to be served by the cashiers, and in supermarkets people are used to queuing at the check-out. Supermarkets have numerous check-outs so queues are brief, but elsewhere it's he who pushes hardest wins. In markets, a loud voice and sharp elbows come in handy.

SALES & DISCOUNTS

Traditional end-of-season sales primarily take place in department stores, although, as most of these stores comprise several floors of 'shops within shops', sales are often confined to one or two individual traders. They flag up their discounts by posting large signs with a figure, e.g. 5 or 7. These rather enigmatic signs don't indicate a 5 or 7 per cent discount, but mean the goods are on sale at 50 or 70 per cent of their original price, so shoppers are getting a 50 or 30 per cent discount; the smaller the number, the greater the discount. Where there are no signs on display, you're expected to bargain in even the most upmarket department store. Ask the sales assistant, 'What is your best price?' or 'What is the discount?' and you'll be amazed at how much you can save.

Supermarkets don't normally discount their goods. Signs saying 'promotion' are intended to draw your attention to a new line rather than indicating a discount. However, as a marketing ploy, supermarkets distribute flyers in local newspapers offering reduced prices on certain products.

You get the best bargains in individual shops, where you can reduce the price of goods by up to 20 per cent with some determined haggling. Ask the seller for his 'best price' or check out the asking price and then offer whatever you think something is worth. The worst that can happen is that they'll refuse your offer. In markets, other than food markets which are competitively priced anyway, discounts can be huge. You may be able to get a famous brand T-shirt down from 85 RMB for just 25 RMB or an antique rug for a quarter of its original asking price – 'antiques' may be overpriced initially to a ridiculous degree. Other than food, don't buy anything in a market without checking prices at a number of outlets, and then press the stallholder for his best price before making an offer.

Note that it isn't polite to haggle just for the fun of it, i.e. with no intention of buying. If you do this, the stallholder may discuss your ancestry loudly – in Chinese – with neighbouring retailers, who may give you an even harder time when you attempt to bargain with them.

TYPES OF SHOP

There are almost no small food shops in China. Greengrocers, butchers, fishmongers and similar shops are mostly gathered together in large

Shopping mall, Beijing

market areas (see below), and this is where most people shop. However, China has embraced the idea of supermarkets, which sell a wide range of everyday goods, except for medicines, although the Western concept of piling your trolley high on a weekly basis is alien to the Chinese, who prefer to visit markets daily to seek out the freshest foodstuffs.

The main types of shops in China include the following:

- **Department stores:** As comprehensive as similar stores elsewhere in the world, many contain branches of international brands such as Dupont, Burberry or Tommy Hilfiger alongside small specialist shops. Well-known department stores include Beijing Hualian and Parkson, although the Chinese equivalent of London's Harrods or New York's Macy's is probably Yan Sha Yo Yi. This department store on Beijing's East Third Ring Road, once a state-owned Friendship Store, is now a shopping Mecca for upwardly-mobile Chinese.

- **Supermarkets:** Chinese-owned stores such as Hualian and Century dominate the market, although foreign retailers such as Carrefour, Wal-Mart and, more recently, Tesco, are edging in. Supermarkets range in size from hypermarkets down to local express stores, and there are some 7-Eleven 'convenience stores', although few open 24 hours a day. Few Chinese people shop late at night and most areas are quiet from 9 or 10pm.

- **Large international franchises:** There are branches of the Swedish home store IKEA, and a great many sports clothing retailers such as Adidas catering to the Chinese taste for casual clothes. However, some international brands have struggled to gain a foothold in the Chinese market, such as British retailer Marks & Spencer, which opened in Shanghai to a wave of indifference – the Chinese thought it was too expensive!

Friendship Stores

These are a throwback to the early '90s, when China had two currencies and foreigners were banned from using RMB and only allowed to use Foreign Exchange Certificates. FECs could be exchanged for goods in Friendship Stores, which were stocked with all the best goods and impossible-to-buy-elsewhere items, and were visited only by foreigners and Party bigwigs. Ordinary people weren't allowed to enter them. Friendship Stores, now privatised, live on today in Beijing, Shanghai, Guangzhou and many other cities, and you can sometimes find goods there that you cannot buy elsewhere, such as English-language books.

- **Local shops:** There are many 'Mom & Pop' corner shops selling everything from rice to razor blades to the local community.

- **Kiosks:** These small street stalls are where people buy their cigarettes, sweets and newspapers. Newsagents' shops are rare in China.

In addition, you'll see a great many pharmacies, many of which are large and stock an astonishing array of medicines and medical aids, such as wheelchairs and blood pressure gauges, together with the herbs and remedies associated with Traditional Chinese medicine. However, they don't sell suntan cream, baby goods or photographic materials, which you must buy from a supermarket. You'll also struggle to buy aerosol deodorant anywhere in China, although roll-on deodorant can sometimes be found. There are a large numbers of shops selling mobile phones, as well as opticians, bakeries and cake shops – and you don't need to go far to find a seller of *baijiu*, the locally-made alcoholic spirit.

Shopping malls are a new phenomenon in China. Smaller shopping centres in cities are popular, but large out-of-town malls, accessible only by car, have yet to take off, not least because there are rarely enough parking spaces.

China is home to the largest shopping mall in the world: the New South China Mall in the southeastern city of Dongguan has over 600,000m² (6.46m ft²) of retail space and even features its own roller coaster. However, despite having room for some 2,350 stores, it's difficult for non-drivers to access and remains almost empty.

MARKETS

From greengrocers and butchers to pet shops and florists, most of China's small shops, particularly those dealing in edible items, can be found in one of China's huge and sprawling markets. Until recently, markets were the equivalent of supermarkets in China – large, purpose-built halls containing every imaginable foodstuff and more – and they're situated where most people prefer to shop.

Busiest are the vegetable markets, where the vegetables are fresher than in supermarkets and there's greater variety. You have to put up with people riding their bicycles and scooters between the stalls, but the choice, quality and the ability to compare prices between different vendors makes it worthwhile. White or brown eggs are usually

Bicycle fruit 'shop'

sold at the vegetable markets (the Chinese prefer white-shelled eggs), and you buy by weight, not size. Also on offer are duck and quail eggs (delicious hard boiled in a salad). There are stalls selling dried fruits and others selling spices and freshly-made noodles. Frequently, there's also a section of the market selling fruit, although there are also a few fruit shops elsewhere. Again, the ability to compare prices and quality is a huge advantage.

Nearby, and sometimes within the same building as the vegetable market, is the meat market. The butchers are mainly women, and mince is frequently prepared by hand on a chopping board. There may be no plastic film over the meat, but there's little wrong with the quality. Pork is the most popular meat, but there's often a separate Muslim meat market where beef and mutton predominate, along with unleavened bread, and not a scrap of pork in sight.

Other interesting markets include:

● **Bird & pet markets:** The Chinese love caged birds and these fascinating markets have an astonishing variety of birds for sale. Most are destined to become pampered pets and high prices are demanded for good singers or talkers. Adjoining the bird market is usually a section for other pets, such as dogs, cats and rabbits, plus other animals including turtles, lizards and crickets. The latter are prized for their 'singing', and a cricket with a good voice can cost up to 200 RMB! There may also be a section for ornamental fish, selling everything from postage stamp-sized turtles in plastic bowls to beautiful tropical fish in well-made aquaria.

● **Flower markets:** Vast markets, often several hectares in size, selling both cut flowers and plants and trees. These markets often occupy huge greenhouses, which can get unpleasantly hot in the summer but have piped heating in the winter.

● **Clothing & textile markets:** The place to go for the cheapest clothes, including copies of famous brands, although some clothing markets target wealthier clientele, such as the Russian Market in Beijing which sells leather and fur coats, including minks and sables. Textile markets sell cloth for home dressmaking, curtains and bed linen.

> One of China's most unique and colourful markets is the Pearl Market in Beijing (Hong Qiao), where pearls and other precious stones are sold at a fraction of the prices charged in Western jewellers. If you tire of looking at diamonds and pearls, there are several more floors selling a cornucopia of attractive and tempting goods.

● **Night markets:** Popular in most cities and towns, night markets sell a wide range of goods but are often visited for the entertainment and food stalls, rather than to do the daily food shop.

You will find antiques markets in China (see page 216) but no flea markets, because the Chinese aren't happy about wearing secondhand clothes or using other people's cast offs.

FOOD

In China, food and medicine go hand in hand. The Chinese believe that you are what you eat and, whereas in the West people accept that fish can be good for the brain, in China they believe that every single thing that you eat or drink has an effect, one way or the other, on your health. As a result, they eat some rather strange things for the benefits they may bring.

It's a fallacy that the Chinese live on rice. Rice is a staple part of southern China's diet and is eaten both boiled and fried, but the people of the north eat more noodles as wheat grows better in the northern climate. Noodles come in a wide variety of shapes and sizes and can also

Crocodile steak anyone?

be made from rice flour. They are served fried or boiled, although boiled noodles are invariably plunged into a bowl of tasty soup, rather than served semi dry on a plate like pasta.

Potatoes are eaten throughout China, often in stews with meat or shaved into thin slivers and stir fried. Other than in fast-food establishments, the Chinese never eat chips and mashed potatoes are unknown.

Bread

There are three kinds of Chinese bread:
- *mantou* – steamed bread which many Westerners find rather heavy going, although sliced it makes fine fried bread;

- *shao bing* – small circular breads, about 12cm (5in) inches across and 1cm (1/2in) thick, which are cooked in a rudimentary oven in the street. Hollow inside, they're filled with hot vegetables and are quite pleasant if toasted;

- *guo kui* – made by Muslim bakers, these circular flatbreads, up to 25cm (10in) in diameter, are often topped with sesame seeds. They are quite hard but tasty. You normally break them with your hand, and the Muslims dunk them in mutton soup.

Traditional crusty bread is difficult to find. Chinese bakers produce a soft 'crusted' white bread, but it tastes sweet, as do so-called French loaves. You can buy decent Danish pastries, *pain au chocolat* and croissants, together with some reasonable bread, in the better supermarkets such as Carrefour, in branches of Delifrance and in coffee shops within Sofitel and Holiday Inn hotels. However, many expats resort to buying bread-making machines, which cost about 600 RMB. Packaged bread mix isn't available, but you can buy dried yeast and strong flour everywhere – ask for the flour that's used for making dumplings.

Meat

The Chinese eat a wide range of meat and poultry, although pork (*zhu rou*) is the most popular. Beef (*niu rou*) is good and can be inexpensive if you go for local cuts; fillet steak imported from Australia costs around 250 RMB a kilo in a supermarket, whereas Chinese beef fillet bought in the meat market costs just 35 RMB per kilo. Muslims eat a lot of lamb (*xiao yang rou*), while mutton is a standby during winter months when it's made into hearty soups and stews. Chicken (*ji rou*) is believed to be particularly nourishing, especially the black-fleshed variety sought after by health-conscious shoppers, and duck is almost the national dish of China, made famous worldwide in the form of Beijing roast duck.

The Chinese also eat rabbit and pigeon, as well as some meats which may be less palatable for Western tastes. Donkey meat is considered a low-priced luxury, while horse is eaten by people in Inner Mongolia. Dog is still bred for the dinner table in some places, and cat (not the domesticated moggie but special civet cats) was popular in Guangdong, but is now off the menu after being blamed for spreading the SARs epidemic. In fact, meat from many wild creatures has been banned because of SARs, including snake, a once-popular delicacy in Hunan and Sichuan.

> **Many cuts of meat and poultry are sold in small pieces so that once cooked they can be picked up easily or pulled apart with chopsticks.**

Fish

Fish (*yu*) tends to be more expensive than meat. Much fish is now farmed, and inland the choice may be limited to freshwater varieties which are full of fine bones. Unfortunately, filleting of fish isn't customary, although in places like Ningbo or Xiamen on the coast, you can find filleted sea fish. Note that fish heads are often sold separately and, because they're believed to be particularly good for you, are priced higher than the rest of the fish.

Shellfish is popular, although oysters are rare. Prawns and shrimp are available everywhere, again usually farmed, and in late autumn and winter

crab is popular, with farmed soft-shelled river crabs especially tasty. Lobster has a curious reputation in China. It's mainly imported from Australia and is expensive at around 600 RMB a kilo. The Chinese don't find it particularly tasty, so people who order it are considered to be rich but rather stupid.

Other sought-after delicacies, such as shark's fin (called shark wing by the Chinese) soup, sea cucumber (*bêche de mer*), abalone and fishes' lips, are normally served only in more upmarket restaurants. The Chinese love them, but Westerners rarely concur. Another 'treat' is frog, usually minced and served in many restaurants, although the huge bullfrogs gazing balefully at you from fish tanks in supermarkets are enough to put you off the idea for life. It doesn't taste particularly nasty, just bland. Small, tortoise-sized turtles are looked upon as a health food, although they look anything but when lying on your plate.

Bok choy

Vegetables

These form a major part of almost every Chinese meal, including breakfast, and are used to balance the taste and texture of meat or fish dishes, or as dishes in their own right. Probably the most popular dish in China today is brown Chinese mushrooms and spring greens (*qing cai mogu*). There is a wide range of vegetables on offer in markets, from local greens – you might call them weeds – to root vegetables, including many types of mushrooms and fungi, bamboo shoots, lettuce, broccoli, cabbage (i.e. *bok choy/pak choi*), asparagus, aubergine (eggplant) and numerous others. One rather unexpected vegetable is the so-called glass noodle, which is made from the starch extracted from peas; another is lemon basil which is delicious boiled. In addition, a surprising variety of flowers are eaten, including yellow chrysanthemums, a yellow lily and the petals from certain flowering trees.

The vegetable that you'll come across most frequently, however, is the humble soya bean. Soya beans can be eaten by themselves boiled, fried or mixed with rice, but are also cooked in many other ways. They are used to thicken sauces or soups, allowed to sprout into succulent bean shoots, turned into soy sauce or *dou ya* (a soya milk drink), or the curd may be boiled to make tofu (*doufu*). Fresh tofu is almost tasteless and very soft, but can be pressed to extract some of the water to make it firmer or deep fried to a golden brown. Tofu is regularly used as a substitute for meat, and some vegetarian restaurants use it to make remarkably good imitation sausages and meat loaf. Even the skin that forms when tofu is being made isn't wasted, but skimmed off, dried and used as a kind of thin pastry, a bit like filo pastry.

Vegetarian Food

In many ways, China is a vegetarian's paradise. For thousands of years, many people have lived on a diet of vegetables and fruit, either for religious reasons or from sheer poverty. The Chinese are very good at preparing vegetables – their way with aubergines is world class – and the menu in any restaurant includes a wide variety of vegetable dishes, including many made from tofu (see above). However, if you're a strict vegetarian, you need to check dishes carefully. To the Chinese, not eating meat smacks of paucity, and so they sneak it into some vegetable dishes in the form of stock or as little slivers. Telling restaurant staff that you're vegetarian can result in chicken or fish dishes appearing on the table, as many people don't count them as real 'meat'; tell them you're Buddhist (say '*Wo xin fuo*') and they'll understand. There are specialist vegetarian restaurants in the major cities.

Fruit

China has a huge variety of fruit, including excellent apples – look for the letters 'SOD' on the label, which means that no chemicals have been sprayed onto the fruit – as well as many exotic specialities such as lychees, dragon fruit and persimmons, which are cheap and delicious in season and even nicer dried. Some Chinese like durian, an extremely pungent fruit which aficionados find fragrant, although Westerners have described it as smelling like dog poo! Fruit is sometimes brought to the table at the end of a restaurant meal as a palate cleanser and to signal the end of the meal.

Dairy Foods

Milk (*niu nai*), butter (*huang you*), margarine (*jinzhi huang you*) and other spreads are available from some supermarkets, together with a huge variety of yoghurt, but the Chinese view dairy products as strictly for children

and milk is often sold in small cartons for toddlers. Many Asian people are lactose intolerant and not able to eat dairy products.

Cheese (*nai lou*) is a sore point with many expatriates; the only cheese readily available is bland, over-processed slices for sandwiches. Some supermarkets stock cans of Danish-made Camembert and Brie, but really tasty cheese is virtually impossible to find and incredibly expensive by Chinese standards; e.g., strong Australian Cheddar at about 50 RMB for 200g, or a similar sized bag of shredded Mozzarella for 40 RMB.

> #### Organic Food
>
> Organic food has yet to take off in China, and you should always wash fruit and vegetables thoroughly to get rid of any residue of pesticides. Though the quality of food in markets is excellent, farmers sometimes add water to meat and vegetables to make them weigh more.

Imported Foods

Just as strong Cheddar is difficult to obtain, so many foreign brands are elusive and expensive. Marmite is impossible to find, although you may be able to track down its Australian cousin Vegemite. Some supermarkets, such as Carrefour, have a strictly limited variety, but otherwise you must seek out a specialist shop where you can find breakfast cereals, muesli (mainly from Germany), cheeses and other foreign foodstuffs. Metro, a German supermarket catering mainly to trade buyers, has branches in many cities, and offers a wide range of imported foodstuffs.

CLOTHES

There is little in the way of specifically Chinese fashion. Although there are some traditional garments, such as the *qipao* (*cheongsam*) and *tangzhuang*, few people wear them. The *qipao*, a skin-tight dress, only suits very slim women, while the *tangzhuang*, a high-collared slim-fitting jacket, sometimes made from silk or highly embroidered, is worn mainly by expatriates who often look silly in it. Dignitaries and government officials may wear the classic Chairman Mao stiff-collared suits in a range of dark and inconspicuous colours, but the vast majority of people wear Western-style clothes, and fashion in China follows the West, even if it's a few years behind Paris and London.

That's not to say that there are no nice clothes in China. There are plenty to choose from, particularly casual and sports clothing, T-shirts and jeans, and sports shoes, and prices in markets are satisfyingly cheap. A number of Western stores have branches in China, including H&M, C&A and Zara, and Chinese yuppies have taken a shine to more upmarket labels such as Savile Row tailor Gieves and Hawkes, which has shops throughout the country.

Many clothes worn by younger people are emblazoned with logos, but you can still find a Chinese influence. The wrap-over high collar and cross-over front with cloth buttons typical of the *qipao* is copied into smart tops for ladies and men that look trendy, and there are slinky slacks with detailed embroidery on the bottom of the legs which look good on tall women.

If you want traditional Chinese clothes, there are specialist outlets in many department stores selling them or you can visit the Silk Market in Beijing, but you're unlikely to find anything that will fit a Western frame. Many Westerners find it difficult to buy **any** clothes in China. If you're 6ft (1.83m) or taller and wear shoes larger than a nine, you may be limited to shopping in stores selling sports clothes and trainers. Women will have problems if they're larger than a size 14 or a size six shoe; a size 12 is considered quite large in China, and many Chinese women are even slimmer. The Chinese follow the continental sizing system, but always try before you buy as clothes sizing can be wildly inaccurate.

Most children's clothes are Chinese-designed and reasonably priced, with choices ranging from cheaper market goods to French boutique fashion. As well as the above-mentioned fashion stores, there are several branches of the British Mothercare chain in China.

There are often dry-cleaning shops next door to supermarkets, and prices are much cheaper than in the West.

Shoe Size Comparisons (Men's & Women's)														
China	33	35	37	37	39	41	41	42	43	43	44	45	46	47	48
Europe	35	36	37	37	38	39	40	41	42	42	43	44	45	45	46
UK	2	3	3	4	4	5	6	7	7	8	9	9	10	11	12
USA	4	5	5	6	6	7	8	9	9	10	10	11	11	12	13

Some Chinese follow the rather bizarre fashion of wearing pyjamas in the street. This started in Shanghai and is now popular throughout central China; they aren't any old pyjamas, however, but best ones saved for wearing out. Pyjamas are one of the bargain buys in China – to wear at home rather than out and about. There are some nice silk pyjamas that aren't expensive and look and feel gorgeous or, if you live in northern China, smart, quilted pyjamas to keep you warm on bitter winter days.

ANTIQUES & COLLECTIBLES

The Western definition of an antique is an item older than 100 years. This classification is much looser in China and unlike in the West, where good antiques are beautifully polished and well presented, most Chinese 'antique' shops display their wares covered in dust or earth to reinforce their 'antiquity'.

One of the major problems with Chinese antiques is forgery. Ever since the first porcelain was produced many centuries ago, people have been producing copies of the original artefacts. Almost every antique that you see is a copy rather than an original, even one with a government seal confirming its authenticity, but is a copy of something made 300 years ago that itself dates back 150 years an antique or not? The answer is yes, even though it isn't exactly what it claims to be.

Genuine antiques fetch huge prices in China, as local citizens try to invest in anything that they expect to grow in value. There are regular television programmes about antiques, and the prices are frequently eye-wateringly high. Many Chinese attend overseas auctions, with the aim of acquiring antiques with a recorded provenance at a price far below that which they would fetch in China. Strangely, genuine Chinese antiques are easier to find in Europe than in China, and much cheaper, and if you know what you're looking for you're more likely to find it in a car boot sale or auction in your home country than in a Chinese antiques market.

Note that you aren't permitted to take a genuine antique out of China without first clearing the export with Customs.

> **Never, ever offer the full price asked for an antique or collectible in China. The original price may be as much as ten or even 20 times higher than the item's value. Always check with two or three vendors before making an offer, as the difference in prices can be startling.**

Apart from antiques, China offers a huge variety of items to collect. They may not be particularly old, but coming from a different culture they're fascinating to many Westerners; and because they're a familiar sight to the locals, they can often be acquired cheaply. There are even recently-made articles, literally straight from the factory, that are so unique that you want to possess them. As well as Chinese classics such as silk, jade and porcelain, it's worth seeking out the following:

● **chopsticks:** some are lacquered and highly decorated or made from precious stones such as jade;

● **cloisonné:** a decorative technique which involves applying coloured enamel to metal objects such as vases and bowls;

● **traditional musical instruments:** popular ones include the *pipa*, which is not unlike a ukulele; the *erhu*, a two-stringed instrument played like a fiddle, with a six-sided sound box that is usually made of wood and topped with snakeskin, and the *dizi*, a Chinese flute.

● **kites:** decorative, cheap and light to carry, making them excellent gifts to take home.

Fake goods abound in China, and you should expect to see many copycat brands and logos. Some are obvious fakes, such as 'Naik' shoes, 'Nokla' phones and 'Polystation' games consoles, but others are identical copies and difficult to tell from the real thing. Most Chinese are content to buy fakes, provided they're reasonably well made and do what they claim to. Pirated software and DVDs sell for a few RMB, and are particularly popular with Chinese shoppers who resent paying high prices for goods made by Western manufacturers. Fake designer clothes are perfectly serviceable, although watches often turn out to be duds.

Chinese furniture – often modern copies of traditional styles – is very well made, and an excellent buy if you're planning to export it when you leave China.

MAIL ORDER SHOPPING

There are no substantial mail-order organisations in China at present, but internet shopping is popular with the younger set and plenty of people use eBay. Visit the Chinese version, Eachnet (⌨ www.eachnet.com), for an idea of what Chinese consumers find tempting. Overseas mail order companies are a good way for expatriates to access items from 'home', from food to fashion, and there are a great many websites offering delivery to China, although you can expect to pay hefty postage charges.

Buying online in China should be no more risky than in any other country, provided the website uses a secure server (https://rather than http://) for all financial transactions.

RETURNING GOODS

If you try to return a faulty item in China, you're most unlikely to get your money back. If you're lucky, you may be offered a replacement or possibly an alternative, but not a refund. Branches of Carrefour have desks specifically for returned items, but they only offer replacement goods. If a retailer refuses to replace your goods, most cities and large towns have a government-run office where disgruntled consumers can complain and seek redress.

WEIGHTS & MEASURES

Although China has adopted the metric system – Imperial measurements are neither used nor understood – a number of old-fashioned weights and measures are still in daily use. For example, no one buys meat, fish or vegetables by the kilogram (*gong jin*); they're invariably sold by the *jin,* which used to be a pound and now equates to 500g. Because tea is so light, it's sold by the *liang* which is one tenth of a *jin* or about 50g. In addition, 1,000 kilograms is called a *ton* in pinyin, rather than a tonne.

Distance is measured in kilometres (*gong li*), but many people measure it by the *li* or half kilometre. A metre (*mi*) is said to be made up of three *chi*, which is a wooden ruler about a foot long used in classrooms.

Areas are measured officially in hectares, but most people still refer to areas of land in *mu*, with six *mu* being equal to an acre, and 15 *mu* equal to a hectare. Liquids are measured in regular litres, and temperatures in Centigrade.

For a metric/Imperial conversion table, see table below.

In China, quantities are usually measured in tens rather than dozens, although roses are most commonly sold in 20s. While larger numbers, such as money, are divided into units of 10,000 (called a *wan*) rather than 1,000, thus a million is called 100 wan (*yi bai wan*). This, in particular, can be confusing at times.

Metric/Imperial Conversion

Weight

Imperial	Metric	Metric	Imperial
1 UK pint	0.57 litre	1 litre	1.75 UK pints
1 US pint	0.47 litre	1 litre	2.13 US pints
1 UK gallon	4.54 litre	1 litre	0.22 UK gallon
1 US gallon	3.78 litres	1 litre	0.26 US gallon

Capacity

Imperial	Metric	Metric	Imperial
1 UK pint	0.57 litre	1 litre	1.75 UK pints
1 US pint	0.47 litre	1 litre	2.13 US pints
1 UK gallon	4.54 litres	1 litre	0.22 UK gallon
1 US gallon	3.78 litres	1 litre	0.26 US gallon

Note: An American 'cup' = around 250ml or 0.25 litre.

Dali City, Yunnan

Yading National Reserve, Sichuan

10.
ODDS & ENDS

A country's culture is influenced by many factors and reflected in myriad ways. Among China's main influences are its geography and climate which vary greatly and are considered here, along with other cultural manifestations such as crime, the national flag and anthem, government and international relations, attitudes to pets, tipping and toilets.

> 'Like weather, one's fortune may change by the evening.'
>
> Luu Mengzheng (Prime Minister during the Song dynasty).

CLIMATE

The sheer size of China creates an enormously diverse climate, with much of the country subject to extremes of temperature and affected by virtually every type of global weather. The prevailing winds create the two main seasons – cold dry winters and warm wet summers – but it's impossible to generalise about China's climate, as the different regions each have a climate of their own, as described below:

The North & Northeast

Autumn is a beautiful month of bright, dry days but winter comes with a vengeance in December and lasts until late March. Winter can be intensely cold with bitter north winds and snow at times. The night-time temperature in Beijing can fall as low as -20°C (-4°F), and even during the day the thermometer hovers close to freezing. In Heilongjiang province and Inner Mongolia, it stays below zero every day and can drop as low as -40°C (-40°F).

Spring is brief in Beijing, sometimes just five or six weeks between late March and early May, with warm sunny days tempered by a chilly wind; this is kite-flying season and the sky over Tian'anmen Square is alive with beautiful darting objects. Summer comes quickly and with it the rain. Summer temperatures often reach 31°C (88°F), and the rainfall and heat combine to create unpleasant humidity. Further north, spring arrives later and the heat isn't so intense, but much of the north suffers from dust or sand storms, blown from Mongolia's Gobi Desert during the late spring and summer. At times, visibility in Beijing can be almost zero.

> Beijing is on approximately the same latitude as Athens, Lisbon, Kansas and New York. Its geographical similarities with New York, on the edge of a great landmass and close to the coast, means that the two cities share a similar climate.

Wild horses, Bashang Grasslands, Inner Mongolia

The Northwest

This remote area, bordering Outer Mongolia and Kazakhstan, has a desert-type climate: dry, but subject to huge swings of temperature. Urumqi, capital of the Xinjiang autonomous region, has just 330mm (13in) of rain a year. In contrast, Turpan (*Tulufan*) is the hottest place in China, where temperatures regularly reach 47ºC (117ºF). It sits in an oasis, irrigated by underground water tunnels, and the heat and water provide a fertile climate in which the finest grapes are grown. However, there's nothing to help retain any warmth in the winter, and from mid-October to mid-March, the wind sweeps down from the north and it can be bitterly cold. In Xinjiang, the average maximum temperature in winter is -10ºC (14ºF), and it can plummet to as low as -40ºC (-40ºF) at night.

Central China

On the central plains of China and around the Yangtze and Yellow rivers, summers are long and hot. Three central cities, Chongqing, Nanjing and Wuhan, are called the 'three furnaces' by the Chinese and, while the average maximum temperature is 34ºC (93ºF), many days between April and October are much hotter. Shanghai, at the mouth of the Yangtze and on similar latitude to San Francisco, Lahore or Cairo, is very humid. It has roughly twice the rainfall of Beijing at an average of 1,168mm (46in) a year, with the heaviest downpours between April and September.

Winters are short but can be as cold as in Beijing. Shanghai winters are often grey and unpleasant, and few homes have central heating, which is rarely installed south of the Yellow River. Fog is also common, particularly in the provinces of Henan and Shandong.

The South

Guangzhou, the largest city in the south, lies on the Tropic of Cancer and is on the same latitude as Cuba, Calcutta and Dubai. Its humid subtropical climate is influenced by the Asian monsoon season and it rains all year round. Guangzhou's average annual rainfall is a very soggy 2,286mm (90in), and most visitors associate the city with constant rain, from heavy tropical deluges to prolonged drizzle, although when the rain stops the weather can be lovely. While the thermometer doesn't hit the highs reached in the northwest, 38ºC (100ºF) isn't unusual, and while the brief winters only dip to an average 12ºC (54ºF), after all the heat it can feel surprisingly cold.

Shenzhen, Guangdong's second-largest city, and the neighbouring provinces share a similar climate, although further south the island of Hainan is warmer and drier, its sea breezes making the climate far more pleasant.

The Southwest

While Guizhou and the Guangxi Zhuang autonomous region have a similar climate to Guangdong, further west Yunnan and Sichuan are affected by their proximity to the Himalayan plateau: the weather is drier and temperatures cooler. With mountains along its western borders, Yunnan has one of the most pleasant climates in China; winters are short and cool but dry, with some frosty nights, while summers are long and warm but not as humid as the more eastern provinces. In Kunming, temperatures vary between 8°C (46°F) and 29°C (84°F), and the Chinese call it the 'city of eternal spring'. In Sichuan the temperatures are similar, although Chengdu is frequently overcast and enjoys fewer sunny days than Kunming.

Tibet

The Tibetan autonomous region is almost totally dry from October to mid-May. Virtually all of its annual rainfall (457mm/18in) is between June and September, and there's so little rainfall in winter that snow is rare, despite its high elevation. However, winters are bitterly cold and the north winds drive sand and dust storms across the country. Even in the summer months, nights are chilly – sometimes below freezing – but the days are warm and can be deceptively hot. Although the average maximum temperature is officially quoted at 24°C (75°F), it can rise as

	Temperatures & Rainfall			
City	**Average Temperature**		**Average Rainfall**	
	Maximum	**minimum**	**mm**	**inches**
Beijing	31°C (88°F)	-10°C (14°F)	619	24
Chongqing	35°C (95°F)	5°C (14°F)	1,088	43
Guangzhou	36°C (97°F)	12°C (54°F)	2,286	90
Guilin	32°C (90°F)	8°C (46°F)	1,284	51
Harbin	29°C (84°F)	-25°C (-13F)	983	39
Jilin	31°C (88°F)	-18°C (0°F)	711	28
Kunming	29°C (84°F)	8°C (46°F)	967	38
Lhasa	24°C (75°F)	-10°C (14°F)	457	18
Shanghai	32°C (90°F)	1°C (34°F)	1,168	46
Shenzhen	32°C (90°F)	11°C (52°F)	1,928	76
Urumqi	28°C (82°F)	-22°C (-8°F)	330	13
Wuhan	34°C (93°F)	1°C (34°F)	1,257	49

high as 38ºC (100ºF) on occasion. At 3,490m (11,450ft) above sea level, Lhasa is almost literally on top of the world, and as a result enjoys some of the sunniest weather in the world: some 3,000 hours of sunshine a year.

Natural Hazards

China, partly because of its sheer size and geography, and its position in relation to tectonic plates, has more than its fair share of natural disasters. Floods, droughts, typhoons (cyclones) and earthquakes in mountainous areas, particularly in the west of the county, where tectonic plates meet, all wreak destruction across the country.

China endures fewer earthquakes than some other countries such as Iran and Japan, but because of the density of its population, the resultant toll of deaths and injuries can be huge. The world's deadliest earthquake took place in Shaanxi province in 1556, in which 830,000 people are thought to have died, and there have been many more seismic disasters, most recently the Sichuan earthquake in 2008 which measured 8 on the Richter scale and left some 68,000 people dead and 4.8m homeless. Wherever you live in China, you should try to ensure that your accommodation is built to earthquake-proof standards and have a plan of what to do if an earthquake strikes.

The south coast is often ravaged by cyclones or typhoons (*tai feng*) in late spring and early autumn. In addition to the damage from high winds, these can create storm surges and widespread flooding, and are something to be aware of if you live in a coastal area. Flooding is also a danger near major rivers and dams, and can sometimes be a result of a particularly powerful typhoon such as 1975's Typhoon Nina, which caused over 60 dams to fail or collapse in Henan province. The 1931 China floods are still considered to be the

Earthquake damage, Sichuan

world's worst-ever natural disaster, after cyclones and unprecedented rainfall caused the Yangtze, Yellow and Huai rivers to burst their banks, resulting in a death toll that has been estimated as high as 4m.

The aftermath of these natural disasters has, in the past, led to epidemics which killed as many or more people than the catastrophe itself, with cholera, rabies and Japanese encephalitis among the most dangerous infectious diseases.

> According to a report published in *TIME Magazine*, the two most polluted cities in the world are both in China: Linfen in Shaanxi province, in the heart of the coal-mining belt, and Tianying in Anhui province, the centre of the lead industry.

Drought is also an increasing problem in China, particularly in the western provinces. In 2009/2010, lack of rainfall in Yunnan and Guizhou provinces left crops ruined and 16m people without access to drinking water, and also sparked forest fires.

Climate change is a big issue in China. However, while the rest of the world worries about the long-term effects such as those posed by the shrinking of the Tibetan glaciers, the Chinese are concerned about the current high pollution levels in its cities, a result of industrial production and China's love affair with the car. While the government has pledged to reduce carbon emissions, many cities can be unpleasant during foggy winters or humid summers, particularly if you're prone to asthma.

CRIME

China is a very safe place for an expatriate to live. Crime does exist but there's little violent crime, and most ordinary citizens are far more concerned about the high levels of white-collar crime and widespread corruption involving government officials. However, the wide gulf between rich and poor is substantial and getting wider each year. Migrant workers in the cities are regularly cheated out of their hard-earned wages by their employers, therefore it isn't surprising if some turn to petty theft and, as a foreigner, you're an obvious target.

Always carry your passport and money somewhere secure, preferably in a money pouch underneath your clothes; getting a replacement passport is a lot of hassle. Be careful anywhere crowded, such as railway or bus stations, where some thieves use a blade to open a body bag or a rucksack. Don't ever take a thick wad of notes out of your pocket and flash it around, even though many *nouveau riche* Chinese do this. And don't do anything you wouldn't do in your own country, such as walking alone through a rough area after dark or hiking through the countryside on your own. Never forget that, as a foreigner, you're rich in some people's eyes; for example, the monthly salary of a foreign teacher is more than some rural people can make in a year.

The Chinese are careful with their possessions and always lock their bicycles and cars. Many houses and apartments have outer steel doors and bars on the windows. In Guangzhou they put bars on the windows of every floor, even on 20-storey buildings, as

Chain your bike!

thieves have been known to gain entry by abseiling down from the roof!

When serious crime occurs, the punishment can be draconian. There are 64 offences for which the death penalty can be imposed – execution is either a bullet in the back of the head or a lethal injection. During 2009, the death sentence was carried out on people found guilty of murder that took place during rioting, for kidnapping and selling young children, and for selling melamine to milk producers after contaminated milk led to the death of several children. Drivers have even been sentenced to death after killing people in road accidents while under the influence of alcohol. Foreigners aren't immune from the death sentence; in recent years, a number of foreigners have been executed in China after being found guilty of major drug offences.

China is deadly serious in its fight against drugs, and each year people are executed for smuggling, manufacturing or selling drugs. Yunnan is a drugs hot spot because of its proximity to the Golden Triangle, an area which overlaps Laos, Myanmar, Thailand and Vietnam, and is a centre for the production of opium. If someone offers you drugs in a dance hall, walk away.

Resident expatriates are unlikely to find themselves accused of political crimes, despite some expats fantasising about being spied on in China. However, if you do something blatantly contrary to local customs, such as lecturing your students on what you perceive to be the failings of the Communist Party of China or attempting to convert them to Christianity, your behaviour may be reported to the Public Security Bureau. Both foreign employees and students can be asked to leave the country for talking too vociferously about their views on politics or religion.

FLAG & ANTHEM

Anthem

The National Anthem of the People's Republic of China is the *March of the Volunteers*, written in 1934 by poet and playwright Tian Han and set to music composed by Nie Er. The composition, a stirring march, was first adopted as the anthem in

1949, but was only made official in the Chinese constitution in 2004. During the Cultural Revolution, it was replaced with *The East is Red*, an ode to Chairman Mao and the Communist Party, which was played through loudspeakers every dawn across China. Deng Xiaoping restored the *March of the Volunteers* to national anthem status in 1978. The Chinese are proud of their anthem and know all the words, and at many schools students sing it each morning before classes commence.

National Anthem

(*Yiyongjun Jinxingqu*/March of the Volunteers)

Qilai! Buyuan zuo nuli de renmen!
Ba women de xuerou, zhucheng
women xin de changcheng!
Zhonghua minzu daoliao zui weixian
de shihou.
Mei ge ren bei pozhe fachu zuihou de
housheng.
Qilai! Qilai! Qilai!
Women wanzhongyixin,
Maozhe diren de paohuo, qianjin!
Maozhe diren de paohuo, qianjin!
Qianjin! Qianjin! Jin!

Arise! All who refuse to be slaves!
Let us use our flesh and blood to build another form of Great Wall!
As the Chinese people faces its greatest peril,
Every person is forced to expel his very last cry.
Arise! Arise! Arise!
Our million hearts beating as one,
Brave the enemy's fire, March on!
Brave the enemy's fire, March on!
March on! March on! On!

Flag

The Five Star Red Flag (*Wu Xing Hong Qi*) became the national flag of the People's Republic of China in 1949, and was first used at the ceremony in Tian'anmen Square on 1st October to declare the People's Republic. The main colour is red to represent the blood of the martyrs of the revolution, and is the colour of communism worldwide. On the red background there are five stars in yellow (or gold), a colour said to be symbolic of communism's bright future. The large star represents the Communist Party of China, while the four smaller stars which look towards it signify the four social classes which then made up China: the workers, the peasantry, the urban petty bourgeoisie (or small businessmen) and the national bourgeoisie (or business leaders).

The flag was designed by Zeng Liansong who beat 38 other finalists in a design competition. In Beijing's Tian'anmen Square, the Chinese flag is solemnly hoisted at dawn each day (and lowered each evening) in a ceremony watched by crowds of people. The Chinese flag is accorded a great deal of respect, which is upheld by law, and you never see its image on towels or underwear.

GEOGRAPHY

China is the fourth-largest country in the world, after Russia, Canada and the United States of America. However, if disputed territories including Taiwan and territories to the far west are included, China is slightly larger in landmass than the US (many Chinese believe it's second in size only to Russia).

It's a hugely diverse country, with a topography which descends gradually from the western highlands down to the sea in the east. The north and west are comprised of wide empty plains, inhospitable deserts and high mountain plateaus over 4,000m (13,123ft) above sea level, while the south and east are lower and more fertile although still varied, ranging from desert scrubland to subtropical forests. Physically, it's a land of extremes. It has the world's highest peak, Mount Everest (called *Zhumulangma Shan* by the Chinese), and its third-longest river, the River Yangtze (*Chang Jiang*).

China has land boundaries with 14 countries. Clockwise from the south its neighbours are Vietnam, Laos, Myanmar (Burma), India, Bhutan, Nepal, Pakistan, Afghanistan, Tajikistan, Kyrgyzstan, Kazakhstan, Mongolia, Russia and North Korea. Its coastline faces the Yellow Sea in the north, and the East and South China Seas, all of which are part of the Pacific Ocean.

The most dominant feature of China is its mountains, which cover a third of its landmass. As well as the Himalayas in Tibet, its most impressive ranges include the Kunlun and Tian Shan ranges in the northwest, the Greater Khingan range in the northeast and the Qinling mountains which range from west to east in central China. Smaller but no less impressive are the high karst peaks along the Li River (*Li Jiang*) and the unusual conical mountains of Luoping in Yunnan province. Almost every city is within easy reach of mountains, and the Chinese treat some of them as sacred. The Taoists nominated the Five Sacred Mountains some 2,000 years ago, while Four Sacred Mountains are revered by the Buddhists. They vary in height from over 3,000m (9,843ft) – including Emei Shan in Sichuan and Wutai Shan in Shanxi – to just 300m (984ft): Putao Shan in Zhejiang. All are places of pilgrimage for the Chinese.

Melting snow and ice from glaciers on the mountain ranges, including the Himalayas, feed the principal rivers of China. China has some 50,000 rivers, but the best known are the Yangtze (*Chang Jiang*), the Yellow River (*Huang He*), the Mekong River (*Lancang Jiang*) and the Pearl River (*Zhu Jiang*). Surrounding these rivers are vast flood plains, through which these rivers have changed paths repeatedly over the centuries, which form the agricultural heart of China. The great plains of the Yellow River are where the Han dynasty created its Middle Kingdom, and Chinese civilisation has grown and blossomed along these mighty waterways.

Vital Statistics

Land area: 9,596,961km² (3,705,407mi²)

Coastline: 14,500km (9,010mi)

Land borders: 22,117km (13,743mi)

Highest point: Mount Everest (*Zhumulangma Shan*), 8,850m (29,035ft)

Lowest point: Turpan Basin (*Tulufan Pendi*), 154m (505ft), the second-lowest place in the world after the Dead Sea

Longest river: Yangtze River (*Chang Jiang*), 6,400km (3,920mi)

Largest natural lake: Qinghai Lake (*Qinghai Hu*), 4,489km² (1,733mi²), a saltwater lake on the Tibetan plateau.

GOVERNMENT

China is one of the last few remaining communist states. Despite the rapid progress made since the death of Mao Zedong, it's still effectively run by the Communist Party of China (CPC) which oversees its administrative and legislative decisions, appoints its judiciary and military, controls its media and provides its head of state. This is a very different system from the parliamentary democracies espoused by most Western countries, but it enjoys widespread support: a Pew Research Centre survey in 2008 revealed that 86 per cent of Chinese were satisfied with their government and economy.

The Constitution

China's most recent constitution has been in place since 1982, and reflects Deng Xiaopeng's desire to modernise his country; interestingly, one article in the constitution describes China as a 'socialist state under the people's democratic dictatorship' which intimates that the ordinary people are in charge under the CPC's leadership. The constitution sets out the structure of its government and includes a number of civil rights, such as freedom of religion and freedom of speech.

Political Parties

There's only one political party of any importance: the Communist Party of China. While some minor parties exist, such as the Revolutionary Committee of the Kuomintang – formed by nationalists who chose not to leave for Taiwan in 1948 – they have little or no real authority. The CPC is the largest political party in the world, with some 78m members.

'Leading cadres at all levels should always maintain a spirit of moral character and be aware of the temptations of power, money and beautiful women.'

Hu Jintao (President of China)

Government

Power is divided between three bodies: the Communist Party of China (CPC), the state itself and the

Great Hall of the People, Beijing

People's Liberation Army (PLA), which is China's military. The CPC is controlled by the Politburo Standing Committee which comprises between five and nine members, all male, and is the highest decision-making authority in China. Current members include President Hu Jintao and Premier Wen Jiabao.

The primary organs of state power are the National People's Congress (NPC), the president and the State Council, which consists of the premier, vice premiers and ministers. The president (formerly called the chairman) is China's head of state. Although the position is theoretically that of figurehead rather than leader, the presidency is generally taken up by the CPC's General Secretary, therefore the Chinese president has more power than many other republican heads of state. The premier, sometimes referred to as China's prime minister, heads the State Council. Both leaders can serve for up to ten years.

The CPC has a large say in the make-up of the NPC which decides China's laws. The NPC meets with the Chinese People's Political Consultative Congress (CPPCC) each year at the Great Hall of the People in Tian'anmen Square. In 2010, 2,889 deputies attended and were elected for five years. Some 70 per cent of NPC delegates are members of the CPC, and most (but not all) positions of significant power are held by members of the CPC. The CPC also has control over the State Council and President, both of which are appointed by the NPC.

NPC delegates are elected by the Provincial People's Congress (PPC) who, in turn, are elected by a lower level Congress who themselves are elected by a local People's Congress. The latter is elected by the electorate and anyone over the age of 18 is eligible to vote. In most cases, the number of candidates is limited. In the case of the NPC, this is limited to only 110 candidates for every 100 seats and for the PPC just 120 candidates for each 100 seats. On the lower tiers, an unlimited number of candidates can compete for a maximum of 50 per cent of the seats.

Local Government

Within China, governmental power is decentralised to quite an extent, and much of the administrative power lies with a succession of local government authorities, each of which devolves some of its power down to the next. These are as follows:

● **Provincial government:** the highest rung of local government. There are 34 provincial governments: one for each of the 23 provinces, including the claimed province of Taiwan; the five autonomous regions, Guangxi Zhuang, Inner Mongolia, Ningxia, Tibet and Xinjiang; the four major municipalities, Beijing, Chongqing,

Shanghai and Tianjin, and the two special administrative regions of Hong Kong and Macau.

- **Prefectures:** 333 second-division governments, representing large urban areas.

- **Counties & districts:** 2,862 third-division governments, representing the administrative areas, both urban and rural, which China has been divided into for over 2,000 years.

- **Townships:** these comprise a total of 41,638 smaller areas, the equivalent of municipalities or communes.

- **Village & neighbourhood Committees:** the most local level of administration, these still have a considerable amount of power. For example, a village head often decides what all the farmers in the area will plant each year. There are 704,386 committees in total, each representing up to 20,000 people.

The Judiciary

The court system is based on civil law and modelled on the French and German legal systems. At the top is the Supreme People's Court, and below it several levels of people's courts which decide both civil and criminal cases. There are separate military courts. Cases are decided by a judge and two jurors who work together, hearing the case and deciding the verdict and, if necessary, the penalty. Jurors are either nominated by their employer or may put their own name forward, but are appointed by the National People's Congress and serve for five years, moving between courts as required. There are roughly 27,000 appointed jurors in China at any one time.

INTERNATIONAL RELATIONS

Since China began to open up to the West under Deng Xiaoping, it has progressively strengthened its international role by taking a stronger stance in the United Nations (UN) and providing personnel to help the UN police war-torn areas, and by joining a large number of international organisations, such as the World Trade Organisation, and involving itself in trade and political bodies, both in Asia and worldwide. However, it always tries to keep a relatively low profile and to obtain its objectives by soft power.

In the past, China has been involved in border disputes with a number of countries, including Russia, India and Vietnam, and some have developed into serious armed encounters. In addition there have been minor clashes over the Diaoyu Islands with Japan and with the US over territoriality in the China Seas. Relations with Russia and India are now cordial, but China has a more awkward relationship with Japan, which is a major economic partner but also a potential military threat – Chinese memories are long when it comes to Japanese atrocities during the Second World War. Another thorny issue is the island of Taiwan.

> **Both the People's Republic of China and the Republic of China (Taiwan) claim ownership of the name 'China', and the PRC also claims Taiwan and its neighbouring islands, and this issue remains unresolved.**

The West, while welcoming the changes in China, cannot help but feel nervous at its seemingly unstoppable growth and the ease with which it manufactures goods and exports them throughout the world. Many Western nations are critical of China's human rights record and with the way it transacts with other countries which have a poor human rights record. China counters this by stating that it considers the rights of society as a whole over the rights of the individual, and that the poor state of some Western societies suggests that they could learn a few things from China.

In many ways, China's position in the world is unique and the West can benefit from it. Its position as an ally of North Korea and a trading partner with South Korea meant that China was a great assistance to all parties involved in the Six Party Talks with North Korea on nuclear disarmament, and it may well be needed as a crucial negotiator in future.

PETS

China doesn't enjoy a good reputation for its treatment of animals. It has long seen them primarily as a source of food, and the idea that they may have feelings is pretty alien; the extraction of bile from caged bears to use as medicine is often cited as an example of Chinese cruelty.

Dogs have had a particularly difficult time in China. In 1949, the communists banned the keeping of dogs as an 'extravagance' during a time of food shortages and stray dogs were shot on sight. Even today, some city authorities limit the number and size of dogs which can be kept as pets, and restrict the times they can be walked on the streets. They also impose a high licence fee –

up to 1,000 RMB a year – and require expensive annual vaccinations against rabies (hydrophobia). Fear of rabies, which is a major health problem in China, has led to culls of not just stray dogs but also pets.

> **Chinese people who cannot afford their own dog can visit a dog zoo, where they can rent a dog for an hour and walk it around the grounds.**

Despite this, there are pet markets in almost every town and city, and extraordinarily expensive pedigree dogs are now a fashion accessory for the *nouveau riche*. Ordinary Chinese, who have neither the space nor the money to keep a dog or cat, opt instead for ornamental fish or caged birds, hamsters, tortoises and even crickets. Beijingers keep their crickets in little porcelain pots hung from their owner's neck, and tucked into their shirts to keep the insects warm in winter.

One of the nicest sights in China is a group of elderly men sitting and chatting in a park while their songbirds hang in their cages from a nearby tree and sing. If you later see these same old

Pekingese dog

men swinging their bird cages strongly as they walk, the birds grimly hanging on to their perches, don't worry; they're improving the strength of the bird's legs, its balance and therefore its health!

It's as well to be aware of the cost and restrictions if you wish to own a dog (or cat) in China. It's relatively easy to acquire a pet – many foreigners adopt strays and, in many cases, take them back to their own country. You can import a pet into China, but you should check the local restrictions first, as these vary from one city to another. Note that each person can only import one dog or cat. If you come from a country with quarantine restrictions, such as the UK, and later return there, your pet will have to go into quarantine for six months.

RELIGION

From the earliest recorded days, Chinese people have followed some form of religion or faith. Over 3,000 years ago, many people had animist beliefs, whereby they prayed to natural features such as mountains and rivers. This is similar to the shamanism practiced by Native Americans, and is still practised today in rural areas, particularly in parts of Mongolia and Tibet. Travel through the mountains anywhere in China and you'll see stones heaped in cairns, perhaps with a cloth on top fluttering in the wind, erected by farmers for their gods.

The first active religion to gain hold in China was Taoism (or Daoism), a system of philosophical and religious thoughts and traditions which was founded by a government official called Lao Tse around 600BC. This was followed by Confucianism, based on the words, morals and ethics of

Confucius (*Kong Fuzi*) who was born in 551BC. Like Taoism, Confucianism is considered by many to be a philosophy rather than a religion, and many Chinese follow the tenets of both Taoism and Confucianism within their daily lives, without claiming to be strict followers of either.

Veneration of Ancestors

Confucius introduced the idea of filial piety, and many Chinese stay loyal to their parents long after death. This is marked by a show of respect for deceased relatives. Many families impoverish themselves to provide a 'suitable' resting place for their parents' remains, often marked with a beautifully carved headstone, which together can cost as much as 150,000 RMB. There's a belief that the departed have spiritual powers, hence the term 'ancestor worship'. For most Chinese, though, their actions are based on honour and admiration rather than religious beliefs.

Around the time of Confucius, Siddhartha Gautama – the Buddha – founded Buddhism in India. This found its way to China in AD67, and spread throughout the country between the 3rd and 6th centuries. It found a natural religious partner in Taoism, although more practically-minded Confucians took longer to accept it. Today, these three religions form the principal beliefs of the majority of the Chinese people. There are Taoist, Confucian and Buddhist temples throughout the country, and it's often not easy for foreigners to tell which temple belongs to which religion.

Subsequently, other religions have followed. Christianity was initially brought to China in the 7th century by the Nestorians from Syria, travelling along the Silk Road. There are believed to be about 3m practising Catholics and some 4m Protestants among the total of perhaps 14m people with Christian beliefs.

Mohammed founded Islam in the 7th century, and the religion made its way to China soon after via sea traders arriving in southern China and also by way of the Silk Road. There are Muslim communities in all the major cities and in many towns and villages, and the further west you travel, the more visible they become. In Xinjiang there's a large Uyghur population of Muslims of Turkic descent. In all, the Muslim community in China is believed to total between 2 and 3 per cent of the population.

With so many traders travelling between China and the Middle East, it isn't surprising that Judaism also made its way to China. A Jewish settlement was established in Kaifeng, in Henan province, not far from the end of the Silk Road at Xi'an, around the end of the 10th century, and they practiced their religion there until around 1850. However, they became closely integrated with the local people and, after they lost their synagogue several times to floods from the Yellow River, the settlement effectively ceased to exist.

Following the founding of the People's Republic of China in 1949, all religions were proscribed (i.e. forbidden): temples and churches were closed and monks and priests were imprisoned as enemies of the people. Religion was said to be the opium of the people, holding them back in a feudal manner. For nearly 2,000 years, Taoism, Confucianism and Buddhism had shaped the way people thought, yet the Communist Party of China (CPC) sought to turn Confucianism upside down, with the uneducated masses effectively ruling the more academically gifted. Even as recently as 1974, during the Cultural Revolution, a campaign was launched to wipe out the teachings of Confucius. All such attempts have been doomed to failure. The Chinese, in their hearts, still believe in the philosophy put forward by Confucius.

Anti-religious policies softened in the '70s as the Cultural Revolution faded away. Religious followers are no longer persecuted, other than the followers of Falun Gong (see below). Today, the temples are busy, mosques are being built and there are many fine old stone-built churches where services are held to packed congregations.

Christianity, in particular, is a growing religion. In the '80s, the average congregation consisted of a handful of elderly Chinese ladies, but now more and more young people attend Christian churches, and both baptisms and marriages are regularly solemnised in church. Some Catholic services are carried out in Latin, and attending Mass in China is an enjoyable occasion; people put on their Sunday best and it's a real social event. Although it tolerates people's adherence to the Catholic faith, the CPC still has issues with the leadership of the Roman Catholic Church. The Vatican stands alone as the only country in Europe to recognise Taiwan as a separate country from China, and asserts its right to appoint Catholic bishops in China. Neither is acceptable to the Chinese government, and currently there's a stalemate between the two.

> **It's difficult to source accurate statistics on religion in China, but as a rough guide there are 160m Buddhists, 120m Taoists/ Confucians, 26m Muslims and 14m Christians.**

Falun Gong

A number of new religious movements are growing across China, among them Falun Gong, which is the only religion to be banned by the Chinese government. The ban took place after mass demonstrations outside the CPC's headquarters at Zhongnanhai and in Tian'anmen Square in the '90s, during which Falun Gong followers proclaimed their faith vociferously. The Chinese government interpreted the protests

as an attempt to usurp its powers, and cracked down hard. Falun Gong is a way of life as much as a religion, and puts great emphasis on morality – its central tenets are said to be truthfulness, compassion and forbearance – but those in authority have described it as an 'evil cult'. The followers of Falun Gong now practise their faith privately, and while they're no longer being persecuted to the same degree as before, the police still keep an eye on them and the subject is still highly contentious in China. Foreigners are advised to leave it well alone!

TIME DIFFERENCE

Time is unusual in China in that, although the country extends across five international time zones, the whole of the country works officially to the same time: Beijing time. When it's 9pm in Beijing, it's 1pm in London and 8am in New York. The use of a single time zone means that, in theory at least, people who live in the far west of the country are obliged to get up and start work in the early hours of the morning. They don't, of course, and there's a sort of unofficial Xinjiang local time which is two hours behind Beijing. Should you have reason to travel to Xinjiang and have a meeting scheduled for a particular time, always check whether this is set in Beijing time or local time. There's no such thing as Summer Time. China doesn't change its clocks in spring or autumn, and is

Falun Dafa emblem

always eight hours ahead of Greenwich Mean Time.

TIPPING

Tipping is officially against the law in China. There's no need to tip hairdressers, hotel porters, toilet attendants or waiters, although a few expensive restaurants add a percentage to their bill which could be construed as a 'service charge'. Just occasionally, if a taxi driver has been exceptionally helpful, it may be appropriate to tip him, but normally it's totally unnecessary. If you tell someone to 'keep the change' they may smile and keep it, but only in major cities such as Beijing or Shanghai. Anywhere else, they're likely to hand it back to you in the belief that you've made a mistake.

TOILETS

Other than in the centre of major cities, public lavatories in China are almost unfailingly unpleasant. Most are of the squat type, and they frequently have only low partitions between customers or no partition at all! Much the same applies to toilets in schools and universities, department stores, restaurants and office blocks, and there's **never** any loo roll. Why there are so many squat toilets is a mystery, as all private houses and apartments built in the last 30 years have sit-down lavatories, and all hotels with en-suite arrangements are similarly equipped. However, once you get the hang of squatting, at least you don't have to perch on a dirty seat. If you're caught short in a public place, your best solution is to use the toilet in the lobby of an upmarket hotel or at an American-style, fast-food outlet; most are passable and some are very clean. Nevertheless, wherever you go, **always** carry a small packet of toilet paper with you.

Bird's Nest Stadium, Beijing

lake, Wudang Shan, Hubei

APPENDICES

APPENDIX A: EMBASSIES & CONSULATES

People's Republic of China

L isted below are the contact details for the embassies and high commissions of the main English-speaking countries in China. For a list of other foreign missions in China, see 🖥 www.embassiesinchina.com.

Australia: Embassy, 21 Dongzhimenwai Dajie, Sanlitun, Beijing, 100600 PRC (☎ 010-5140 4111, 🖥 www.china.embassy.gov.au). There are also Australian consulates in Guangzhou and Shanghai.

Canada: Embassy, 19 Dongzhimenwai Dajie, Chao Yang District, Beijing, 100600 PRC (☎ 010-5139 4000, 🖥 www.canadainternational.gc.ca/china-chine). Canadian consulates are located in Chongqing, Guangzhou and Shanghai.

Ireland: Embassy, 3 Ritan Dong Lu, Beijing, 100600 PRC (☎ 010-6532 2691, 🖥 www.embassyofireland.cn). There's also an Irish consulate in Shanghai.

New Zealand: Embassy, 1 Ritan Dongerjie, Chao Yang District, Beijing, 100600 PRC (☎ 010-8532 7000, 🖥 www.nzembassy.com/china). There are NZ consulates in Guangzhou and Shanghai.

South Africa: Embassy, 5 Dongzhimenwai Dajie, Beijing 100600 PRC (☎ 010-8532 0000, 🖥 www.saembassy.org.cn/index.asp). There's also an SA consulate in Shanghai.

United Kingdom: Embassy, 11 Guang Hua Lu, Jian Guo Men Wai, Beijing, 100600 PRC (☎ 010-5192 4000, 🖥 http://ukinchina.fco.gov.uk/en). British consulates are situated in Chongqing, Guangzhou and Shanghai.

USA: Embassy, 55 An Jia Lou Lu, Beijing, 100600 PRC (☎ 010-8531 3000, 🖥 http://beijing.usembassy-china.org.cn). American consulates are located in Chengdu, Guangzhou, Shanghai, Shenyang and Wuhan.

Abroad

L isted below are the contact details for Chinese embassies in the principal English-speaking countries. A full list of Chinese missions abroad can be found on the PRC's Ministry of Foreign Affairs website (🖥 www.fmprc.gov. cn/eng/wjb/zwjg/2490).

Australia: Embassy of the People's Republic of China, 15 Coronation Drive, Yarralumla, ACT 2600, Canberra (☏ 02-6273 4780, 🖥 au.chineseembassy. org/). There are consulates in Melbourne and Sydney.

Canada: Embassy of the People's Republic of China, 515 St Patrick Street, Ottawa, Ontario K1N 5H3 (☏ 0613-789 3434, 🖥 www.chinaembassycanada. org/eng/). Consulates are located in Calgary, Toronto and Vancouver.

Ireland: Embassy of the People's Republic of China, 40 Ailesbury Road, Ballsbridge, Dublin 4 (☏ 01-269 1707, 🖥 ie.china-embassy.org/). Residents of Northern Ireland should contact the Chinese embassy in London (see below).

New Zealand: Embassy of the People's Republic of China, 2-6 Glenmore Street, Kelburn, Wellington (☏ 04-472 1382, 🖥 nz.chineseembassy.org/nz/). There is also a consulate in Auckland.

South Africa: Embassy of the People's Republic of China, 965 Church Street, Arcadia 0083, Pretoria (☏ 012 431 6500, 🖥 www.chinese-embassy.org.za/). There are also consulates in Cape Town and Johannesburg.

United Kingdom: Embassy of the People's Republic of China, 49-51 Portland Place, London W1B 1JL (☏ 020-7299 4049, 🖥 www.chinese-embassy.org. uk/). Consulates are located in Edinburgh and Manchester.

USA: Embassy of the People's Republic of China, 3505 International Place, NW, Washington, DC 20008 (☏ 0202-495 2266, 🖥 www.china-embassy.org/ eng). There are consulates in Chicago, Houston, Los Angeles, New York and San Francisco.

The business hours of embassies vary and they close on their own country's national holidays as well as on Chinese or local public holidays. Always telephone to confirm the business hours before visiting.

APPENDIX B: FURTHER READING

English-language Newspapers & Magazines

The Beijinger (🖳 www.thebeijinger.com). Free monthly magazine.

Beijing This Month (🖳 www.btmbeijing.com). Free monthly lifestyle and culture magazine.

Beijing Today (🖳 www.beijingtoday.com.cn). English weekly edition of the *Beijing Youth Daily*.

Business Beijing (🖳 www.btmbeijing.com). Free monthly business magazine.

City Weekend (🖳 www.cityweekend.com.cn). Free weekly listings and classified advertisements with editions in Beijing, Guangzhou and Shanghai.

Economic Observer (🖳 www.eeo.com.cn/ens). English edition of the weekly Chinese newspaper.

Expat (🖳 www.theexpat.com). Singapore-based monthly magazine available throughout China.

Global Times (🖳 www.globaltimes.cn). English-language version (launched in 2009 to compete with overseas media) of the Chinese CPC newspaper. Also publishes two local English-language sections, *Metro Beijing* and *Metro Shanghai*.

Time Out Beijing & Time Out Shanghai (🖳 www.timeout.com/cn/en/beijing). Monthly what's-on guides from the publishers of the listings bible.

See also Media on page 244.

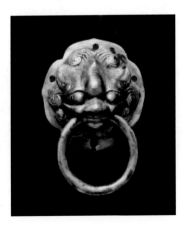

Books

Aselection of books about China and Chinese culture is listed below; the book's title is followed by the name of the author and the publisher's name in brackets. Finding copies of these books in China may be difficult – your best bet is the Foreign Language Bookstore in Wangfujingdajie, Beijing or try a branch of The Bookworm (⌨ www.chinabookworm.com). Books are also available by mail order from websites such as Amazon UK (⌨ www.amazon.co.uk) or Australia's China Books (⌨ www.chinabooks.com.au). There are also a number of English-language bookshops in Hong Kong.

Culture

The Arts of China, Michael Sullivan (University of California)

The Big Book of China: a Guided Tour through 5,000 Years of History, Qicheng Wang (Long River)

The China Book, a People, a Place, a Culture, Li-Yu Hung (Black Dog – available from ⌨ www.chinabooks.com.au)

Chinese Calligraphy, Zhongshi Quyang & Wen C Fong (Yale University)

China: Its History and Culture, William Scott Morton (McGraw Hill)

China's Imperial Past: an Introduction to Chinese History and Culture, Charles O. Hucker (Stanford University)

How to Read Chinese Paintings, Maxwell K. Hearn (Yale University)

Mao's Last Dancer, Li Cunxin (Penguin)

The River at the Centre of the World, Simon Winchester (Penguin)

A Social History of the Chinese Book, Joseph Peter McDermott (Hong Kong University)

Three Thousand Years of Chinese Painting, Professor Richard Barnhart et al (Yale University)

History

A Brief History of Chinese Civilisation, Conrad Schirokaver (Wadsworth)

A Brief History of the Dynasties of China, Bamber Gascoigne (Robinson)

Cambridge Illustrated History of China, Patricia Buckley Ebrey (Cambridge University Press)

China; a Cultural, Social and Political History, Patricia Buckley Ebrey (Wadsworth)

China: A New History, John King Fairbank & Merle Goldman (Belknap)

Chinese Civilisation: A Source Book, Patricia Buckley Ebrey (Free Press)

Getting Rich First, Duncan Hewitt (Chatto & Windus)

Sources of Chinese Tradition, William Theodore De Bary (Columbia University)

Understanding China, John Bryan Starr (Hill & Wang)

Language

1,000 Chinese Words (Berlitz)

BBC Mandarin Chinese Phrase Book & Dictionary, Dr Qian Kan (BBC Active)

Beginner's Chinese, Yong Ho (Hippocrene)

China Phrasebook, Michael Cannings (Lonely Planet)

Chinese-English Visual Bilingual Dictionary (Dorling Kindersley)

Colloquial Chinese, Kan Qian (Routledge)

Chinese Language for Beginners, Lee Cooper (Tuttle)

First Thousand Words in Chinese, Heather Amery (Usborne)

Learn to Write Chinese Characters, Johan Bjorksten (Yale University)

The Times' Essential English-Chinese Dictionary (Federal)

Literature & Biographies

Life and Death in Shanghai, Nien Cheng (Penguin)

Red Sorghum, Mo Yan (Arrow)

Wild Swans, Jung Chang (Harper Perennial)

Living & Working in China

China CEO: a Case Guide for Business Leaders in China, Juan Antonio Fernandez & Lui Shengjun (John Wiley)

China CEO: Voices of Experience, Juan Antonio Fernandez & Laurie Underwood (Wiley)

Chinese Business Etiquette, Scott P. Seligman (Warner)

Doing Business in China: How to Profit in the World's Fastest Growing Market, Ted Plafker (Business Plus)

How to Live and Do Business in China, Ernie Tadla (Trafford)

Mr China, Tim Clissold (HarperBusiness)

One Billion Customers: Lessons from the Front Lines of Doing Business in China, James McGregor (Free Press)

Tourist Guides & Travel Literature

Behind the Wall, Colin Thubron (Vintage)

Berlitz Pocket Guide – China, Ken Bernstein (Berlitz)

China Survival Guide: How to Avoid Travel Trouble and Mortifying Mishaps, Larry Herzberg (Stone Bridge)

China: The 50 Most Memorable Trips, J D Brown (Frommer's)

Eyewitness Travel: China, Peter Neville-Hadley (DK Publishing)

Fodor's Exploring China, Christopher Knowles (Fodor's)

Lonely Planet Beijing City Guide, Damien Harper (Lonely Planet)

Lonely Planet China, Damien Harper (Lonely Planet)

Riding the Iron Rooster: By Train Through China, Paul Theroux (Penguin)

River Town: Two Years on the Yangtze, Peter Hessler (John Murray)

The Rough Guide to China, David Leffman et al (Rough Guides)

Miscellaneous

A Field Guide to the Birds of China, John MacKinnon & Karen Phillipps (OUP)

Atlas of Birds of China, Chian Yan Wen (Henan Science & Technology Publishers)

APPENDIX C: USEFUL WEBSITES

This appendix contains information about some of the most useful websites covering China and the Chinese people. All are in English or have English-language options unless otherwise stated. Note that Chinese websites can be unreliable and links don't always work, therefore you may need to refresh or re-type the address in the address bar.

Accommodation

AsiaXpat (💻 www.asiaxpat.com). Pan-Asian hub with links to Beijing, Guangzhou and Shanghai, including property advertisements and more.

The Beijinger (💻 www.thebeijinger.com). Loads of classified adverts, including accommodation to rent in Beijing.

Century 21 (💻 www.century21cn.com/english). 'Estate agency' franchise with branches throughout China.

City Weekend Magazine (💻 www.cityweekend.com.cn). Accommodation to let in Beijing, Guangzhou and Shanghai.

Craigslist (💻 http://geo.craigslist.org/iso/cn). Classifieds in a number of Chinese cities, including accommodation to rent.

Lezone Real Estate (💻 www.bj-realestate.com). Apartments and serviced apartments to rent in Beijing.

Wuwoo Real Estate Service (💻 www.wuwoo.com). Beijing-based property agency website featuring English-language content and a useful map.

Business

All Roads Lead to China (💻 www.allroadsleadtochina.com). Business analysis, insights and news.

American Chamber of Commerce (💻 www.amchamchina.org). Website of the US Chamber of Commerce in China, including some useful forums.

Australian Business Foundation (💻 www.abfoundation.com.au). Includes guidance to the business start-up procedures in China.

Australian Chamber of Commerce (💻 www.austcham.org). Also represents New Zealand companies.

Australian Trade Commission (Austrade, 🖥 www.austrade.gov.au). A site promoting trade and investment between Australia and other countries.

Business Link (🖥 www.businesslink.gov.uk). UK government website, including a section on international trade with information on doing business in China.

British Chamber of Commerce (🖥 www.britcham.org). With branches in Beijing, Guangzhou and Shanghai, the website includes a job-search function and also represents Irish companies.

Canadian Chamber of Commerce of South China (🖥 www.cancham.org. cn). Based in Guangzhou.

Canadian-China Business Council (CCBC, 🖥 www.ccbc.com). A Canada/ China bilateral trade and investment facilitator.

China Briefing (🖥 www.china-briefing.com). Monthly magazine and daily news service about doing business in China.

China-British Business Council (🖥 www.cbbc.org). The largest membership organisation for all UK companies doing business in China.

European Union Chamber of Commerce (🖥 www.europeanchamber.com. cn/view/home). Representing the countries of the European Union.

Ministry of Commerce (🖥 http://english.mofcom.gov.cn). Information for those wishing to do business in China.

State Administration of Foreign Experts' Affairs (🖥 www.safea.gov.cn). Useful website for those wishing to work or do business in China, including details of job fairs and information on work permits.

Culture

About Chinese Culture (🖥 http://chineseculture.about.com). A cornucopia of culture, ancient and modern, plus news, articles and more.

China Highlights (🖥 www.chinahighlights.com/travelguide/culture). Useful articles on Chinese culture within the website of an established travel agency.

China Today (🖥 www.chinatoday.com). With links to many aspects of life in China, from culture and traditions to investments and statistics.

Expats in China (🖥 www.expatsinchina.com). Cultural and literary forum for expats interested in China.

Travel China Guide (🖥 www.travelchinaguide.com/intro/arts). Section on Chinese arts and crafts, from kites to porcelain. The page on Beijing opera is excellent, and explains the various characters' roles.

Government

China Culture (🖥 www.chinaculture.org). English-language information from China's Ministry of Culture, including current cultural events.

China Internet Information Centre (🖥 www.china.org.cn). Chinese news resource collated from a number of official sources.

China Today (🖥 www.chinatoday.com/gov/a.htm). Includes a list of government websites.

e-Beijing (🖥 www.ebeijing.gov.cn). Official website of the government of Beijing.

Ministry of Foreign Affairs (🖥 www.fmprc.gov.cn/eng/default.htm). China's relations with the rest of the world.

Ministry of Education (🖥 www.moe.edu.cn/publicfiles/business/htmlfiles/ moe/moe_2792/index.html). Statistics and information.

People's Bank of China (🖥 www.pbc.gov.cn/publish/english/963/index. html). China's central bank.

Language

Beijing Normal University (🖥 www.bnulxsh.com/english/index.htm). Offers both full university courses and short courses for language learners.

Beijing University of Language and Culture (🖥 www.blcu-china.org). The only university in China to specialise in teaching the Chinese language and culture.

China Study Abroad (🖥 www.chinastudyabroad.org). Offers a range of courses based in Beijing, Dalian, Hangzhou, Kunming, Nanjing, Qingdao, Shanghai, Tianjing and Xi'an.

Fudan University, Shanghai (🖥 www.fudan.edu.cn). The leading university in Shanghai, offering a range of courses from full degrees to short courses.

New Concept Mandarin Limited (🖥 www.newconceptmandarin.com). Immersion courses in Beijing, Guangzhou, Nanjing, Shanghai, Shenzhen and Suzhou, as well as online courses and DVDs.

Omniglot (🖥 www.omniglot.com/writing/mandarin.htm). An in-depth look at Mandarin Chinese with many useful links.

Peking University (🖥 www.pku.edu.cn). Based in Beijing, one of China's top universities which also offers language courses.

Tsinghua University, Beijing (🖥 www.tsinghua.edu.cn). Four different courses available, with accommodation provided if required.

Zhongwen (🖥 www.zhongwen.com). Rick Harbaugh's guide to Chinese characters and how they evolved over the centuries.

Living & Working

Allo Expat (🖥 www.beijing.alloexpat.com). Comprehensive info for expats in Beijing, including a useful expat forum.

China Expat (🖥 www.chinaexpat.com). City guides and art, business, culture, history and travel in China.

Job China (🖥 www.jobchina.net). Mainly jobs for teachers but also some other vacancies.

Lost Laowai (🖥 www.lostlaowai.com). China expat and travel community.

Meijob.com (🖥 http://english.meijob.com). Search engine with some good contacts in industry and education.

My China Career (🖥 www.mychinacareer.com). Job-search website including relatively high level positions in most industries.

My China Start (🖥 http://expats.mychinastart.com). Useful website for newcomers.

Shanghai Expat (🖥 www.shanghaiexpat.com). Comprehensive information for expats in Shanghai.

State Administration of Foreign Experts' Affairs (🖥 www.safea.gov.cn). Useful website for those wishing to work or do business in China, including details of job fairs and information on work permits.

Media

China Central Television (🖥 http://english.cctv.com). The website of China's national broadcaster.

China Daily (🖥 www.chinadaily.com.cn). The only national English-language daily newspaper in China.

China.org (🖥 www.china.org.cn). Comprehensive official information and news site containing a wealth of information in many languages.

Go Chengdoo (🖥 www.gochengdoo.com/en). Lively e-zine aimed at Western expats, with reviews of local news, sights, restaurants and events in Chengdu.

Go Kunming (🖥 www.gokunming.com/en). A similar service for expat residents of Kunming.

People's Daily (🖥 http://english.peopledaily.com.cn). English-language version of China's most-read newspaper.

Shanghai Daily (🖥 www.shanghaidaily.com). English-language version of one of China's major newspapers.

Shenzhen Daily (🖥 www1.szdaily.com). One of China's leading English-language newspapers.

South China Morning Post (🖥 www.scmp.com). Hong Kong daily newspaper.

Xinhua (🖥 www.xinhuanet.com/english2010). News from China's national news agency.

See also English-language Newspapers & Magazines on page 237.

Miscellaneous

Beijing Municipal Health Bureau (🖥 http://english.bjhb.gov.cn). Health news from the Chinese capital, with links to hospitals.

China-Japan Friendship Hospital (🖥 http://english.zryhyy.com.cn). Provided medical services to the Beijing Olympics in 2008.

China Meteorological Administration (🖥 www.cma.gov.cn/english/forecast_gn.php). Local weather forecast.

China Today (🖥 www.chinatoday.com). Comprehensive general information.

Chinese Yellow Pages (🖥 www.yellowpages-china.com). Details of companies, importers, exporters, manufacturers and vendors.

DEFRA (🖥 www.defra.gov.uk/wildlife-pets/pets/travel/quarantine/index.htm). The UK government's information on quarantine.

Eachnet (🖥 www.eachnet.com). China's version of eBay.

International Centre for Veterinary Services Beijing (🖥 www.icvsasia.com). Information for pet owners in Beijing, including veterinary services.

International SOS (🖥 www.internationalsos.com). International healthcare provider with clinics in Beijing, Nanjing, Shekou and Tianjin.

Passport for Pets (🖥 www.passportsforpets.co.uk). Can advise on and organise pet travel from the UK and Ireland to China; used by UK and Irish governments.

Peking Union Medical College Hospital (🖥 www.pumch.cn). Another hospital which provided care during the 2008 Olympics.

Pet Relocation (🖥 www.petrelocation.com). The resources section includes the latest rules on importing your pet to China.

Weather (🖥 http://weather.china.org.cn/english).

Wikipedia (🖥 http://en.wikipedia.org/wiki/people%27s_republic_of_china). Dedicated portal from the community encyclopaedia.

Teaching English

ChinaJob (💻 www.chinajob.com). Government-backed organisation primarily recruiting teachers of English.

ELS Teacher Café (💻 http://china.eslteachercafe.com). Forum for English-language teachers in China.

Middle Kingdom Life (💻 http://middlekingdomlife.com/guide). Information-packed guide to living and working in China, compiled by an American professor and headmaster based in Guangzhou and Jilin.

Teach English Abroad (💻 www.teachabroadchina.com/travel-in-china-forum). Includes job postings and classified adverts.

Travel & Tourism

Air China (💻 www.airchina.com). One of China's leading airlines, based in Beijing.

Cathay Pacific (💻 www.cathaypacific.com). Hong Kong's leading airline and one of the world's best.

China Airlines (💻 www.china-airlines.com). The flag carrier of Taiwan/Formosa.

China International Travel Service (💻 www.cits.net). State-owned travel organisation established for more than 50 years.

China National Tourist Office (💻 www.cnto.org). The official government tourist website.

China Travel (💻 www.chinatravel.com). Claims to be the world's largest China travel information site.

China Travel Service (💻 www.chinatravelservice.com). The national organisation for travel within China.

Going to China (💻 http://goingtochina.com). Chinese travel and tourism resource.

Just China (💻 www.justchina.org). China travel guide.

Monkey Shrine (💻 www.monkeyshrine.com). Travel company specialising in travel on the Trans-Siberian railway.

Railways of China (💻 www.railwaysofchina.com). An unofficial overview of China's railways.

Travel China Guide (💻 www.travelchinaguide.com/cityguides). Information on China's major cities.

Beijing Opera

APPENDIX D: MAP OF PROVINCES AND OTHER ADMINISTRATIVE AREAS

Provinces

Anhui
Fujian
Gansu
Guangdong
Hainan
Hebei
Heilongjiang
Henan
Hubei
Hunan
Jiangsu
Jiangxi
Jilin
Liaoning
Qinghai
Shaanxi
Shandong
Shanxi
Sichuan
Taiwan (claimed by China as a province)
Yunnan
Zhejiang

Municipalities

Beijing
Chongqing
Shanghai
Tianjin

Special Administrative Regions

Hong Kong
Macau

Autonomous Regions

Guangxi
Inner Mongolia
Ningxia
Tibet
Xinjiang

APPENDIX E: USEFUL WORDS & PHRASES

Below is a list of words and phrases you may need during your first few days in China. They are, of course, no substitute for learning Chinese, which you should make a priority. All words are written in pinyin which is the approved way of transliterating Chinese phonetically using the Latin or Roman alphabet. A guide to pronunciation is provided in Chapter 5.

Pronouns

I	*wo*
you (singular)	*ni*
he/she/it	*ta*
we/us	*women*
you (plural)	*nimen*
they/them	*tamen*

You can change any of the above into a possessive by adding '*de*', e.g. mine (*wo de*), his (*ta de*), theirs (*tamen de*).

Asking for Help

Do you speak English?	*Ni shuo yin yu ma?*
I don't speak Chinese	*Wo bu hui jiang zhong wen*
Please could you speak slowly?	*Qin jiang man dian?*
I don't understand	*Wo ting bu dong*
Do you understand?	*Dong ma?*
I want …	*Wo xiang yao …*
I need …	*Wo xu yao …*

Communications

Telephone & Internet

phone line	*dianhuaxian*
mobile phone	*shou ji*
no answer	*mei ren jie*
engaged/busy	*zhan xian*
internet	*yinte wang*
computer	*diannao*
email	*dian zi you jian*
internet café	*wang ba*

Post

post office	*youdianju*
postcard/letter/parcel	*ming xin pian/xin han/bao guo*
stamps	*you piao*
How much does it cost to send a letter to Europe/USA/Australia?	*Yi feng ji dao ou zhou/mei guo/ audaliyia de xin yao duo shao qian?*

Media

newspaper/magazine	*bao kan/za zhi*
Do you sell English-language newspapers?	*You ying wen bao zhi chu shou ma?*

Courtesy

yes	*shi* (this literally translates as 'is' and implies 'that's it, that's right')
no	*bu* (this means 'not so'; to explain that you don't have something, say *mei you*)
excuse me/sorry	*du bu qi* (used when apologising or trying to pass someone)

I don't know	*wo bu zhi dao*
I don't mind	*wo bu jie yi*
please	*qing*
thank you	*xie xie*
you're welcome	*bu ke qi* or *bu yong xie*

Countries

Australia/Australian	*aodaliya/aodaliya ren*
Canada/Canadian	*jianada/jianada ren*
France/French	*faguo/faguo ren*
Germany/German	*deguo/deguo ren*
Ireland/Irish	*ai'erlan/ai'erlan ren*
Netherlands/Dutch	*helan/helan ren*
New Zealand/New Zealander	*xinxilan/xinxilan ren*
Spain/Spanish	*xibanya/xibanya ren*
UK/British	*yingguo/yingguo ren*
USA/American	*mei guo/mei guo ren*
Which country are you from?	*Ni shi nage guojia de?*
I'm British/American/ Australian	*Wo shi yingguo ren/meiguo ren/audaliyia ren*

Days & Months

Monday	*xing qi yi*
Tuesday	*xing qi er*
Wednesday	*xing qi san*
Thursday	*xing qi si*
Friday	*xing qi wu*
Saturday	*xing qi liu*
Sunday	*xing qi tian* or *xing qi ri*

January	*yi yue*
February	*er yue*
March	*san yue*
April	*si yue*
May	*wu yue*
June	*liu yue*
July	*qi yue*
August	*ba yue*
September	*jiu yue*
October	*shi yue*
November	*shiyi yue*
December	*shi'er yue*

Driving

car insurance	*che xian*
driving licence	*jia shi zheng*
hire/rental car	*zu che*
How far is it to … ?	*You duo yuan … ?*
Can I park here?	*Zhe neng ting che ma?*
unleaded petrol (gas)	*qi you*
Fill up the tank please	*Jia man qi you*
I need … RMB of petrol (gas)	*Jia … renminbi qi you*
air (for tyres)	*jia man qi* or *gei tai jia qi*
water/oil	*shui/you*
car wash	*xi che*
My car has broken down	*Wo de che huai le*
I've run out of petrol (gas)	*Wo de che mei you le*
My tyre is flat	*Wo de che tai bian le*
I need a tow truck	*Wo xu yao yi ge tuo che*
bicycle/electric bicycle	*zixingche/diandong zixingche*

Emergency

Emergency!	*jin ji qing kuang*!
Fire!	*zhao huo le*!
Help!	*jiu ming*!
Police!	*jin cha*!
Stop thief!	*zhua zei*!
Watch out!	*xiao xin*!

Finding your Way

Where is … ?	*… zai nali*?
Where is the toilet?	*Cesuo zai nali*?
Where is the nearest … ?	*Zhui jin de … zai na li*?
How do I get to … ?	*Zen me zou … *?
Can I walk there?	*Wo neng zou dao na li ma*?
How far is … ?	*You duo yuang … *?
I'm lost	*Wo mi lu le*
left/right/straight ahead	*zuo/you/yizhi zou*
opposite/next to/near	*dui mian/pang bian/fu jin*
north/south/east/west	*bei/nan/dong/xi*
airport	*jichang*
bus/plane/taxi/train	*gonggongqiche/feiji/chuzuche/huoche*
minibus	*xiao mian bao che*
bus stop	*gong jiao che ting che dian*
Please turn on the meter	*qing da biao*
train/bus station	*huo che zhan/gong jiao che zhan*
What time does the bus arrive?	*Shen me shi hou da ba dao zhe*
What time does the train leave?	*Shen me shi hou huo che chu fa*
ticket	*piao*
bank/embassy/consulate	*yinhang/da shi guan/ling shi guan*
market/supermarket	*shichang/chao shi*
police station	*jingchaju*
hotel/restaurant	*binguan/fandian*

Note that the words *binguan*, *fandian*, *jiudian* and *dajiudian* can all refer to either a hotel or a restaurant.

Greetings

Hello	*ni hao*
how are you	*ni hao ma*
good morning	*zao shang hao*
good afternoon	*xiawu hao*
good evening	*wan shang hao*
good night	*wan'an*
goodbye	*zaijian*

Health & Medical Emergencies

I feel ill	*Wo gan dao bu shu fu*
I feel dizzy	*Wo gan dao tou yun*
I need a doctor	*Wo xiu yao kan yi sheng*
I need an ambulance	*Wo xiu yao jiu hu che*
doctor/nurse/dentist	*yi sheng/hu shi/yia yi*
surgeon/specialist	*shou shu/zhuan jia*
hospital/health clinic/A&E	(emergency room) *yiyuan/zhen suo/ji_zhen*
chemist's (pharmacy)	*yaodian*
optician's	*yang ke*
prescription	*chu fang*

In a Bar or Restaurant

waiter/waitress!	*nan fu wu sheng/nu fu wu sheng*!
menu	*cai pu*
bill	*mai dan*
well done/medium/rare meat)	*ba cheng shou/wu cheng shou/san* (for cheng shou
vegetarian	*su shi zhe*
meat/fish	*rou/yu*

Numbers

zero	*ling*
one	*yi*
two	*er* (when stating a number, e.g. of an apartment it's *er*; when stating a quantity, e.g. two fish, the word used is *liang*, e.g. 'two fish' is *liang yu*)
three	*san*
four	*si*
five	*wu*
six	*liu*
seven	*qi*
eight	*ba*
nine	*jiu*
ten	*shi*
eleven	*shi yi*
twelve	*shi er*
thirteen	*shi san*
fourteen	*shi si*
fifteen	*shi wu*
sixteen	*shi liu*
seventeen	*shi qi*
eighteen	*shi ba*
nineteen	*shi jiu*
twenty	*er shi*
twenty one	*er shi yi*
thirty	*san shi*
forty	*si shi*
fifty	*wu shi*
sixty	*liu shi*
seventy	*qi shi*
eighty	*ba shi*
ninety	*jiu shi*
100	*yi bai*
200	*er bai*

500	*wu bai*
1,000	*yi qian*
5,000	*wu qian*
10,000	*yi wan*
One million	*yi bai wan*
One billion	*yige yi*

Paying

How much is this?	*Duoshao qian?*
The bill, please.	*Mai dan.*
Do you take credit cards?	*Shi yong xin yong ka ma?*

Socialising

Pleased to meet you	*Hen gao xing jian dao ni*
My name is …	*Wo de ming zi jiao …*
What's your name?	*Ni jiao shenma ming zi?*
Are you married?	*Ni jiehun le ma?*
Have you got children?	*Ni youmeiyou hai zi?*
This is my husband/wife	*Zhe shi wo de zhang fu/qi zi*
This is my son/daughter	*Zhe shi wu de er zi/nu er*
This is my friend/colleague.	*Zhe she wo de peng you/tong shi*
What's your job?	*Ni gan shenma gongzuo?*
How old are you?	*Ni dou da le?*
How are you?	*Ni hao ma?*
Very well, thank you	*Fei chang hao, xie xie*

Shopping

What time do you open?	*Sheng ma shi jian ying ye?*
What time do you close?	*Sheng ma shi jian xia ban?*
I'm just looking (browsing)	*Wo kan kan*
Have you got any…	*You mei you …*

Can I try it on?	*Wo ke yi shi shi ma?*
I need size … bigger/smaller/longer/shorter	*Wo yao … chi cun shao da dian/shao xiao dian/shao chang dian/shao duan dian*
May I have a bag, please?	*You dai zi ma?*
How much is this?	*Duoshao qian?*

Time

yesterday	*zuotian*
today	*jintian*
tomorrow	*mingtian*
the day after tomorrow	*houtian*
week	*xingqi*
month	*yue*
year	*nian*
minute	*fenzhong*
hour	*xiaoshi* (the hour on a clock is *dian*, e.g. 'two o' clock' is *er dian*)
What's the time?	*Jidian le?*

Yungang Grottoes, Datong (Shanxi)

INDEX

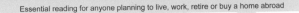

Survival Books

Essential reading for anyone planning to live, work, retire or buy a home abroad

Survival Books was established in 1987 and by the mid-'90s was the leading publisher of books for people planning to live, work, buy property or retire abroad.

From the outset, our philosophy has been to provide the most comprehensive and up-to-date information available. Our titles routinely contain up to twice as much information as other books and are updated frequently. All our books contain colour photographs and some are printed in two colours or full colour throughout. They also contain original cartoons, illustrations and maps.

Survival Books are written by people with first-hand experience of the countries and the people they describe, and therefore provide invaluable insights that cannot be obtained from official publications or websites, and information that is more reliable and objective than that provided by the majority of unofficial sites.

Survival Books are designed to be easy – and interesting – to read. They contain a comprehensive list of contents and index and extensive appendices, including useful addresses, further reading, useful websites and glossaries to help you obtain additional information as well as metric conversion tables and other useful reference material.

Our primary goal is to provide you with the essential information necessary for a trouble-free life or property purchase and to save you time, trouble and money.

We believe our books are the best – they are certainly the best-selling. But don't take our word for it – read what reviewers and readers have said about Survival Books at the front of this book.

Order your copies today by phone, fax, post or email from:
Survival Books, PO Box 3780, Yeovil, BA21 5WX, United Kingdom.
Tel: +44 (0)1935-700060, email: sales@survivalbooks.net,
Website: www.survivalbooks.net

Buying a Home Series

Buying a home abroad is not only a major financial transaction but also a potentially life-changing experience; it's therefore essential to get it right. Our Buying a Home guides are required reading for anyone planning to purchase property abroad and are packed with vital information to guide you through the property jungle and help you avoid disasters that can turn a dream home into a nightmare.

The purpose of our Buying a Home guides is to enable you to choose the most favourable location and the most appropriate property for your requirements, and to reduce your risk of making an expensive mistake by making informed decisions and calculated judgements rather than uneducated and hopeful guesses. Most importantly, they will help you save money and will repay your investment many times over.

Buying a Home guides are the most comprehensive and up-to-date source of information available about buying property abroad – whether you're seeking a detached house or an apartment, a holiday or a permanent home (or an investment property), these books will prove invaluable.

For a full list of our current titles, visit our website at www.survivalbooks.net

Living and Working Series

Our Living and Working guides are essential reading for anyone planning to spend a period abroad – whether it's an extended holiday or permanent migration – and are packed with priceless information designed to help you avoid costly mistakes and save both time and money.

Living and Working guides are the most comprehensive and up-to-date source of practical information available about everyday life abroad. They aren't, however, simply a catalogue of dry facts and figures, but are written in a highly readable style – entertaining, practical and occasionally humorous.

Our aim is to provide you with the comprehensive practical information necessary for a trouble-free life. You may have visited a country as a tourist, but living and working there is a different matter altogether; adjusting to a new environment and culture and making a home in any foreign country can be a traumatic and stressful experience. You need to adapt to new customs and traditions, discover the local way of doing things (such as finding a home, paying bills and obtaining insurance) and learn all over again how to overcome the everyday obstacles of life.

All these subjects and many, many more are covered in depth in our Living and Working guides – don't leave home without them.

The Expats' Best Friend!

Culture Wise Series

O ur **Culture Wise** series of guides is essential reading for anyone who wants to understand how a country really 'works'. Whether you're planning to stay for a few days or a lifetime, these guides will help you quickly find your feet and settle into your new surroundings.
Culture Wise guides:

- Reduce the anxiety factor in adapting to a foreign culture
- Explain how to behave in everyday situations in order to avoid cultural and social gaffes
- Help you get along with your neighbours
- Make friends and establish lasting business relationships
- Enhance your understanding of a country and its people.

People often underestimate the extent of cultural isolation they can face abroad, particularly in a country with a different language. At first glance, many countries seem an 'easy' option, often with millions of visitors from all corners of the globe and well-established expatriate communities. But, sooner or later, newcomers find that most countries are indeed 'foreign' and many come unstuck as a result. **Culture Wise** guides will enable you to quickly adapt to the local way of life and feel at home, and – just as importantly – avoid the worst effects of culture shock.

Culture Wise – The Wise Way to Travel

The essential guides to Culture, Customs & Business Etiquette

Other Survival Books

The Best Places to Buy a Home in France/Spain: Unique guides to where to buy property in Spain and France, containing detailed regional profiles and market reports.

Buying, Selling and Letting Property: The best source of information about buying, selling and letting property in the UK.

Earning Money From Your French Home: Income from property in France, including short- and long-term letting.

Investing in Property Abroad: Everything you need to know and more about buying property abroad for investment and pleasure.

Life in the UK - Test & Study Guide: essential reading for anyone planning to take the 'Life in the UK' test in order to become a permanent resident (settled) in the UK.

Making a Living: Comprehensive guides to self-employment and starting a business in France and Spain.

Renovating & Maintaining Your French Home: The ultimate guide to renovating and maintaining your dream home in France.

Retiring in France/Spain: Everything a prospective retiree needs to know about the two most popular international retirement destinations.

Running Gîtes and B&Bs in France: An essential book for anyone planning to invest in a gîte or bed & breakfast business.

Rural Living in France: An invaluable book for anyone seekingthe 'good life', containing a wealth of practical information about all aspects of French country life.

Shooting Caterpillars in Spain: The hilarious and compelling story of two innocents abroad in the depths of Andalusia in the late '80s.

**For a full list of our current titles, visit our website at
www.survivalbooks.net**

PHOTO

www.dreamstime.com

Pages 14 © Gautier, 16 © Yaopengyue, 19 © Acik, 20 © Annalia, 22 © Mamahoohooba, 24 © Seesea, 39 © Dawnbal1, 41 & 68 © Assignments, 49 © Kiankhoon, 52 © Kitch, 55 © Nigsphotos, 61 © Hemul, 63 © Emily2k, 67 & 132 & 204 © Hanhanpeggy, 70 © Elenray, 74 © Yuri_arcurs, 75 © Perkmeup, 77 © Jeancliclac, 79 © Nikolais, 80 © Baks, 81 © Andreynikolajew, 88 © Ecoasis, 91 © Fyletto, 94 © Tracy0703, 96 © Mauriehill, 98 © Elena Platonova, 105 © Mailthepic, 108 © Lieska, 126 © Pemotret, 128 © Christineg, 131 & 258 © Bertrandb, 137 © Ecophoto, 138 © Avava, 140 © Phildate, 148 © Leesniderphotoimages, 151 © Ecophoto, 152 © Bowie15, 166 & 171 © Hupeng, 175 © Alexey Arkhipov, 177 © Ptlee, 178 © Suto Norbert, 181 © Larryye, 182 © Gmv, 188 & 196 © Sergeibach, 190 © Photoclicks, 193 © Chenws, 199 © Sunmdn, 213 © Graphics1976, 215 © Guochun, 216 © Jiajianzheng, 218 © Icolourfulstone, 223 © Ene, 224 © Mbighin, 233 © Sofiaworld, 234 © Studio, 247 © Bendao, 258 © Oddlens.

CREDITS

www.shutterstock.com

Pages 10 © xfdly, 12 ©Paul Merrett, 18 © Trombax, 34 © Jack.Qi, 36 ©fang CHEN, 40 © 43 © Philip Lange, 50 defpicture, 51 ©chungking, 56 © karam Miri, 59 © Yuri Shirokov, 64 ©zhu difeng, 65 & 212 © BartlomiejMagierowski, 73 © Benjamin Loo, 78 © agophoto, 82 © Pan Xunbin, 84 © Jack.Qi, 87 © Roman Sigaev, 93 © Kobby Dagan, 106 © Hung Chung Chih, 110 © zhu difeng, 112 © Craig Hanson, 118 ©Shi Yali, 120 © gary718, 123 © Shi Yali, 124 © BrandonHot , 135 © mary416, 142 © Gautier Willaume, 145 © grafica, 157 © zhu difeng, 159 © Victoria Roxana Fiorenzi, 160 © Kobby Dagan, 161 © Photobank, 162 © Kobby Dagan, 163 © EML, 167 © Lee Prince, 168 © Nataliya Hora, 172 © michaeljung, 185 © yeo2205, 186 © oksana. perkins, 195 © Barnaby Chambers, 200 & 205 © claudio zaccherini, 206 © @cam, 208 © Sam Chadwick, 209 © Swapan, 211 © sevenke, 220 © iBird, 222 © Brian K Tan, 226 © testing, 228 © Tish1, 237 © Adulsak S.

www.wikipedia.com

© 27, 28, 29, 31, 33, 44, 45, 47, 48, 53, 89, 103, 115, 117, 146, 155, 165, 198, 203, 207, 230, 231.

1,⁴/₁₄ 14 c 3/19 3/19
19/14

Culture Wise Series

Culture Wise - The Wisest Way To Travel